.721

ALSO BY GARY WEBSTER

*Tris Speaker and the 1920 Indians:
Tragedy to Glory* (McFarland, 2012)

.721
A History of the 1954 Cleveland Indians

GARY WEBSTER

McFarland & Company, Inc., Publishers
Jefferson, North Carolina, and London

LIBRARY OF CONGRESS CATALOGUING-IN-PUBLICATION DATA

Webster, Gary, 1956–
   .721 : a history of the 1954 Cleveland Indians / Gary Webster.
      p.   cm.
   Includes bibliographical references and index.

   ISBN 978-0-7864-7655-8
   softcover : acid free paper ∞

   1. Cleveland Indians (Baseball team) — History.
   2. Baseball — Records — Ohio — Cleveland — History.
I. Title.
GV875.C7W43 2013
796.357'64097713209045   2013035469

BRITISH LIBRARY CATALOGUING DATA ARE AVAILABLE

© 2013 Gary Webster. All rights reserved

No part of this book may be reproduced or transmitted in any form or by any means, electronic or mechanical, including photocopying or recording, or by any information storage and retrieval system, without permission in writing from the publisher.

On the cover: (left to right) Cleveland players Larry Doby, Al Smith, Hal Newhouser and Bobby Avila in 1954 (Cleveland State University)

Manufactured in the United States of America

McFarland & Company, Inc., Publishers
  Box 611, Jefferson, North Carolina 28640
  www.mcfarlandpub.com

Table of Contents

Preface   1
1. Hank and Al   5
2. A Slow Start   53
3. Picking Up the Pace   65
4. Avoiding the Swoon   81
5. Seeing Stars   97
6. Can't Shake the Yanks   115
7. Magic Numbers   133
8. The Catch, the Homer and Other Calamities   153
Epilogue   167
Appendix A. The Players' Statistics   175
Appendix B. The 1954 Schedule   178
Chapter Notes   183
Bibliography   188
Index   189

Preface

When the topic of conversation among baseball fans turns to the greatest individual teams of all time, there are some conspicuous absences.

One is the 1906 Chicago Cubs, who still hold the sport's record for highest winning percentage with a staggering .763. Even though those Cubs boasted four Hall of Famers in shortstop Joe Tinker, second baseman Johnny Evers, first baseman (and manager) Frank Chance, and pitcher Mordecai (Three Finger) Brown and won 116 games while dropping just 36, they blew their chance to be considered the best team ever by losing the World Series to the cross-town "Hitless Wonders" White Sox, who somehow managed to win the American League pennant despite a pathetic .230 team batting average. A season for the ages went down the drain in six October afternoons.

The 2001 Seattle Mariners laid waste to the American League's West Division, matching the Cubs' record of 116 victories and seemingly clinching the division title sometime around the Fourth of July. Little more than a decade has passed since manager Lou Piniella's crew established the league record for wins in a single season, but they're barely an afterthought when fans argue about the best teams ever. The Mariners struggled to win their Division Series against the Cleveland Indians in five games and were eliminated from the League Championship Series in six games by the New York Yankees. A team that didn't even reach the World Series, regardless of how many games it won during the regular season, doesn't figure in the debate over the best team of all time.

When was the last time anyone mentioned the 1969 Baltimore Ori-

Preface

oles, who breezed to the first-ever American League East Division title with 109 victories and then flattened the Minnesota Twins in three straight games in the League Championship Series? The 1969 Orioles are only remembered as the team the "Miracle Mets" defeated in the World Series. And no one ever thinks of the Miracle Mets as the greatest team ever. Except maybe overly enthusiastic Mets fans.

To be considered the best team in the history of a professional sport, a team must have won that sport's championship, explaining why the 1954 Indians find themselves in the company of the 1906 Cubs, the 2001 Mariners and the 1969 Orioles, among others, when fans debate which team was the best in major league history. All were big winners during the regular season and big busts in the post-season, whether that post-season consisted only of the World Series or today's multi-tiered playoff system.

Clevelanders should look back with pride on the accomplishments of their 1954 Indians, whose 111 victories remains the franchise record and was the American League record for 44 years, until the Yankees eclipsed it with 114 wins in 1998. The 1927 Yankees' record of 110 regular season victories stood for only 27 years. The 1954 Tribe's .721 winning percentage is still the league's all-time best. The Indians snapped the Yankees' streak of five consecutive pennants and denied Casey Stengel's only team to win 100 or more games a flag. The Indians rode the right arms of Bob Lemon, Early Wynn and Mike Garcia, still one of the best starting pitching staffs ever assembled, and boasted of the American League batting champion in second baseman Bob Avila. What Clevelanders remember, however, is how their seemingly invincible Indians were humiliated in the World Series by the New York Giants, failing to win even a single game. The Tribe wouldn't win another pennant for 41 years.

How did it happen?

A study of the statistics indicates the Indians were a classic example of a team that was greater than the sum of its parts. Despite a roster which included five future Hall of Famers, the 1954 Indians wouldn't be confused with the 1927 Yankees' fabled Murderers' Row. In his declining years, Tribe Hall of Famer Bob Feller, who won 13 games as a spot starter

Preface

in 1954, insisted that the 1948 World Series champion Indians were a much better team and the collapse against the Giants shouldn't have been as startling as it was. Other players suggested that manager Al Lopez was obsessed with breaking the 1927 Yankees' record and drove the team too hard to achieve that goal, leaving them exhausted at season's end and rendering the World Series anti-climactic. Maybe they slumped at the worst possible time, as Lopez suggested. Or maybe the Giants were a better team.

I don't claim that this book will uncover reasons for the Indians' World Series swoon that has baffled baseball historians for nearly 60 years. But it will tell the story of a talented team whose accomplishments deserve better than to be relegated to the dumpster of history.

1

Hank and Al

An American League baseball team has called Cleveland, Ohio, its home since the circuit was born in 1900. A lot of players, managers, coaches and executives have been associated with the franchise in that time, but few, if any, have been as controversial, and as polarizing, as Hank Greenberg. And few, if any, have been as underappreciated as Al Lopez.

Greenberg joined the Indians three weeks before the club's magical journey to the 1948 World Series championship began. Greenberg reportedly invested $100,000 in the team and was given the title of "second vice president" by owner Bill Veeck. Veeck's first vice president, Harry Grabiner, had been part of the original ownership group that purchased the Indians in June of 1946. Because Greenberg, who had been released by the Pittsburgh Pirates after the 1947 season but hadn't officially retired, had been working out with the Indians in Tucson, Arizona, there was speculation that he planned to continue his career in Cleveland. Greenberg did nothing to discourage that speculation.

"I don't want the players to get the idea that I am going to beat anybody out of a job," said the former Detroit Tigers slugger who had slammed 58 home runs in 1938. "I'm going to stay in condition and if they need me, I'll play. I would hate to tell you anything definite about my playing status at this time because I might change my mind tomorrow. All I can say is this: as long as I'm able I will help out in the field in some capacity, even if it is collecting the balls during batting practice."

Asked if he might serve as a coach, Greenberg answered, "I think the purpose of this club or any club is to win the pennant. If my coaching will help, then I'll do it." Greenberg said he was interested in joining Veeck's group when he heard the Indians were available in 1946, but wasn't ready to retire as a player. "Since I left the Tigers, though, I've been looking for something just like this. I like the Cleveland club very much. Naturally, I wouldn't be buying into it if I didn't. It's a good ball club and I think we have a chance for the pennant."[1]

Greenberg's career as an active player was over and he saw no action with the Indians. He was right about the club's pennant prospects, however. Though most of the so-called "experts" picked the Tribe to finish behind the New York Yankees and Boston Red Sox, Cleveland captured only its second pennant in franchise history and dispatched the Boston Braves in a six-game World Series. Greenberg spent the summer of 1948 building a player development system that he believed would keep the Indians in contention for years to come.

When Veeck shocked the Cleveland community — which had turned out in record numbers to cheer the Indians in 1948 and kept the Municipal Stadium turnstiles moving to the tune of more than 2.2 million paid admissions in 1949, even as the club slipped to third place — by selling the team to a group of northeastern Ohio business leaders in November of 1949, Greenberg stuck around. It was revealed during the course of the negotiations between Veeck and the group headed by insurance executive Ellis Ryan that Greenberg had not invested any money in the Indians and owned no stock. But he'd become a valued member of the front office, and within hours after taking control of the Tribe, Ryan, the club's new president, elevated Greenberg to the position of general manager previously held by Veeck and signed him to a three-year contract.

"Greenberg has a fine record with the Indians and we are happy to have him with us," Ryan said in announcing Greenberg's promotion. "I understand the club never had a farm system of this magnitude until he helped develop it. I don't want him to decrease that activity. I want him to continue operating the farm system in addition to being general manager."[2] Veeck had been an experienced baseball executive before buying the Indians. Ryan sold insurance. None of the other members of the new ownership group were baseball men, so Ryan promised that Greenberg

1. Hank and Al

would be given a "free hand" to run the ball club without interference. Ryan also expressed the opinion that, in order to return the Indians to the top of the American League, some trades would be necessary.

Greenberg took advantage of the opportunity to prove that he was, indeed, in charge of the club. While not dismissing the possibility of making some deals, Greenberg noted that "the fact is that I think we've reached the point where it's time we started building solidly with young material from our farms. We've produced more really promising ball players on our farms this year than any other club in the majors. That's where our plans for the future are."[3] Greenberg's aversion to making trades would quickly become a point of contention between him and most of the writers who covered the Indians for Cleveland's three daily newspapers.

Although a new general manager usually exercises the prerogative to choose the team's field manager, Greenberg was content to allow player-manager Lou Boudreau to finish the two-year contract Veeck had awarded him after the 1948 World Series victory. Greenberg did mention the possibility that Boudreau, whose range at shortstop had been diminished not only by the broken ankle he suffered in 1945, but by 13 years of playing the infield's most demanding position at the major league level, might switch to third base in 1950. Boudreau didn't take the hint, playing in just two games at third base and only 61 at shortstop as his Hall of Fame playing career neared an end.

The 1950 Indians improved their record from 89–65 to 92–62 in Boudreau's ninth season as manager, but fell from third place to fourth, six games behind the Yankees. Boudreau was finished as a player, but the writers who covered the Indians were confident Greenberg would retain him as the club's manager, albeit for only one year and at a considerably reduced salary. Veeck had signed Boudreau for two years at $65,000 per season in 1948, and it was speculated that he'd have to accept a pay cut of roughly $20,000 to serve as a bench manager in 1951. Harry Jones, the baseball beat writer for the Cleveland *Plain Dealer*, told his readers on November 7, 1950, that a new contract for Boudreau awaited only Boudreau's signature.

Four days later, Jones told the same readers that Boudreau had been fired and Al Lopez would call the shots from the Indians dugout in 1951.

General manager Hank Greenberg (left) and his hand-picked manager, Al Lopez. Together, they produced a lot of victories and a lot of tension (Cleveland State University, *Cleveland Press* collection).

Hours after making the managerial change, Greenberg was the featured speaker at the annual banquet of the Associated Grocery Manufacturers Representatives at Cleveland's Hotel Hollenden. It was reported by *The Plain Dealer* that Greenberg was greeted by cries of "Boudreau, Boudreau, Boudreau!" by the assemblage but received a standing ovation when his speech was through.

"[The fans] want a winning team and my job is to provide it," Greenberg said. "We knew we had as manager a man who was probably the most popular player in the history of the Cleveland baseball club. You people want a winner. I take great pleasure in being partly responsible for bringing a new manager to Cleveland." Greenberg added that he hoped Indians fans would give Lopez "a chance to prove he is the best manager in baseball today."[4]

1. Hank and Al

The standing ovation notwithstanding, Greenberg failed to convince at least one of the attendees of the wisdom of the move. "You'll be sorry!" he was told by a bellicose fan in the crowd, and Greenberg acknowledged the possibility that the fan was right.

Greenberg and Ryan explained that the delay in dismissing Boudreau and hiring Lopez was caused by Lopez's lack of availability at the end of the 1950 season. Lopez had spent the final year of his playing career, 1947, with the Indians, and had asked for and been granted his release by Veeck in order to accept the job of managing the Pirates' Indianapolis farm team in the American Association. Veeck briefly considered firing Boudreau and hiring Lopez to manage the Tribe, but thought better of it. Lopez piloted Indianapolis to the 1948 American Association pennant and finished second in 1949 and 1950. His 1949 team won the Little World Series, defeating the International League champion Montreal Royals, the Brooklyn Dodgers' top farm team.

Ryan and Greenberg decided to change managers only if Lopez was available. If not, Boudreau would be retained. Their first inquiry about Lopez to Indianapolis owner Frank McKinney was rebuffed. Lopez had signed a contract to manage Indianapolis in 1951, and it was rumored that he was the top candidate to replace Pirates manager Billy Meyer, if Meyer was dismissed after a dismal last-place finish. When Dodgers general manager Branch Rickey was forced out by club owner Walter O'Malley and landed in Pittsburgh, he showed little interest in Lopez. Meyer was retained, and the Indians inquired about Lopez again. McKinney released Lopez from his contract, and he signed a two-year deal to manage the Tribe (at $40,000 per season) on November 10.

"I think I can handle the Cleveland club, and I will do all I can to get a winning team," Lopez said. "I'm glad to come back to Cleveland. I had a lot of fun that year I was here and I made a lot of friends. I hope to make a lot more."[5]

The fan backlash against Boudreau's firing was less intense than in 1947, when Veeck, who admired Boudreau as a player but wasn't particularly enamored with him as a manager, tried to trade him to the St. Louis Browns for shortstop Vern Stephens. When word of the swap reached Cleveland, Veeck was besieged by enraged fans who swore never to pass through Municipal Stadium's turnstiles again if the Indians' beloved shortstop was traded. Ever the showman, Veeck made a grandiose display of bowing to public pressure (in truth, the Browns pulled out of the deal, deciding to send Stephens to the Red Sox instead) and signing Boudreau to a two-year contract. Though Greenberg's dismissal of the winningest manager in franchise history (and Boudreau's 728 victories are still tops among Cleveland field bosses) aroused some ire among the paying customers, most realized that Boudreau's playing days were over and were willing to give Lopez a chance.

Boudreau's firing didn't arouse much angst among the press, either. Gordon Cobbledick, the sports editor of *The Plain Dealer*, who would become Greenberg's harshest critic, had no problem with the decision to change managers. "They [Greenberg and Ryan] did it because they believed it would make the Indians stronger. Is that bad?" Cobbledick wrote on November 11.

Greenberg and Ryan had the manager they wanted, and Lopez rewarded them by guiding the Indians to a pair of second-place finishes in 1951 and 1952, trailing the Yankees by five and two games, respectively. The strong showing earned Lopez a one-year contract extension, but in 1953 the Indians finished second again, a disappointing 8½ games out of first. The natives in northeastern Ohio who, in Greenberg's words, "want a winning team," were growing restless and impatient with Hank and Al.

It was only fitting that the Yankees clinched the pennant, their fifth straight, in front of a friendly crowd at Yankee Stadium at the expense of their closest pursuers. New York's 8–5 victory on September 14 eliminated the Indians and left the visitors nervously looking over their shoulders at the Chicago White Sox. First place was out of reach, and there was a very real possibility that the downcast Indians might surrender second place to the White Sox over the season's final ten games. Such a development would've ruined Lopez's record: in his first five seasons as a manager (three with Indianapolis, two with Cleveland) his teams had never finished lower than second. A third straight runner-up finish with the Indians was suddenly in jeopardy.

The night after clinching, Yankees manager Casey Stengel held court with "his writers" and had a dire prediction for the other seven American

1. Hank and Al

League teams. "In 1954 we could have the best team we ever did have. It will be a pleasure for me to be back managing it, too. Yes, sir and yippee." There had been rumors that Stengel, despite having one year remaining on his contract, would step down after the 1953 season. The Old Professor soon put those idle rumors to rest.

"Sure, at one stage of my career here, I did think of quitting. It was at the end of the 1951 season. But now, after five years, my interest is at its peak. What would I do out at Glendale [California, Stengel's off-season home] if I were to quit? Where in the world of sport is there a more interesting job than I have?"[6] Ironically, Stengel was correct in predicting his 1954 squad would be even stronger than the 1953 pennant-winners. It would be the best team Stengel managed in New York, at least in terms of regular season victories. But the 103 games the Yankees would win in 1954 wouldn't be enough to capture a sixth straight flag.

"The way we played today, we'll need a major overhaul," said Lopez, the Indians' discouraged manager.[7] The question that would dominate Cleveland's sports scene for the next two weeks was whether that major overhaul would start with the hiring of a new manager.

The Indians' elimination was met with a minimum of weeping and wailing in Cleveland since the team had fallen 10½ games behind after being swept in a four-game series at Municipal Stadium by the Yankees in mid–June and never got closer than five games out of first place (and that only briefly) the rest of the way. The Cleveland print media had long since conceded the pennant to New York. That didn't mean no one was going to be held accountable for the Indians' inability to chase the Yankees all the way to the wire as they had in 1952, however. Cobbledick placed the responsibility squarely on Greenberg's shoulders, noting that in spring training Greenberg had ventured the opinion that the Indians were stronger than they'd been in 1952, while the Yankees were weaker. Though Greenberg made no promises, Cobbledick interpreted that analysis to mean Greenberg was predicting a pennant.

Cobbledick had a simple explanation for the Indians' continued failure to overtake the Yankees. New York had better personnel, and a much smarter and more capable general manager than Greenberg in the person of George Weiss, who took control of the Yankees' front office

.721

when Ed Barrow, the architect of the New York dynasty, retired in 1945. The Yankees kept operating with machine-line precision with Weiss at the helm. Greenberg, in Cobbledick's opinion —formulated after having watched him in action for four seasons— was no George Weiss. That was why the Indians kept finishing second. And as the Tribe tried to maintain its hold on the runner-up spot in the waning days of the 1953 season, Cobbledick saw no reason to believe Cleveland could reverse the trend the following year.

Before the Indians departed New York to continue their final road trip of the year in Philadelphia, Lopez picked the Yankees to win yet another World Series from the Brooklyn Dodgers. "I figure it'll go seven games with the Yanks winning because their club is just a little better. I rate the pitching about even. The Yanks have an edge in personnel, though."[8] Lopez was a former Dodger who had played for Stengel when he managed the team in 1934 and 1935.

With nine games left in the 1953 season, three questions remained regarding the Indians. First, could they hold off the White Sox and finish second? Second, would Lopez return as manager in 1954? Third, if Lopez, whose contract, according to the newspapers, expired after the final out of the season's final game, chose not to come back to Cleveland, would Greenberg follow him out the door?

Harry Jones, clearly a Lopez supporter, presented the case for keeping the Tribe's skipper. Jones devoted a column to the accomplishments of the only other managers in modern major league history to finish second in three consecutive seasons ... although not their first three seasons, as would be the case with Lopez if the Indians could hold off the White Sox. Jones pointed out that neither Joe McCarthy, whose Yankees finished second to the Washington Senators in 1933 and to the Tigers in 1934 and 1935; nor John McGraw, whose Giants were runners-up to the Chicago Cubs in 1918, the Cincinnati Reds in 1919, and the Brooklyn Robins in 1920; nor Eddie Dyer, who managed the St. Louis Cardinals to second-place finishes in 1947, 1948 and 1949, were fired or resigned after their club's third consecutive bridesmaid finish. Jones noted that McGraw's and McCarthy's teams both ran off a string of four straight pennants afterward.

1. Hank and Al

McGraw, in 1920, had been at the helm of the Giants since 1902. He owned part of the team and was so firmly entrenched in New York that the Statue of Liberty stood a better chance of being dislodged from its perch than McGraw did of being fired. McCarthy's Yankees won the World Series in his second season (1932), but the three straight runner-up finishes that followed didn't sit well with owner Jake Ruppert, who sternly warned his manager after the 1935 campaign that he hadn't been hired to finish second. Dyer, whose Cardinals won it all in 1946, his rookie year in the dugout, resigned after St. Louis slipped to fifth place in 1950. Jones's message was intended for both Greenberg and Lopez, but if Lopez chose not to re-up in Cleveland for 1954, it would be his decision. He was still Greenberg's guy, and Hank wanted him back. Greenberg was reported to be en route to Philadelphia to meet with his manager, but he refused to discuss Lopez's status with the press until season's end.

The Indians clinched second place with a two-game sweep of the White Sox in Comiskey Park on September 22 and 23. Bob Feller's 8–3 victory in the first game was his tenth of the season and 249th of his illustrious career. Lopez would start Feller in the season's last game to give him the chance to notch career victory number 250.

"I'm a much better pitcher now than I was last year, and I think I can do better next year," Feller said, looking ahead, as all the Indians were, to 1954. "I've been throwing a sinker. It's got me out of plenty of jams. I knew how to throw a sinker before. It's the same kind of pitch [Bob] Lemon uses. But I always was afraid it would injure my arm. This spring, I worked on two pitches, the knuckler and the sinker. I developed a way of throwing the sinker so that it was easy on my arm. It was all in the follow through."

Feller thought he could pitch effectively "at least another three years. That is, if the Indians will have me." He was grateful to Lopez for giving him a shot at winning his tenth game, since ten victories meant "being half a 20-game winner."[9]

Earning Feller a landmark victory wouldn't be all that was at stake for the Indians during the season's final weekend. With second place clinched, Lopez gave his regulars the option of sitting out the three-

.721

game series with Detroit at Municipal Stadium ... all of his regulars except third baseman Al Rosen, who had a legitimate chance to win the American League's Triple Crown. Rosen had the RBI title locked up, but was battling Philadelphia's Gus Zernial for the home run leadership and Washington's Mickey Vernon for the batting crown.

In order to give Rosen as many plate appearances as possible, Lopez penciled him in as the leadoff batter in all three games. Rosen responded with a sizzling nine hits in 15 at-bats. Rosen's two homers in the Friday night game gave him 43, enough to edge out Zernial, who finished with 42. But Vernon's five hits in his last eight at-bats gave him a final average of .337 (technically, .3371) to Rosen's .336 (technically, .3355). A hit in his last plate appearance would've given Rosen the batting championship and the Triple Crown, but he couldn't leg out a slow roller hit to Detroit third baseman Jerry Priddy with two out in the ninth inning of the last game of the season. Priddy threw Rosen out by a step. Although 9,579 fans disagreed with umpire Hank Soar's call, Rosen had no complaints. "Soar called the play right," Rosen said in the clubhouse. "I missed the bag."[10]

Lost in the drama of Rosen's bid for the Triple Crown was Feller's attempt to win his 250th career game. The Tigers pounced on Feller for three first-inning runs and scored seven in the seven frames Feller pitched. The Indians lost, 7–3. Feller would have to wait until 1954 to notch the milestone victory.

Lopez didn't have much to say to reporters after the loss that left the Indians with a record of 92–62. His contract having expired, he prepared for a trip to New York, where he was to meet Greenberg the following day. Most Clevelanders expected Lopez to reject Greenberg's offer of a new contract and look for employment elsewhere. Sports editor Franklin "Whitey" Lewis of the Cleveland *Press* offered the opinion that the Indians were hoping Lopez would leave, suggesting that they blamed him for the club's inability to overtake the Yankees. Lewis wrote that if Greenberg truly wanted Lopez to return, he would've offered the manager a new contract weeks before.

Hal Lebovitz, who covered the Indians for the Cleveland *News*, also speculated that Lopez would leave and said the Reds were among his many potential suitors now that he was a free agent. *The Plain Dealer*,

1. Hank and Al

in an opinion lacking a byline, said Lopez would probably reject Greenberg's offer of a one-year deal when they met on the day after the season ended, and that if Lopez left, Greenberg's days were most likely numbered, because the team's ownership wanted the manager to stay and met with him in September to try to convince him that Cleveland was where he belonged.

The front page headline of the *Press* on September 28, the day of Lopez's meeting with Greenberg, said SOMEBODY'S LEAVING — LOPEZ OR GREENBERG? As it turned out, the answer to that question was neither.

Lopez's meeting with Greenberg lasted roughly half an hour. When it was over, the two men met with reporters to announce that Lopez had signed a contract to manage the Indians through the 1955 campaign, at a salary of $40,000 annually. It was the third contract Lopez had signed with the Tribe, each calling for the same salary. Pundits noted that Lopez was now under contract for one more year than the man who'd brought him to Cleveland in 1950.

Lopez didn't get a raise as a reward for three straight second-place finishes, but he apparently was able to wring a few concessions from his boss before agreeing to pilot the Indians for two more seasons. Although Lopez was Greenberg's hand-picked choice to manage the Indians, and both men denied that a rift had developed between them in the three years they'd worked together, their philosophies as to how to win ball games differed significantly. Greenberg, one of the sport's premier sluggers as a player, liked the long ball and offered Tribe players tips (which Lopez resented), encouraging them to swing for Municipal Stadium's fences. Lopez, as befit a former catcher, believed games were won with pitching and defense. Greenberg apparently agreed to stop serving as batting coach without portfolio.

There was also the matter of a television set the club had removed from the manager's office, apparently on orders from the general manager, because Greenberg thought Lopez spent too much time watching it and not enough time on the field with the players. Lopez paid for a new TV out of his own pocket, with his angry players contributing. Lopez insisted he wouldn't have been upset had Greenberg come to him first and explained his displeasure.

.721

The news conference at which the announcement was made contained the standard blather from both the general manager and the manager. "I think he has done a terrific job in the three years he has managed the club and at no time was consideration given to replacing him," said Greenberg. "I'm sorry I waited until now and let this thing drag out so long, but I have always felt that the time to re-hire a manager is at the end of a season. I simply told Al we wanted him to come back, and he said he would."[11]

Said Lopez, "I'm very happy. I like the ball club, I like the people of Cleveland, and I'm happy about the whole thing."[12]

Greenberg put the cherry on the sundae. "I've said it before and I'll say it again. Lopez, in my opinion, is the best manager in the business."[13] That opinion was shared by Stengel, who had beaten Lopez out of three consecutive pennants. "He's the greatest manager in the game," Stengel told Greenberg. "He's the only guy who can beat me. Give him some help and he'll beat everybody."[14]

The rumor that Lopez would leave Cleveland for Cincinnati was more than just a rumor. Reds general manager Gabe Paul admitted that "I asked Greenberg for permission to talk to Lopez. Greenberg refused that permission."[15]

Lopez admitted that his club needed help if it was to overcome the Yankees, particularly at first base. "We can't count on Luke [Easter], and Bill Glynn isn't the answer. We've got to try and come up with somebody.... With a few changes we might be able to do what we failed to accomplish in the three years I've been here."[16] Lopez didn't identify the accomplishment that had eluded him, and he didn't have to.

With his manager in the fold for two more years, it was time for Greenberg to attend to the business of adding the pieces to his ball club that would enable it to dethrone the mighty Yankees in 1954. He started by purchasing the contract of first baseman Glenn "Rocky" Nelson from the Dodgers. The 29-year-old Nelson had seen action with the Cardinals, Pirates and White Sox since 1949 and played in 37 games for Brooklyn in 1952. He had no future with the Dodgers due to the presence of Gil Hodges and spent the 1953 season with Brooklyn's Montreal farm team, winning International League MVP honors. Greenberg believed the Indi-

1. Hank and Al

ans needed more punch than had been provided by Glynn in 1953. Glynn batted just .243 and hit only three home runs, not nearly enough production from a corner infielder on a contending team.

Among Nelson's admirers was Bobby Bragan, the reigning minor league Manager of the Year for piloting the Hollywood Stars to the Pacific Coast League pennant in 1953. "Don't see how the Dodgers could let him get away," Bragan said while managing the Cuban winter league team Nelson played for. "He was the best hitter in the minors last year. And I think he's going to hit for Cleveland, too. I'd bet anything on it.

"One thing about Rocky, he isn't gonna get scared. They don't call him Rocky for nuthin'. He knows this is his big chance, maybe the last one he'll ever get, but that don't bother him none. He's as cool as they come and he won't choke up."[17]

Nelson had impressed the brain trust of the Athletics, who planned to pluck him from the Dodgers in baseball's annual draft of minor leaguers had the Indians not acquired him. "He was my number one choice," said manager Jimmy Dykes. "The manager of our farm team at Ottawa and our scouts say he's quite a player. They told me to get him. He's much better than anything you have at first right now."[18]

"We'll go to spring training with three first basemen. The one who shows up best wins the job," said Lopez. "We bought Nelson because after much study we decided he was the best available in the minors. He's a better hitter than Glynn, but not as good a fielder."[19]

Nelson continued to mash minor league pitching in the Little World Series as his Montreal Royals took on Kansas City. Nelson batted .769 through four games before leaving the club to visit his critically ill father in West Portsmouth, Ohio. He made his first visit to Municipal Stadium on October 12 to meet with Greenberg, although the two didn't discuss a contract.

"I can hit, all right," Nelson assured reporters anxious to interview the Indians' new slugger. "Trouble is I never got a chance to show my stuff in the big time. The Cardinals sent me down to Columbus and I start to rap the apple like Ty Cobb. I'm bangin' away at .428 or somethin' like that. So the Cards get excited and yank me back. With me in the line-up we win 10 straight games. So what do you think happens? I'm benched."[20] For the record, the Cardinals never won ten in a row while Nelson played for them. They went nine straight without a loss in 1949, when Nelson played in 82 games and batted .221, and had a pair of seven-game winning streaks in 1950, when Nelson hit .247 while seeing action in 76 games.

Nelson, a left-handed hitter, had grown accustomed to hitting balls into the right field seats at Montreal Stadium, just 293 feet from home plate. He was shocked by the vast expanse of outfield at Municipal Stadium, but breathed easier when told the temporary fence installed each baseball season had been removed for football.

Greenberg may have been hoping that Nelson could hold down first base while 17-year-old phenom Frank Leja learned his craft in the minors. Leja, a strapping six-foot-four, 210-pound mega-prospect from Holyoke, Massachusetts, stunned the Indians on the day they obtained Nelson by signing a $100,000 contract with ... who else ... the Yankees. Greenberg had been certain Leja would accept an offer from the Indians. "I told him that no matter what the Yankees offered, we'd go higher. But he never called back after talking to the Yankees."[21] Leja's decision turned out to be a blessing for Cleveland. Because baseball's bonus rule required a team signing a player for more than $5,000 to keep that player on the big league roster for two seasons, Leja wasted 1954 and 1955 sitting on the Yankees' bench, playing in 19 games and contributing one hit in seven trips to the plate. Sent to the minors at the Yankees' earliest opportunity, Leja never wore a New York uniform again and didn't return to the majors until 1962, when he was sent to the plate 16 times by the expansion Los Angeles Angels and failed to get a hit. Leja's career totals: one hit in 23 at-bats. Stengel couldn't resist gloating after stealing Leja from New York's closest competitor. When asked if it was the size of the bonus the Yankees offered that convinced Leja to snub the Indians, Stengel sneered. "Money? All we promised him was a World Series cut for the next five years," grinned the manager.[22] And Leja did cash a World Series check in 1955. Only four fewer checks than the Yankees had promised.

The Yankees disposed of the Dodgers in the 1953 World Series, as Lopez had predicted, although they needed only six games rather than

1. Hank and Al

seven. When it was over, echoing *The Plain Dealer*'s Cobbledick, reporter Jack Hand of the Associated Press posed the question of who could keep the Yankees and Dodgers from meeting in a third straight World Series in 1954. Hand's answer was: nobody. Hand predicted that both 1953 pennant winners would repeat in the coming season. In fact, in Hand's opinion, the Yankees figured to pile up pennants for the foreseeable future.

Nobody in October of 1953 was suggesting that Lopez's Indians would be the team to beat in the American League in 1954. Least of all the Cleveland media, led by Cobbledick, who explained succinctly why the Indians had finished as American League runners-up three straight years. In a column on November 1, Cobbledick expressed surprise that Feller had told a group of baseball fans in Buffalo, New York, a few days earlier that the Indians were intimidated by the Yankees. Cobbledick wasn't buying it and produced statistics to refute Feller's accusation.

Cobbledick noted that the Indians and Yankees had split their 1953 season series, each club winning 11 times. He lauded the Tribe for taking 11 of its last 15 meetings with New York after dropping the first seven games (including the sweep in Cleveland in mid–June that effectively ended the pennant race). The Yankees had captured the 1952 season series from Cleveland, 12 games to 10, meaning that during the previous two seasons, the Yankees had beaten the Indians 23 times and the Indians had beaten the Yankees 21 times. Cobbledick saw no evidence in those numbers to indicate that the Indians weren't sufficiently aggressive when playing the Yankees, as Feller had suggested.

Returning to the cold, hard facts, Cobbledick noted that it was the Indians' failure to handle two also-rans, the Red Sox and Senators, that cost them the pennant, or at least making a stronger run at New York than they did. The fourth-place Red Sox, managed by former Indians boss Lou Boudreau, won 13 of their 22 meetings with Cleveland. The Indians were 11–11 against the fifth-place Senators. Had the Indians merely taken the season series from Boston and Washington, they would've added four victories to their total and finished a more respectable 4½ games out of first place, which may have placated the fans and the press somewhat.

Feller did say something to the gathering in Buffalo that Cobbledick agreed with. Feller expressed concern that the Indians were closer to falling back in the pack than they were to overcoming the Yankees, and suggested fourth place might await the Tribe in 1954 if Ted Williams could fashion a typical Williams season for the Red Sox and the White Sox could acquire another front-line pitcher. Cobbledick agreed that the Indians were on the brink of sinking into the second division if they didn't make some significant moves of their own. Something Greenberg, in the opinion of Cobbledick in particular, but other Cleveland writers as well, was far too reluctant to do.

Hal Lebovitz agreed with Cobbledick. The Indians, in Lebovitz's opinion, didn't tremble at the sight of the Yankees pinstripes. They couldn't finish ahead of New York because they lacked the talent. Lebovitz compared the starting lineups of the two teams and concluded that only at third base, with Rosen, did the Indians have a sizable advantage. At every other position, the Yankees were better. The equalizer, according to Lebovitz, was the Tribe's pitching.

"When [Early] Wynn, Lemon and [Mike] Garcia are right," Lebovitz wrote, "nobody can beat them. Not even the Yanks."[23] But the Tribe's "Big Three" was getting old, and asking it for the kind of effort that would be needed to overhaul the Yankees in 1954 figured to be too much.

A few cracks in the world champions' armor were showing as the off-season progressed. Pitcher Johnny Sain and pinch-hitter deluxe Johnny Mize had both retired following the World Series victory over the Dodgers, and Stengel, representing the Yankees at the annual minor league convention in Atlanta in late November, was at a loss as to how to replace them.

> We may have to get some pitching somewhere and some pinch-hitting, too. But we're pretty well fixed everywhere else. Tell you the truth, I don't think anyone will trade us a pitcher. I don't see where I'm gonna get a guy to win me 14 games next year [as Sain had in 1953.] I've got to get 'em back, but where? Maybe the kids will help, but I can't count on 'em. And those other fellas [starters Ed Lopat, Allie Reynolds and Vic Raschi] aren't getting any younger. They're gonna have to report in shape next spring and stay that way 'cause I've got to give the kids a good chance.[24]

1. Hank and Al

Al Rosen, the 1953 American League MVP (presenter unidentified). Rosen got off to a strong start in 1954, but struggled with injuries from Memorial Day on (Cleveland State University, *Cleveland Press* collection)

One New York writer with an overly active imagination thought he knew where Stengel could get the pitching he needed to overcome Sain's loss. The writer speculated that George Weiss was negotiating with Greenberg to acquire Garcia. "A real joke!" snorted Lopez. "The last guy we'd give the Yanks is Garcia. They'd really be unbeatable if they had him."[25] (Sain would come out of retirement and spend 1954 in the Yankee's bullpen, and pitched for Kansas City in 1955 before hanging up his cleats for good.)

As to the competition, Stengel, like Feller, was worried about Boudreau's Red Sox. "That Boston outfit is liable to scare hell out of anybody, and I don't see where Cleveland is going to be any weaker. With that pitching they ought to be plenty tough again."[26]

The Indians' minor league system earned plaudits at the convention. Of the eight teams the Indians owned outright or had a working agreement with, six had won pennants in 1953, and three had captured their league's playoff championship. *The Plain Dealer* noted with pride that only one Yankees farm team had won a pennant.

"I think the record speaks for itself. It certainly looks as though we can hope for the future," said Greenberg.[27] How many of those farmhands would be ready to strengthen the Indians in 1954?

The Indians needed no improvement at third base. Rosen became the American League's first unanimous choice as Most Valuable Player, earning all 24 first-place votes by virtue of his near-miss quest for the league's Triple Crown. He was the first Cleveland player to be named MVP since Boudreau in 1948. The only other Indian to have been deemed most valuable was George Burns in 1926. Burns batted .358, tied Sam Rice for the league lead in hits with 216, set a league record for doubles with 64, and drove in 114 runs while leading the Tribe to an unexpected second-place finish, three games behind the Yankees. No Indian has won the award since Rosen, who said,

> This is the greatest thing that has ever happened to me but I don't want it to be the last. The main thing I want to do now is help the Indians win a pennant. I'd also like to win the Triple Crown and, of course, I'd like to be a two-time winner of the Most Valuable Player award. I don't want to win the batting championship at the expense of the team, though. I mean, my

1. Hank and Al

job is to drive in runs, not get a lot of singles and doubles. I've got to keep going for that long ball.

Rosen said he thought he could hit .340 in 1954, which might be good enough to win the batting title that eluded him "unless Ted Williams has a great year." Rosen also said he was occasionally asked if he thought he could break Babe Ruth's single-season record of 60 round-trippers. He didn't. "That's a lot of homers," he said. "I'll settle for 50."[28] Rosen's 43 homers in 1953 would prove to be his high-water mark and remained the team record until 1995.

The MVP award capped a banner year for the Cleveland third baseman. He'd come within one base hit of winning the Triple Crown and had been rewarded by the club with a new contract shortly after the season ended. Rosen would be paid $40,000 in 1954, an increase of $15,000 over his 1953 salary. "Rosen was unquestionably the outstanding ball player in the American League in 1953 and he really earned an increase," said Greenberg.[29] The general manager added, "Many people have already conceded the 1954 flag to the New York Yankees but we're going to work as hard as possible to improve our club and wreck those premature predictions."[30]

The *News* had informed its readers on November 9 that Rosen, preparing for a career after baseball in an era when a single contract didn't set up a player financially for life, had been hired by the Cleveland investment firm of Baxter, Williams and Company "and will receive training as an investment counselor." Lest any Indians fans become unnerved by the news, it was reported that "he will also continue with the Indians."

Though the Indians didn't make a trade during the minor league convention, they weren't idle. They purchased 22-year-old right-handed pitcher Don Fracchia, who'd been voted the top hurler in the Double-A Texas League after winning 15 games and losing 12 for the last-place Beaumont club. Beaumont team president Allen Russell described Fracchia thusly: "he's not very fast, but he gets 'em out."[31] Fracchia cost the Indians $7,500. He never pitched in the big leagues.

Greenberg failed to make a trade at the minor league meeting, but it wasn't due to lack of effort. He had his sights set on Washington outfielder Jackie Jensen, who hit .266 with ten homers and 84 RBI in 1953. The Indians were set in center field with Larry Doby and in left field with Dale Mitchell, but right field had been a revolving door that Greenberg thought Jensen could close. He was startled when the Senators traded Jensen to Boston on December 8, in exchange for outfielder Tom Umphlett and pitcher Mickey McDermott.

"I don't understand it," Greenberg moaned.

> I've been after [Senators owner Clark] Griffith for two months, but he simply wouldn't listen to any offer for Jensen. Now, out of a clear sky, he trades him to Boston. It's pretty discouraging. I think Mr. Griffith could at least have told us that the Red Sox had made an offer for Jensen and given us the opportunity of making a counter proposal. Apparently, he just didn't want us to have him.[32]

Although Greenberg insisted he was open to trading any member of the Tribe's "Big Three" starting pitching staff, he wasn't interested in swapping 17-game winner Early Wynn to the White Sox in exchange for first baseman Ferris Fain, a two-time American League batting champion with the Athletics. Fain's average plummeted to .256 after being traded to Chicago, and he'd hit just eight homers total while leading the league in average in 1951 and 1952. Greenberg wanted more pop from his first baseman and apparently believed Nelson would provide it. Hanging on to Wynn proved to be wise, as his 23 victories would pace the American League in 1954.

The winter meetings ended and Greenberg had nothing to show for his efforts but the acquisition of Fracchia. Cobbledick wasn't impressed and asked how long Tribe fans would pay their way into Municipal Stadium to watch the same old faces finish second ... or possibly lower. He applauded the Red Sox for adding Jensen to a team that had come home a highly respectable fourth (84–69) in 1953 and commended the third-place White Sox for adding outfielder Willard Marshall, obtained from Cincinnati. Though Cobbledick doubted that either deal would affect the balance of power in the American League, he praised the Red Sox and White Sox for trying to strengthen themselves. Greenberg, so far, had done nothing, in Cobbledick's opinion, to give Clevelanders hope that the Indians would be improved in 1954.

1. Hank and Al

As for Cobbledick's question about whether fans would buy tickets to watch another second-place club in 1954, the front office was concerned about lagging attendance as well. Fewer fans had filed through the Municipal Stadium turnstiles each season beginning with 1949, the year after Bill Veeck's Indians electrified northeastern Ohio by winning the pennant and World Series. Since setting the major league record with a paid attendance of 2,620,627 in 1948, the Tribe's gate had steadily decreased to 1,069,176 in 1953. Close (or, as in 1953, not so close) but no cigar was wearing thin with Clevelanders. And Greenberg's bosses had their eyes on the bottom line.

Stengel didn't think anyone would be willing to provide the pitching help the Yankees needed following Sain's retirement. He should've known better. Weiss always plugged the holes in the New York lineup, and he engineered an 11-player, blockbuster deal with the Athletics that figured to give his manager the starting pitcher he wanted and the pinch-hitter he'd need with Mize no longer on the bench. On December 16, Weiss shipped a pair of first basemen, Vic Power and Don Bollweg, and outfielder Bill Renna to Philadelphia in exchange for first baseman (and ex-Indian) Eddie Robinson and third-year pitcher Harry Byrd. Six minor leaguers were also involved in the deal.

"We strengthened ourselves in the departments we needed help the most," Weiss said, noting that while he parted with some young talent, none of the players he sent to the Athletics figured prominently in New York's plans for 1954.[33]

Greenberg, who was about the only American League executive who hadn't made the A's an offer for Byrd, insisted the deal wouldn't alter the Indians' preparations for the coming season. "I haven't given it much thought. It doesn't concern our club," the Tribe's GM insisted.[34]

Greenberg may not have been concerned, but other club bigwigs were. One unidentified executive reportedly walked the halls of the team's offices repeatedly asking "how can the A's do a thing like that? It just doesn't make sense. The Yankees must have given them a bundle of money."[35]

White Sox general manager Frank Lane, whose bid for Byrd was rejected, conceded that the deal appeared to be lopsided in favor of the

Yankees, but said the young players the A's obtained could help turn around that floundering franchise. According to *The Plain Dealer,* Lane offered the A's $50,000 and four players. The *News* reported Lane's offer as $150,000.

Byrd was the player the Yankees wanted, even though the 27-year-old right-hander had led the American League in defeats with 20 (against 11 victories) for a Philadelphia club that won just 59 games in 1953. Byrd had been the league's Rookie of the Year in 1952 with a 15–15 record and 3.31 earned run average. His ERA had ballooned to 5.51 in 1953, but the Yankees no doubt felt Byrd's numbers would improve significantly with a much stronger team behind him.

Robinson was a lifetime .276 hitter with 145 career home runs to his credit. In his only season with the Athletics, Robinson batted just .247 but slugged 22 homers and drove in 102 runs. In spite of those numbers, plus the fact the Yankees gave up two first basemen in the trade, Robinson hadn't been acquired to play in the field. New York needed a full-time pinch-hitter, and Robinson filled the bill nicely. He would lead the American League in both pinch-hitting appearances and pinch-hits in 1954.

Greenberg may not have been panicking over the deal, but columnists for Cleveland's newspapers were. Ed McAuley of the *News* wrote that whatever hope fans around the American League, particularly in Cleveland, might have had that Sain's retirement would significantly weaken the Yankees pitching staff and leave them vulnerable had been removed by Byrd's acquisition. McAuley's colleague, Ed Bang, who had covered the Indians for more than 40 years, concurred. Bang wrote that the Byrd trade was almost enough to convince him to go out on a limb and predict the Yankees would win their sixth straight pennant and world championship.

There was a dissenting opinion in the *News's* sports department. Howard Preston refused to concede the pennant to New York nine days before Christmas. Preston, admitting he was expressing a minority viewpoint, said he considered Byrd to be just a pitcher with great potential, and asked why Robinson had been traded by the Indians, White Sox, Senators and Athletics? Preston saw no reason to cancel the 1954 season and award the championship to the Yankees.

1. Hank and Al

Cobbledick was just as concerned as McAuley and Bang, asking whether Weiss had forced the Athletics to agree to the trade by putting a loaded gun to the head of the team's decision makers. Cobbledick wasn't happy that the Indians were the only team that had finished in the American League's first division in 1953 but not yet made a trade during the off-season. Whitey Lewis, too, was aggravated with Greenberg and echoed Cobbledick's opinion that attendance would continue to plunge in 1954 if the Tribe's general manager didn't provide some hope that the club would seriously contend for the pennant.

Not that there weren't deals waiting to be made. Cobbledick had been reporting for weeks that the Baltimore Orioles, who had been the St. Louis Browns until October, were ready and willing to swap catcher Clint Courtney to the Tribe for catcher Joe Ginsberg and outfielder Al Smith, if only Greenberg would pick up the phone and call Orioles general manager Art Ehlers. Cobbledick was baffled as to why Greenberg wouldn't make the call.

"I won't let Ehlers dictate the terms," explained Greenberg. "I'll make what I consider an equitable deal."[36]

When it came to trading, Greenberg wasn't the only timid Tribesman. Cobbledick conceded that Greenberg didn't deserve all the blame for failing to pull off even one significant trade in his four years as general manager. Cobbledick admitted that, without providing specifics, Al Lopez undoubtedly turned thumbs down on some deals Greenberg wanted to make, labeling the Tribe manager even more cautious than his boss. Cobbledick then explained Greenberg's unique trading philosophy. Greenberg, in the columnist's opinion, rarely made trades because his fellow general managers were too smart to deal with him. Greenberg's odd trading credo called for always getting the better of his trading partner and never trading an opposing team a player it could actually use, while demanding in return a player the Indians needed. If Cobbledick was correct, it was little wonder Greenberg's deals were few and far between.

January passed uneventfully until the annual Ribs and Roasts dinner, at which skits written and performed by Cleveland media members (mostly writers) lampooned all of the city's sports personalities, not just those who wore Indians uniforms (or worked in the club's front office.) Before the frivolity began, Rosen was honored as the Tribe's "man of the year," and Lopez took to the dais to provide a note of optimism amid the prevailing gloom, which had deepened after the Cleveland Browns lost the National Football League championship game to the Detroit Lions in late December, allowing a 16–10 lead to slip away in the contest's closing minute.

"Seriously, I think our ball club will be better," the manager told the gathering. "I don't know whether the Yankees will fold, but we realize they're tough. But we'll be a lot better than we were last year. We are figuring on finishing first."[37]

Lopez's boss noted that Cleveland's $550,000 payroll in 1954 would be the highest in the major leagues. To those who insisted the club needed new faces, Greenberg pointed out that "only 11 men who were with the Indians in 1950 will make the trip with the squad of 46 going to spring training." Getting into the spirit of the occasion, Greenberg said "I am going to take the advice of the baseball writers." He then paused. "As long as it agrees with my ideas."[38]

The good feeling of the Ribs and Roasts having soon passed, Cobbledick wasted no time taking Greenberg to task for some of the comments he made at the dinner. Acknowledging it was true that only 11 players remained from the roster Greenberg inherited when he took the general manager's job, Cobbledick noted that those 11 players formed the Tribe's nucleus: Lemon, Wynn, Garcia, Feller, Rosen, Easter, Avila, Doby, Hegan, Kennedy and Mitchell. The players Greenberg had added to that nucleus consisted of, in Cobbledick's opinion, "a bunch of guys named Joe." Greenberg, according to Cobbledick, was guilty of "the unforgivable [sin] of standing pat on a team that's not good enough."[39]

The mantra from Cleveland's sportswriters that Tribe fans were weary of the same old faces never let up during the winter of 1953–1954. Cobbledick beat the drum loudest, but Ed Bang joined in frequently, urging Greenberg to pull the trigger on a deal, if only for the sake of getting the writers off his back briefly.

Greenberg finally swung a deal on January 20, but it was so unim-

1. Hank and Al

portant Cobbledick didn't even bother commenting on it in his daily column. Greenberg swapped light-hitting (and unhappy) catcher Joe Tipton to the Senators for light-hitting (and unhappy) catcher Mickey Grasso. Tipton was unhappy with his lack of playing time behind Jim Hegan and had requested a trade, threatening to retire rather than play another season with the Indians. Grasso was unhappy because Clark Griffith, unimpressed with his back-up catcher's .209 batting average, wanted to slash Grasso's salary by $3,000. Greenberg signed Grasso for the same $14,000 he'd been paid in 1953, and Grasso said he was certain he'd hit better in Cleveland than he had in Washington.

Greenberg didn't cut Grasso's salary, but he wasn't as generous with some of the men who had contributed to the second-place finish of the previous season. The Indians announced on January 12 that Doby agreed to terms for 1954 with less muss and fuss than expected. Doby had held out in 1953 and accepted a 1954 salary of between $25,000 and $30,000, which represented a cut from the previous year. "I expected some trouble, too," the center fielder said. "Hank was very nice and I'm satisfied. I just want one thing — to have a good year. I know I had a disappointing one in '53."[40] Bob Kennedy reluctantly agreed to a contract that called for "a sizable slash" from his 1953 salary, the direct result of a .236 batting average and a meager 22 RBI, poor numbers even for an outfielder known for his glove and not his bat.

Lemon and Wynn weren't as agreeable as Doby and Kennedy to having their salaries decreased. Both pitchers received contracts calling for less money than they'd been paid in 1953. Both returned the documents to Greenberg minus their signatures. Greenberg explained his philosophy regarding contracts.

> By this time, the players know how we do business. We don't try to outsmart them into signing for less than we think they're worth. The first figure we offer a man is the one we think he deserves. Occasionally, a player will argue his way into a better contract, but in the long run he'll collect about as well as if he never put up an argument. A player who demands, and gets, more than we think he is worth puts himself under the obligation of having an extra good season. And the inferior ones even up and the player's total income is about what it would have been if he had accepted our first offers.[41]

.721

Greenberg justified the offers by pointing to the Tribe's declining attendance figures, which resulted in declining revenue. One unidentified Indian saw Greenberg's point. "If we can't draw the money at the gate, we can't go on getting it in the paycheck," the anonymous player was quoted as saying. "But I've been reading the papers pretty closely and I haven't seen where Greenberg cut his own salary as an economy measure. I figure he's at least as responsible for the falling attendance as we are."[42] Greenberg, however, wasn't working on one-year contracts as the players were. He was in the third year of a three-year pact. However, with that contract expiring at the end of the upcoming season, his performance in the front office, as reflected by the team's performance on the field, would be under review by the team's board of directors. The board would pass judgment on Greenberg sooner than expected.

Greenberg wasn't carrying the Ebenezer Scrooge bit overboard. He signed George Strickland and pitcher Dave Hoskins to 1954 contracts calling for pay increases. Strickland had been a pleasant surprise in 1953, fielding slickly at shortstop and batting .284 with four homers and 47 RBI. He would never approach those offensive numbers again. Hoskins, a product of Greenberg's treasured farm system, had won nine of 12 decisions with a 3.99 ERA in 1953 and appeared to be a building block for the Tribe's pitching staff of the future.

"No first year pitcher in the league won more games [nine]," Greenberg noted when Hoskins' signing was announced. "He represents insurance against any possible decline in our pitching."[43] No one could have known at the time that 1954 would be Hoskins' last season in the major leagues, and he wouldn't win another game.

The demand for new faces in the Cleveland dugout grew louder when Greenberg returned from baseball's winter meeting in New York empty-handed. "The offers were worse than ever, if that's possible," the general manager lamented. "For instance, Boston offered me outfielder Hoot Evers. In return, all they wanted was a regular player (presumed to be Bob Avila.) Frank Lane offered me Freddie Marsh and Luis Aloma. I couldn't back with players like those. We'll just have to go into spring training with what we've got and see what happens. Maybe it's time for us to get lucky and come up with somebody good out of our system."[44]

1. Hank and Al

Marsh might have been a useful spare part for the Tribe — depending on the player or players the Indians would've had to part with to acquire him. Marsh hit .306 in 62 games for Chicago in 1954. Aloma posted an 18–3 record from 1950 through 1953 with the White Sox, but didn't pitch in the majors after 1953.

The Indians added a familiar face to their formidable mound crew in mid–February, inviting former Tigers ace (and Greenberg's old teammate) "Prince" Hal Newhouser to spring training. The former MVP, whose 29 victories led Detroit to the 1945 pennant and World Series championship, had been suffering from a sore arm since 1951 and was released by the Tigers in July of 1953, with a record of 0–1 and an inflated 7.06 ERA. He became a free agent after clearing waivers and was in Florida trying to work out the kinks in his left arm when Greenberg offered him a chance to make the Tribe's staff. Doctors had examined Newhouser and couldn't find anything wrong with him, and he jumped at the chance to make a comeback at age 32.

"I'll just be a rookie getting a try-out," said Newhouser. "I won't discuss a contract until I see if my pitching is good enough to make the team. I know the Indians have one of the best staffs in the business, but I hope to make the grade and preferably as a starter, but if not as a reliever."[45]

"He's a great competitor and if his arm is all right he'll be a tremendous help to us. It certainly is worth the trial," said Greenberg.[46] The general manager revealed that he'd contacted Newhouser about joining the Indians after he was released by Detroit.

> I asked him to come to Cleveland and told him if he was having any arm trouble we'd be happy to try to have it repaired. I told him I thought he was still young enough to have plenty of pitching left in his arm. After all, he won't be 33 until May. Newhouser said the doctors could find nothing wrong with his arm. He said he wanted to rest up and give his arm a whirl during the winter. He went down to Tampa several weeks ago. He worked out for three weeks. I called him down there and he said he felt fine and that his arm was strong. But, he said he wouldn't make a decision until he got back to Detroit. He said he didn't want to sign a contract unless he was certain he could help us. I'm really tickled about his decision.[47]

Greenberg's intuition about his former teammate was right on the money. Newhouser's left arm had one more good season left in it, and while he wasn't able to crack the Tribe's starting rotation, he gave the club a much-needed effective southpaw reliever.

With the start of spring training just days away, Greenberg appeased his critics by making a trade he hoped would shore up the Indians' weakest position: right field. On February 19, he swapped a pair of right-handed minor league pitchers, Bill Upton and Leroy Wheat, to the Athletics for veteran outfielder Dave Philley. The 33-year-old Philley immediately moved to the head of the line for the right field job. Philley was available because he felt his 1953 statistics (.303 batting average, nine homers, 59 RBI) for the woeful Athletics entitled him to a substantial raise over his $18,000 salary. According to the *Press*, Philley wanted his 1953 salary increased by $10,000, a sizable chunk of money to the nearly bankrupt Athletics. Connie Mack's son Earle, who was running the club along with his brother Roy, claimed to have offered Philley an increase of $6,000. Philley said the Athletics offered just $3,000 more than he'd earned the previous season.

"We've got another solid outfielder who ranks with the best in the American League," said Greenberg as he announced the deal. "In spite of the leg injury that handicapped him much of last season, he still played in all of Philadelphia's games. He is very fast and will improve our team speed."[48] Greenberg said he'd spoken with Philley and didn't think the new Indian's contract demands would be a problem. Philley signed two days later. Terms weren't reported, but since Greenberg hadn't cut Grasso's salary, it's reasonable to think he was generous with Philley, who brought a lifetime batting average of .273 to the Indians.

The deal proved to be little more than a salary dump for the financially strapped Athletics, who were preparing for what would prove to be their final season in Philadelphia. Wheat posted an 0–2 record in 11 games over two years, and Upton pitched in just two games with no decisions.

Garcia became the first member of the Tribe's "Big Three" to agree to contract terms on February 20, signing for $30,000. Greenberg saw no reason to give Garcia more money despite his 18–9 record the previous year. That didn't bode well for Lemon, who was 21–15 in 1953, and Wynn, who was 17–12. Greenberg wasn't as concerned with a pitcher's total number of victories as he was with winning percentage, and since Garcia's .667 hadn't earned him a raise, Lemon and Wynn figured to be headed for lengthy holdouts.

Garcia, nicknamed "Big Bear," was happy to be in the fold. "I didn't take a cut and I'm well satisfied. I've been working out for three weeks and am eager for training to start."

As the players reported to Hi Corbett Field in Tucson, Arizona, where the Tribe had trained since 1947, rumors swirled that it would be their last spring in the desert southwest. The *Press* quickly punctured those rumors, reporting that they had been floated by the wily Greenberg in order to frighten the baseball fans of Tucson into thinking they might lose the Indians, and hopefully increasing attendance at the exhibition games. The newspaper reported that it was unlikely the Indians would leave Tucson for Daytona Beach, Florida, where their minor leaguers trained, and it was correct. The Indians stayed in Tucson through the 1992 season.

Veteran outfielder Dale Mitchell signed his 1954 contract on February 21 and had a warning for Philley. "Mitch told me neither Philley nor anyone else is going to chase him to the dugout, and I'm glad he feels that way," Greenberg said. "If we have three outfielders capable of keeping Philley on the bench it'll be all right with me. The more competition we have at every spot the better ball team we'll have."[50]

Philley thought he could be just what the doctor ordered for the Tribe. "The way I look at it, this club needs one thing: the determination to win. I thought the last couple of years the Indians could win if they wanted to bad enough. Now I don't want to sound boastful, but I'll add my share of determination and maybe it'll be just what the club needs. I know I want to win. I ought to. I've played on second division clubs long enough."[51]

Grasso expressed a similar sentiment after being traded to the Indians. "Cleveland had a darn good team last year, it just needed a player who could light a match under the rest of the team. I might be the guy."[52]

Philley's and Grasso's comments didn't ruffle any feathers among the Indians. And they weren't alone in expressing the opinion. Although Cobbledick had earlier defended the Indians against Feller's accusation that they lacked aggressiveness when they tangled with the Yankees, he thought the new additions may have been on to something. After suggesting earlier that the Indians couldn't finish ahead of the Yankees because the Yankees were a better team, Cobbledick expanded on Philley's and Grasso's comments and claimed several American League players (whom he didn't identify, although he said some of them wore pinstripes) had suggested over the years that the difference between the two teams was that the Indians just didn't seem to want to win as badly as the Yankees did. He expressed the hope that fiery competitors such as Philley and Grasso could change the club's culture of passivity.

First to arrive in camp was first baseman Bill Glynn, who showed up a day early. "I didn't want to take any chances on being grounded by bad weather and getting here late. I've got my work cut out for me, so I figure I better be here on time. I've been reading where Luke [Easter] says the job is going to be his until somebody takes it away from him and I see where Nelson had a great winter in Cuba. All I can say is I'll do my best."[52] Glynn blamed his poor 1953 showing offensively on a shoulder injury sustained in spring training that hampered his ability to swing a bat all season.

Although pitching was supposed to be their weakness, the Yankees stunned the baseball establishment by unloading Vic Raschi to the Cardinals in late February after a salary dispute. In exchange, New York was to receive $75,000, some in cash and some in players. The deal was made shortly after Allie Reynolds had signed a contract for $41,500, making him the highest paid pitcher in Yankees history. Raschi was paid $40,000 in 1953 and was holding out for more. George Weiss felt the time had come to send a message to the defending world champions.

"I don't want to make Raschi the whipping boy, but there is an attitude of complacency on the club. Some of the players have become independently wealthy through the winning of five straight world championships."[53] Weiss wanted to make sure everyone wearing pinstripes knew who was in charge, and chose to make an example of Raschi. The message was clear: five consecutive world championships notwithstanding, any Yankee with an inflated opinion of his value to the club (at least as Weiss saw it) was expendable.

1. Hank and Al

Lopez heard the news when he arrived at Tucson's airport. "No kidding! Say, that is a surprise. I heard that Weiss was pretty mad about all those hold-outs, but I never thought he would sell Raschi. Well, he's going to be a tough man to replace. Raschi was still a good pitcher last year. Gave us plenty of trouble, anyway."[54]

Rosen was happy to see Raschi change leagues. "That's the best news I've heard in a long time. My average ought to go up a few points now," the reigning league MVP chuckled.[55] Stengel, who had been fretting about how to replace the 14 victories he lost when Sain retired, now had to concern himself with replacing Raschi's 13 wins from 1953 as well. It appeared unlikely that the arrival of Harry Byrd alone would be enough to pick up the slack.

Greenberg was asked why the Indians didn't make a bid for Raschi after he'd been put on waivers by Weiss, thus indicating his availability. "We had a chance to get Raschi but we didn't want him," said the Tribe GM of a pitcher whose lifetime record was a sparkling 120–50. "I don't know what other clubs in the league could afford to buy him, so I am not surprised that he was waived out of the league."[56] Every American League club passed on Raschi, knowing Weiss had no intention of parting with him for a mere $10,000. The Indians may have been the only team that could, as Greenberg explained, pay Weiss's asking price for Raschi and then meet the pitcher's salary demands, a total package in the $120,000 range. It was also doubtful Weiss would've been willing to send Raschi to the Yankees' closest competitor. The Yankees may have been arrogant, but they weren't stupid.

Taken at face value, Greenberg's comment that Raschi, a pitcher with a career winning percentage of .706, couldn't help the Indians appears to have been the kind of statement that often made writers and fans furious with the general manager. But Greenberg had reasons for not bidding for Raschi, and he detailed them in the *News*.

> I didn't claim him because I didn't think we could use him. He's a right-hander. Besides our top men, we have a couple of right-handers who will win as many games for us as Raschi would. Now here's a fellow 35 years old, with a leg that has given him a lot of trouble. He won 13 games last year, but he completed only seven. He couldn't have won 13 for any other

.721

 club. And now he's a year older. Does that sound like the kind of pitcher you'd want to buy for a lot of money, and then give a $40,000 contract?[57]

Apparently not in Greenberg's opinion, although the argument could've been made (but no Cleveland writer made it) that, had Weiss been willing to sell Raschi to the Indians, his acquisition, even if it helped the Tribe only marginally, figured to substantially weaken the team it had to overcome to win the pennant. For the record, Greenberg was proven right about Raschi's best days being behind him. He was 8–9 with a 4.73 ERA for the Cardinals in 1954 and 0–1 in 1955 before being waived and hooking up with the Kansas City Athletics, for whom he won four games and lost six. Raschi's career record against the Indians was 22–9, and he'd won seven of nine decisions against them in 1952 and 1953. Rosen wasn't the only Indian who wouldn't miss him.

That Greenberg had some holdouts of his own to deal with was driven home on February 24, when Lopez presided over the club's first spring workout. Lemon, Wynn and Feller were absent. It was Feller's first holdout in his lengthy career in Cleveland, which dated back to 1936. Feller laughed at the thought and said that he and Greenberg simply hadn't discussed his contract at all during the off-season and he was certain they'd have no trouble reaching an agreement when Feller arrived in Tucson. He was right. The *Press* reported that Feller signed for $30,000, less than he'd earned in 1953. Feller's highest salary had been $82,000 during the world championship season of 1948, when his earnings were augmented by an attendance clause in his contract. The Indians drew 2.6 million fans to Municipal Stadium that season.

As for the absences of Lemon and Wynn, Greenberg sounded as if their holdouts were the least of his worries. "I'll probably call Lemon and Wynn before long and get this thing settled," the general manager said. "They're going to sign sooner or later and I'd hate to see them miss the first few days of training."[58]

Both of Greenberg's calls proved to be fruitful. Wynn reluctantly agreed to terms on March 1, reportedly accepting a $6,000 cut from his 1953 salary of $38,000. Renowned as a tough competitor who'd throw a brushback pitch at his grandmother if she was crowding the plate, Wynn wasn't about to forget the acrimonious negotiations he'd had with Greenberg, nor the fact that his salary had been reduced two seasons in a row. "You can't win. Nobody can," Wynn told reporters when he arrived in camp. Told by the scribes that he looked lean and mean, Wynn joked, "I took one look at that contract and couldn't afford to eat." He admitted to having done no off-season conditioning. "I just wasn't in the mood. Having to argue like that takes the heart out of you."[59] Wynn was asked why he caved in so quickly.

> Well, I hate to say anything since somebody in Florida wrote that I'd like to train in Tampa and wouldn't mind being traded to the White Sox. I never said that, but you know how those things are. Once they're in the paper, it's hard to rub them out. Hank Greenberg was really sore about that one. Then Hank made me his latest offer, I talked it over with my wife and we decided we liked Cleveland too well to take any chance on being sent elsewhere. It's a good town and we've made a lot of friends there.[60]

Wynn wasn't about to forget two years of hard-nosed contract negotiations with Greenberg. "I'll have a good season," he vowed. "I'll show him."[61]

Lopez didn't want an angry Wynn grousing during training camp.

> When you sign your contract, forget about it," he counseled the pitcher. "Don't carry a grudge around all season long. I know you were unhappy last year. Maybe that didn't have anything to do with the fact that you didn't win as many games as you did the season before, but I know a guy can't do his best when he's not in the right frame of mind. So get your contract problems settled once and for all and forget about 'em. You can have a great year if you set your mind to it.[62]

Two days later, Lemon reached agreement with Greenberg after what was described as a "heated" phone call. Lemon's 1954 salary of $42,000 made him the highest paid hurler in the American League, but was $2,000 less than he'd been paid in 1953. He reported to Tucson in a better frame of mind than Wynn, calling his brief holdout "just one of those things."[63]

Amid all the acrimony, at least between Greenberg and two of his star pitchers, a light note was needed, and Rosen's 30th birthday celebration on March 2 provided it. Two members of Rosen's fan club, Tucson chapter, baked a cake and delivered it to Hi Corbett Field. Spud Goldstein, the

Tribe's traveling secretary, kidded Rosen that "you don't look a day over 35."[64]

To break the tedium before the exhibition season began on March 6, the Indians played three intra-squad games, with coaches Red Kress and Tony Cuccinello calling the shots while Lopez watched. So informal was the first of these encounters that Mitchell and Easter played for both teams. Kress's squad won the first game, 4–0; Cuccinello guided his team to a 6–4 victory to square the series, and then won bragging rights with a 3–0 victory over Kress's men in the rubber match.

One reason the Yankees had won five consecutive world championships was Weiss's thoroughness and attention to detail. Even though it was almost impossible for two ball clubs to be more familiar with each other than the Indians and Yankees, New York dispatched scouts Roy Hamey and Babe Herman to Arizona to keep an eye on the Tribe. Lopez thought the Indians should send a scout to Florida to check out the Yankees, but they didn't. Hamey didn't see much improvement in the Indians. "Philley will help in right field, but I don't see anything else different."[65]

Bill Veeck, a man of leisure after having been forced by the other American League club owners to sell the Browns as a condition of permitting the team to move to Baltimore to become the Orioles, visited Tucson the first week of March and tried to sell Greenberg and Lopez on the attributes of Leroy (Satchel) Paige, who was still fondly remembered in Cleveland for his contribution to the 1948 world champions. Paige had pitched for Veeck's Browns in 1953, and Veeck thought he'd be a welcome addition to the Indians' bullpen.

"Get one thing clear. This doesn't mean a thing to me except that I'd like to see somebody beat the Yankees and I think the Indians are the only club which has a chance. The Indians need a relief pitcher — and Paige is the best. For two or three innings he's as good as he ever was."[66] Paige had won three and lost nine for the Browns in 1953, eight of the defeats in relief. Greenberg and Lopez weren't interested, and neither was any other team. Paige's legendary career was over, with the exception of one inning for Kansas City in 1965, which helped Charles O. Finley draw a few extra fans to watch a last-place club.

1. Hank and Al

The Indians scheduled 35 exhibition games for the spring of 1954, two dozen of them against Leo Durocher's New York Giants, continuing the longest spring training rivalry in baseball. The Indians and Giants had been battling since 1934, with the exception of the World War II years when travel restrictions forced teams to train close to home. The Indians had won 124 games, the Giants 112. Spring games between the Tribe and Giants were unlike games against any other exhibition opponents. Harry Jones noted that Cleveland and New York played for keeps on the diamonds of Arizona and elsewhere as they barnstormed their way to their respective homes, and Jones's counterpart with the *Press*, Frank Gibbons, wrote that the Indians and Giants put on a spring show unlike any other.

A crowd of 5,266 ventured to Hi Corbett Field to witness the first of 24 scheduled encounters pitting the Indians against the Giants, and they got their money's worth and then some. The Giants rallied for three ninth inning runs to grab a 10–9 victory. It was noted in newspaper game accounts that Giants manager Durocher pulled out all the stops to achieve the victory.

Greenberg was pleased with what he'd seen under the Arizona sun. "It's a good group. I think it's the best group we've ever had. I think we've got a good club now. The new men seem to be doing all right. There's a greater spirit of competition here than I've ever seen before," he told reporters before departing for the team's minor league training camp in Daytona Beach.[67]

The Indians' bats were booming in the Arizona heat. Cleveland scored a staggering 64 runs (9, 23, 15 and 17) in its first four exhibitions. On the negative side, the Indians committed a ghastly 15 errors in those same four games. Jones assured his readers the Tribe was neither as prolific offensively nor as pathetic defensively as the early returns seemed to indicate.

On the topic of gloves, it was noted early in the exhibition season that players in both Arizona and Florida were forgetting the new rule requiring players to carry their gloves with them to the dugout when they weren't on the field. Since the advent of gloves in the 1880s, players had left their leather at their positions when their team was at the plate.

After two unidentified American League managers asked that the rule be scrapped, league president Will Harridge made the spring training rounds to poll the players as to their opinions. According to the *News*, the Indians had no problems with the new rule. Lopez said he hadn't heard any complaints. The rule stuck.

The Indians weren't as good as they looked offensively early in the exhibition season, but what about Rudy Regalado? A 23-year-old Californian with just one year of minor league ball under his belt, Regalado wasn't even supposed to be in Tucson. "I wasn't going to bring him here. But he wrote and asked to come here for a few days and I told him it would be all right," said Greenberg.[68] Regalado took advantage of Greenberg's generosity and made it impossible for the Indians to send him to Florida to train with his fellow minor leaguers. Regalado stroked 13 hits in 22 at-bats in the Tribe's first four exhibitions for a .591 average. "Rudy the Red-Hot Rapper" quickly became the talk of training camp.

Aside from Regalado, the other players under the microscope were Nelson and Newhouser. "I don't see how Nelson can miss if he plays the kind of first base for Cleveland that he did for me all last year," said Walter Alston, the rookie manager of the defending National League champion Dodgers, who had managed Nelson in Montreal in 1953.[69] But Nelson was struggling in Tucson, and Regalado's breathtaking break from the gate drew additional attention to Nelson's poor early showing. Lopez was giving Nelson the benefit of the doubt. Having failed to stick with four other teams, Nelson knew this was his last shot at the big leagues, and Lopez thought he was pressing. "I want to give him a chance to relax and get started. I don't know whether he can hit up here, but I know he can field. He hasn't been fielding too well, and that's what makes me think he's feeling the pressure."[70]

Nelson had come to camp echoing a familiar refrain. "In my opinion, I've never been given a thorough trial. I've never had a chance in the big leagues to stay in the line-up long enough at one time to show what I could do." Aware that the Athletics were interested in him, Nelson said he was happy the Indians had purchased his contract. "I'm glad Cleveland got me. I prefer the first division. This is a great opportunity, of course. I am not making any predictions. I know I have to beat out

1. Hank and Al

two good men, Luke Easter and Bill Glynn. But I also know I have always hit above .300 in the minors. I think I can do all right in the majors—if they leave me in there."[71]

Lopez, whose specialty was handling pitchers, chose to bring Newhouser along slowly, not using him in a game until March 13. "I haven't felt the slightest pain," Newhouser said before his first test under game conditions. "A year ago, I was hurting from my shoulder to my fingertips. I've been throwing for over a month now, in Florida and here, and lately I've been throwing pretty hard. I'll admit I was pretty doubtful when I came out here. I've been living with this arm so long I had resigned myself to its being no good. Now I don't know. Let's wait awhile. But right now I'm feeling more optimistic than I have for years."[72]

Used in relief against the Giants, Newhouser surrendered ten hits and six runs in three innings of work as the Indians lost, 16–6. Lopez seemed unconcerned. "I thought he looked pretty good. He threw pretty well considering this was his first time out. Actually, the first big test will come tomorrow. If his arm feels good then I'd say he won't have any more trouble with it."[73]

Pitching coach Mel Harder, a 223-game winner for the Indians during a 20-year career, was satisfied with Newhouser's first appearance in a game since the summer of 1953. "He had a good overhand motion," said Harder. "He threw with his shoulder, a good sign. He seemed very free in his last inning and broke off a couple of good curves. I was quite pleased."[74]

Newhouser took the rocky outing in stride. "My arm felt all right. I didn't like seeing them hit all those line drives, though. I was afraid somebody might get hurt."[75]

Newhouser was pitching for a job. Garcia's spot in the starting rotation was secure, but he raised a few eyebrows when he was hammered by the Orioles in his second appearance of the spring. Scheduled to pitch three innings, the Big Bear was lifted after he allowed seven runs in just two innings of work. For the spring, Garcia had pitched four frames and been strafed for 17 runs.

"I've been concentrating on holding the runners on base this spring and I've been getting a lot of practice," the pitcher cracked. "Every time

I look up, there's another man on base." Garcia attributed his troubles to the fact that, for the first time in his major league career, he hadn't done any throwing during the winter. "So apparently my arm is just not strong yet. I think I'm throwing as hard, but the ball doesn't travel as fast."[76]

The biggest news of training camp was made off the field, when the Indians announced that Greenberg had been signed to a new, two-year contract. He and Lopez were now under contract through the 1955 season. The decision to offer Greenberg a new deal had been made by the club's board of directors at their February meeting, but not announced until March 21.

"I made the proposal and the directors unanimously agreed that Greenberg should have a new contract," said Indians president Myron H. (Mike) Wilson. "I suppose you might call it a vote of confidence. We feel he has done a good job. So many people have been writing to the club asking 'what about Greenberg?' we felt it was better to settle the thing before the start of a new season."[77] Greenberg had been signed to his previous contract by the club's previous management. Wilson, who owned just 3 percent of the team's stock as part of the group that bought the Indians from Veeck in 1949, led the group of shareholders who ousted team president Ellis Ryan in 1952 when Ryan decided to dismiss Greenberg. Wilson became club president following Ryan's departure.

Wilson said Greenberg didn't seek the contract extension. "We got to talking one day and he was curious about how long I would stay on as president. I told him as long as I had competent people such as himself and Lopez. I guess that's where the idea got started."[78] As had been the case with Lopez, Greenberg's new contract didn't call for a raise. He'd continue to be paid $65,000 annually.

The extension didn't sit well with Cobbledick, who had come to the conclusion after watching Greenberg run the club for four years that he was a failure. Cobbledick quoted Alva Bradley, the Indians' team president from 1928–1946, who claimed that "I hire the manager. The public fires him," and said that principle, in the opinion of the current team ownership, didn't apply to the front office, since Tribe fans had been making their displeasure with Greenberg known for a couple of years, most obviously at the box office.

1. Hank and Al

Whitey Lewis didn't approve of the board of directors' decision to extend Greenberg's contract either, and said Greenberg's re-hiring was the result of his friendship with Wilson. Wilson, in Lewis's opinion, knew nothing about baseball and proved it by keeping Greenberg on the job.

Ed McAuley and Ed Bang saw things differently. McAuley wrote that Greenberg was obviously doing a better job than six of the other general managers in the American League ... the exception, of course, being Weiss. Bang wrote that the criticism of Greenberg mystified him, and that the positive things he'd done as the Tribe's GM far outweighed his mistakes.

One of the players Greenberg acquired during the off-season, Mickey Grasso, was lost to the Indians for at least three months when he suffered a broken ankle sliding into second base in a game against the Cubs on March 24. Grasso's ankle was shattered in six places. On the plus side, Newhouser, who reported no pain or stiffness in his arm the day after his first spring outing, pitched three scoreless and hitless innings as the Tribe clobbered the Cubs, 12–2. The following day, Regalado continued his torrid spring, belting his sixth and seventh home runs (all of them off Cubs pitching) and adding a pair of singles in a 6–3 victory. Regalado's average had dropped to .447, but he had 17 runs batted in.

According to one source, the deal Cobbledick spent the winter urging Greenberg to make with Baltimore for Clint Courtney almost came to pass. Orioles first baseman Dick Kryhoski told reporters that only an errant pitch from the Giants' John McCall kept him from being sent to Cleveland, along with Courtney, in exchange for Mitchell, Bob Kennedy, Al Smith and Dave Pope in mid–March. McCall's pitch broke Kryhoski's wrist, cancelling the deal. Baltimore general manager Art Ehlers denied Kryhoski's claim, saying "Dick's name has never been mentioned to any club in connection with a deal."[79]

Though the Indians were in the market for a first baseman, sending Mitchell to Baltimore would've left Greenberg searching for a new left fielder, although he may have believed Wally Westlake could handle the position. No thought was being given to trying Regalado in the outfield.

The Tribe broke camp in Tucson on March 25 and headed for Oklahoma City, where it would begin its annual barnstorming tour against the Giants, making its way north by train. In response to the Pittsburgh Pirates announcement that they would travel exclusively by air in 1954, Cleveland's traveling secretary said the club would continue to ride the rails to many of its road games. "We never have made more than one or two flights a season, but this year we will make six or possibly more," said Spud Goldstein. "We looked into the possibility of traveling exclusively by air, but we found that there were too many restrictions. In the first place, you can't load the trunks on a plane so they have to go by train. And because of weather conditions, you must have stand-by rail transportation at all times. The railroads don't like their equipment being tied up that way, either."[80]

The Indians lost both games in Oklahoma City. Lopez continued to give Nelson every chance to claim the first base job, and Nelson continued to disappoint, going hitless in three at-bats in the first game to lower his average to a puny .200 as the Indians dropped a 6–3 decision. One error and two other defensive misplays prompted Jones to declare Nelson the goat of the Indians' 10–4 loss in the second game.

The *News*, in its unattributed "Indian Items" column, went further. Nelson, the newspaper said, "can't possibly be as bad he now appears. Nobody could be that bad!"[81] On the bright side, Regalado, who was playing as well as Nelson was playing poorly, swatted a pair of home runs, giving him nine for the spring. In fairness to Nelson, the *News* pointed out that a howling wind in Tulsa cost him a home run and a triple in a 4–1 loss to the Giants the following day.

Cobbledick spent most of training camp in Arizona, and he didn't like what he saw as the regular season approached. In an effort to confirm his opinion that the Tribe's woes began in the general manager's office, he quoted three players, whom he declined to identify, who were just as unhappy with Greenberg as he was.

"If it hadn't been for Greenberg, we'd have won the pennant the last three years," he quoted one player as saying. "This is the unhappiest ball club I've ever seen. I'll bet there aren't more than three satisfied players in the camp," said another. Finally, Cobbledick quoted another anonymous Indian as saying "off the record, this is a deteriorating ball club. It has tried to stand still for three years, and in this business there's no standing still. You go forward or you go backward. We're going backward."[82]

Among the experts who agreed with Cobbledick and the players he quoted in his column was Boston's Ted Williams, who at the time was just returning to the Red Sox line-up after injuring a shoulder early in training camp. "The Indians? How can they be better? They're an old ball club and they haven't done anything to help themselves."[83] The Splendid Splinter never was one to sugarcoat his opinions.

Cobbledick wasn't alone in his assessment of the Indians, and Lopez was keenly aware of the grumbling. "No team looks good losing," he said after the Indians were drubbed twice in Oklahoma City. "Soon as we start hitting and win a few ball games it'll be different."[84]

Newhouser pitched five impressive innings as the Indians lost to the Giants in Houston, 4–2, on March 31. "Prince Hal" was charged with all four runs, but only one was earned, and New York managed just three hits. The Giants scored three times in the first inning, each tally being unearned due to a pair of errors by Regalado at second base. Jones told his readers Newhouser's performance cemented his spot on the roster, assuming Newhouser wanted to pitch for Cleveland.

With Philley expected to solve the Indians' right field problem, the only position that hadn't been nailed down as the barnstorming tour continued was first base, where Nelson bumbled and stumbled, and Easter and Glynn were regarded as stop-gaps at best. Though Regalado kept swinging a hot bat, Lopez insisted on using him at second base, even though he'd played first at the University of Southern California. That infuriated Cobbledick, who pleaded in his column with the manager to give Regalado a shot. Lopez was adamant about using him elsewhere.

"I just don't picture Rudy as a first baseman," said Lopez. "He's not a small fellow, but he's not as big as a right-handed first baseman ought to be. A left-hander has an advantage at that position, but fellows like Hank Greenberg and Hal Trosky, for example, could do the job on account of their extraordinary reach."[85]

McAuley wasn't as convinced as Cobbledick that Regalado was a bona-fide major leaguer. He agreed with Lopez that Regalado wasn't a first baseman. But he disagreed with Lopez that Regalado was a second baseman. McAuley suggested solving the first base dilemma by replacing Rosen at third base with Regalado and moving Rosen to first. Lopez didn't like that idea, either.

Lopez had a reason not to move Rosen across the diamond. "That would kill off all the incentive Nelson, Glynn or Easter now have. What better time is there to test Nelson than in spring training? There's plenty of time later for shifting around — if it becomes necessary."[86]

Whitey Lewis's candidate for first base was the 38-year-old Easter, who, in the columnist's opinion, had proven he could hit major league pitching. Nelson hadn't. If spring training was any indication, Nelson was proving that he couldn't.

In Florida, the Yankees were having even more trouble winning exhibition games than the Indians. A 9–3 loss to Pittsburgh on March 31 left the defending champions with an 8–16 slate and drew a stern warning from co-owner Dan Topping, who accused his players of being overconfident. "They think that nobody can beat them. The five straight pennants have got them to thinking that way. Well, they'll have to get that idea out of the back of their heads." In the next breath, however, Topping claimed not to be concerned, particularly after meeting with Weiss and Stengel.

"Stengel isn't concerned, so why should I be? There are reasons why some games were lost. Casey preferred to look at young players and see what he had for the future."[87] Topping's manager had been in baseball far too long to worry about how a veteran team such as his World Series champions performed in games that didn't count. The Pirates improved their exhibition record to 12–6 with the victory over New York. Pittsburgh would lose 101 games in 1954, almost twice as many as the Yankees.

As the Indians and Giants continued their travels, Grasso remained in a hospital in Mesa, Arizona. To help his broken ankle heal properly, doctors had inserted a pin in it. Initial estimates that the Tribe's back-up catcher would miss three months now appeared overly optimistic.

1. Hank and Al

There was a strong possibility Grasso's season was over. Fortunately for the Indians, young Hal Naragon, a local product from nearby Barberton, Ohio, had impressed both behind the plate and with the bat. With Grasso likely done for the year, Naragon's chances of sticking with the big league club as Jim Hegan's understudy increased.

Garcia's and Nelson's miserable springs continued while the Indians kept dropping games to the Giants. Nelson was hitless in four trips to the plate in a 4–0 loss on April 2, the first time the Tribe had failed to score in an exhibition game. Nelson's average fell to .170 with the "oh-fer." Two days later, Garcia allowed ten hits and six runs in a five-inning outing as New York won again, 6–1. The pounding included back-to-back home runs by Willie Mays and Monte Irvin. Garcia had given up 29 runs on 41 hits in just 16 innings.

"I'm just getting racked, that's all," the pitcher said. "I'm trying as hard as I can but I can't get anybody out."[88] Lopez thought lack of work was Garcia's problem. "I'm going to use him oftener this week. I may let him pitch a couple innings each day. That ought to straighten him out."[89]

In the same game, Nelson's average plummeted to .161 as he took another collar. "I can't believe he's that bad," said Lopez. "I'm going to rest him a few days, then give him another chance. Maybe he'll snap out of it."[90] Although Nelson's acquisition from Brooklyn had been accompanied by considerable publicity, *The Plain Dealer* revealed that every penny of the $35,000 purchase price for Nelson and Gale Wade, an outfielder who wouldn't make the Tribe's 25-man squad, had gone to Fort Worth, Wade's team. That meant Nelson, the MVP of the International League, had been a mere "throw-in." He spent the spring of 1954 performing like one.

Lopez had a surprise visitor when the Tribe's road show stopped for a game in Dallas, Texas, on April 3. Phil Cavarretta, a Dallas resident and the 1945 National League batting champion who, just a few days before, had been relieved of his duties as manager of the Cubs, asked Lopez for a tryout. Lopez didn't refuse, but told Cavarretta his chances of making the team were virtually nil, so Cavarretta approached Durocher with the same request. Cavarretta worked out with the Giants but eventually stayed in Chicago, signing with the White Sox.

Newhouser's last spring appearance solidified his place on the Cleveland pitching staff. In a 2–1 loss on April 6, Newhouser held the Giants to an unearned run on two hits over five innings. He still wasn't under contract to the Indians, however, and was free to sign with any team that had been impressed with his performance. While there seemed to be little doubt Newhouser would wear an Indians uniform in 1954, a rumor made the rounds that the White Sox were interested and might make him an offer. It was unlikely that Greenberg would get involved in a bidding war for his former teammate's services.

Upon returning to Cleveland after four weeks studying the Tribe's farmhands in Daytona Beach, Greenberg offered his assessment of the upcoming campaign.

> It's been said that we need new faces. We have the new faces. There's Philley, definitely a regular, plus Naragon, Nelson, [Don] Mossi, [Dick] Tomanek, [Jose] Santiago, Regalado and several others. The Indians, I say they have a great chance. Competition for jobs has been the big thing. Right along I've maintained that the Yankees are weaker. Jerry Coleman's legs don't seem to be holding up and they'll miss Vic Raschi.... It looks like a tight race this season — Boston, Chicago, Cleveland or New York — any one of them could do it.[91]

While the Indians concluded their barnstorming tour in Indianapolis, the home of their Triple-A minor league affiliate, on April 11, Newhouser was in Greenberg's office at Municipal Stadium signing a contract. "There was no bartering and I accepted Hank's first proposal. I know the Indians are taking a gamble with me and I certainly hope I'm able to do the ball club some good. My arm feels good now, but, of course, I don't know when the pain might return. I'm ready to work any place — either the bullpen or as a starter."[92] Newhouser said he'd received offers from three other teams, but didn't identify them. The *News* estimated Newhouser's salary at $15,000.

"I'm glad Newhouser is with us," said Lopez, "although I can't truthfully say that I'm certain right now where he will be used. I don't think his place is in the bullpen, especially in the bad weather we usually get early in the season."[93]

1. Hank and Al

As the barnstorming series with the Giants drew to a close, a noted authority on how to play center field, Hall of Famer Tris Speaker, who had managed the Indians to their first World Series title in 1920 while playing the position and batting .388, was asked for his assessment of Willie Mays, the Giants' young outfielder. Mays had played in just 155 games in 1951 and 1952, missing the entire 1953 season due to military service. "He looks like a promising player," was all Speaker had to say.[94]

Lopez thought Mays had plenty to prove. "We've got to wait a few years before comparing him to great ballplayers."[95] According to Frank Gibbons, the Indians weren't all that impressed with Mays, the consensus being that he'd hit about .280 and wasn't as good defensively as Boston center fielder Jim Piersall. Mays would lead the National League with a .345 batting average in 1954, and the Indians would get a first-hand look at his prowess with the glove in the first game of the World Series in late September.

With one exception, the writers who earned their salaries covering the Indians weren't enthusiastic about the 1954 edition. Jones, Lebovitz and McAuley picked the Tribe for another second-place finish, although Lebovitz professed to believe the Indians had their best shot at a pennant since 1948. Lewis thought 1954 would be the year both the Indians and Yankees would tumble, predicting the White Sox would win the pennant, with Cleveland sliding to third place.

Gibbons, however, saw something in Tucson that led him to believe 1954 would be the Tribe's year. He tabbed the Indians to break the stranglehold the Yankees had held on the American League pennant since 1949. He also advised any readers who might actually risk their money based on his prediction that they may want to put a few dollars on the Indians at the place window, too, just to be on the safe side.

Not everyone was as unimpressed by the Indians as the local writers. Bill Corum of the International News Service picked the team to win the pennant, although it was hardly a ringing endorsement. "I pick the Cleveland Indians to take away what amounts to the Yankees' permanent stick of peppermint candy," wrote Corum. "I'm not picking them to win the pennant so much as the Yanks to lose. I'm only guessing that it'll be Cleveland since, if the Yankees lose, somebody else has got to win."[96]

.721

Corum wasn't the only prognosticator who believed the Yankees to be vulnerable. Some of the writers who covered the Bronx Bombers on a daily basis felt the same way. Their opinions were presented to Cleveland fans by the *News* shortly before the season began.

Roger Kahn, *Herald Tribune*: "The Indians will probably finish second from force of habit."

Charles Feeney, *Long Island Press*: "This could turn out to be a disastrous year for the Indians. They failed to win with top notch pitching and now their pitchers may be on the downgrade. I'm picking the Indians to drop to fourth place this year."

Barney Kremenko, *Journal American*: "First base is still a problem, but if that is ironed out favorably, another flag may fly on Municipal Stadium."

Lewis Effrat, *Times*: "Al Lopez, a sound manager, has a chance to bring the Indians home in front this time, but this observer cannot pick them higher than second place. The Yankees figure to top them again."

Joe King, *World Telegram and*

The 1954 American League champion Cleveland Indians. Team elder statesman Bob Feller is seated front left (Cleveland Public Library).

1. Hank and Al

Sun: "Indians add up about the same as last year, with possible added depth in pitching."

Jim McCulley, *Daily News*: "I think the Yanks are due for a fall and will miss Raschi despite the fact that he was on his way down. The flag appears to be up for grabs between the Yanks, Red Sox, Indians and White Sox."

Arch Murray, *Post*: "This should be either a big year or a disastrous one for the Indians. There'll be no half-way finish this time, meaning they'll either go all the way or drop to third or fourth. If the Yankees grow fat-headed and take things too much for granted, the Indians could go all the way."

Ken Smith, *Daily Mirror*: "I have heard less Yankee talk around the Indians than usual and that is the best sign. Previously, they appeared to look for Yankees under their beds. The Indians are still the hope of the world to knock off the champs."[97]

Lopez was asked by the *News* to size up his team as spring training concluded.

> This 1954 edition of the Indians is the best club I have ever managed. It's better than our '52 team which fell short of the pennant by two games. And I'm convinced from what I've seen this spring, we have made quite an improvement over what we had last year at this time. I can't make any predictions that would have any real value because I haven't seen the clubs in Florida. I do feel the league will have better balance this year, with Washington and Baltimore being stronger, and I believe this will work to our advantage. It will force the Yanks to use their better pitchers more often, rather than save them for the contenders as they did in the past.[98]

The *Press* got a more definitive assessment from Lopez. "We will finish no worse than second and will give the Yankees a better fight than last year. The Yankees are bound to be weaker due to the loss of Billy Martin [to military service], Vic Raschi and Johnny Mize. The Indians are bound to be stronger because of Dave Philley, Don Mossi, Dick Tomanek and Rudy Regalado. Hal Newhouser should also help."[99]

The *News* also asked Leo Durocher for his assessment of his club's frequent spring training opponent. "I like the Indians," said the Lip. "They're a real good ball club, well-balanced. The Indians are a better ball club now than they were last spring. I'm discounting completely the

.721

fact that my club has whacked them so often on this tour.... I realize we're not that good and they're not that bad. The Indians simply aren't hitting yet; that's the whole answer." As for his prediction regarding the upcoming pennant race, Durocher was uncharacteristically diplomatic. "It should be a terrific race in your league," he concluded.[100]

Among other prognosticators, 145 players polled by *Sport* magazine picked the Yankees to win another pennant. Thirty-five favored the Indians and 25 liked the White Sox. The Baseball Writers' Association of America predicted a third-place finish for the Tribe, behind New York and Chicago. Legendary sportswriter Grantland Rice, while not predicting a Cleveland pennant, saw trouble ahead for the Yankees. "The outlook at present is that Stengel has the toughest job ahead of him that he has known for the last six years," was Rice's opinion.[101]

The United Press picked the Yankees to win, followed by the Indians, White Sox and Red Sox. In the National League, the defending champion Dodgers were chosen to repeat, trailed by St. Louis, Milwaukee and the Giants. The Scripps-Howard newspaper experts thought the Yankees would grab another flag, with the Indians slipping to third, behind Chicago and ahead of Boston. In the National League, the Dodgers were the choice to finish ahead of Milwaukee, St. Louis and the Giants. No one was particularly impressed by Durocher's team.

Giants shortstop Alvin Dark had seen a lot of the Indians as the two clubs barnstormed their way north, and he liked what he saw.

> Don't worry about your club. I'm not kiddin'. You have a better team now than last year at this time. Pay no attention to what you see here in spring training. It don't mean nothin'. You know Rosen and Avila are goin' to hit during the regular season. I'm tellin' you, your club is improved. Much more depth. You watch and see. To me, your pitching looks very, very good.[102]

The Indians lost their last exhibition game when Mays tripled in the top of the tenth inning and scored on a single by Don Mueller off Bob Chakales, a perpetual prospect who was running out of chances to stick with the Indians. The 5–4 defeat gave the Indians a 13–16 record for the spring, 8–13 against the Giants. The Yankees were even worse, winning eight and losing 19.

The Indians and Giants hadn't seen the last of each other in 1954.

2

A Slow Start

It was probably the same reaction most rookies had when gazing around Cleveland Municipal Stadium for the first time.

"Holy cow! This is a big place!" said Rudy Regalado as he and his new teammates worked out in the 76,000-seat concrete and steel edifice on the southern shore of Lake Erie on April 12.[1] The big place hadn't seen many large crowds in 1953, despite the Indians' second-place finish, and it would be up to Regalado and his teammates to change that in the season that would begin the next day in Chicago.

"Regalado was the big surprise of the training season," Al Lopez told reporters before putting his team through its paces. "The Giants used the best they had all the way against us and his average speaks for itself. Yes, I think he can hit all right."

Lopez had also been impressed with rookie left-handed reliever Don Mossi who, like Regalado, came from out of nowhere to win a roster spot. "Mossi has a fastball that does things. He could be the answer to our need for a left-hander in the bullpen."[2]

Lopez was glad to hear that the Yankees had obtained veteran outfielder Enos Slaughter from the Cardinals the day before. "It shows the Yanks are plenty worried," suggested the manager. "They must be worried about Mickey Mantle and also about their pinch-hitting. Slaughter is a hustler, but he's 38 and just about all through, from what I am told. If they play him in the outfield, they'll have to put a younger man on the bench."[3]

After the workout, Lopez addressed the Cleveland Advertising Club's annual luncheon welcoming the team home. Asked for a prediction as to where the Indians would finish in 1954, the manager said "all I'm hoping is to finish one notch higher."[4]

Bob Feller represented the players at the luncheon and was guardedly optimistic about the Tribe's prospects. "It looks as though we have good material, but getting the right man in the right spot may take a Houdini. I'm glad that Al Lopez has that job and not me."[5]

Cleveland's new mayor, Anthony Celebrezze, offered words of encouragement based on personal experience. "When I decided to run for mayor, none of the experts gave me a chance, either, and look what happened."[6] Celebrezze had been elected in a landslide the previous November.

The Indians won the opening day match-up of anticipated contenders before a record crowd of 31,026 at Comiskey Park on April 13. With left fielder Wally Westlake and shortstop George Strickland contributing home runs, and second baseman Bob Avila adding four hits in six at-bats, the Indians chased White Sox starter Billy Pierce in the seventh inning and cruised to an 8–2 victory behind a complete-game nine-hitter by Early Wynn, who took advantage of his first opportunity to show Hank Greenberg he didn't deserve to have his salary slashed for the second straight year. It was Lopez's fourth consecutive opening day victory as Indians manager.

At Griffith Stadium in Washington, the defending champion Yankees lost to the Senators, 5–3, in ten innings.

Cleveland swept its brief two-game set from the White Sox. Westlake homered for the second straight game; Bill Glynn, who won the first base job almost by default, stroked four hits; and Bob Lemon pitched a complete-game three-hitter as the Tribe won, 6–3. The Indians made quick work of Chicago rookie starter Jack Harshman and appeared to have left their offensive struggles in spring training. "Last week against the Giants we didn't hit at all," said Lopez. "It didn't look as if we were ever going to hit."[7] Lopez was also happy to defeat a pair of lefties. "I am happy to see us take care of these lefthanders so early. Seems to me the big Yankee pitchers now are Whitey Ford and Ed Lopat and they threw left-handed the last time I looked."[8]

Avila said he was never concerned about the Indians' lack of offense.

2. A Slow Start

The Indians charge on to the field in the season opener at Chicago's Comiskey Park. Their victory over the White Sox would be the first of 111 wins (Cleveland Public Library).

"Spring training — phooey! The season's open now. The base hits count!"[9]

The Tribe's two victories didn't impress White Sox owner Chuck Comiskey, the son of the club's founder, Hall of Famer Charles Comiskey. "Nice club you have," he told Cleveland writers. "Ought to come in second again."[10] Comiskey didn't mean second to the Yankees. He meant second to the White Sox.

The fan apathy Gordon Cobbledick wrote of so often during the winter was on display at the Indians' April 15 home opener. Municipal Stadium was just slightly over half full, and the 40,421 patrons left disappointed as the Detroit Tigers spoiled the party with a 3–2 victory. Spectators sat through a 90-minute rain delay, and, according to the *News*, it was the threatening weather that kept the gathering from approaching the 60,000 mark. A storm struck after the Indians had squandered a chance to break a 2–2 tie in the home half of the eighth inning. After they loaded the bases with two out, Dale Mitchell pinch-hit for Westlake, who had, at least temporarily, taken the left field job from him, and flied out.

Lopez chose to send Mike Garcia back to the mound once the deluge had subsided, and Garcia surrendered what proved to be the winning run without allowing a ball to leave the infield. He walked Ray Boone and Walt Dropo to start the ninth. Glynn made a good play on Al Kaline's bunt, forcing Boone at third base. Everyone was safe when Strickland couldn't make a play on Bill Tuttle's grounder to deep short, and Dropo scored as Matt Batts hit another ground ball to shortstop and was tossed out by Strickland. Tigers reliever Ralph Branca surrendered a pinch-hit single to Luke Easter in the home half of the ninth which did no damage. Lopez sent Rocky Nelson to the plate to pinch-hit for Garcia, and Branca induced Nelson to foul out on a 2-and-0 pitch. Lopez was asked if it was wise to give Nelson the green light considering how poorly he'd hit in spring training. Lopez responded that Nelson's job was to get a hit, not to walk.

Al Rosen insisted he'd been interfered with by Kaline as he tried to field Batts' ball. "I was all set to field the ball and make the play at home when I was hit. I know it sounds like an alibi, but I've been in this game too long to make excuses. You noticed I went right for the umpire, but nobody saw a thing."[11] Garcia, who couldn't get anyone out in spring training, took the hard-luck loss. He allowed just four hits and the two ninth-inning walks, which proved to be his undoing, as he authored the Tribe's third straight complete game. Though disappointed with the loss, Garcia was pleased by the way he threw the ball after a miserable spring.

"You're doggone right it bothered me. I was trying to get those batters out and I couldn't. Believe me, I wasn't feeling so confident when the season opened. But at least I proved to myself that I can still throw fast and I had a darn good curve. I'll take my chances any time with the kind of stuff I had today."[12]

April 16 was an off-day for the players, but not the front office. Lopez and Hank Greenberg spent the day at Municipal Stadium working the phones, seeking to make a trade. Speculation had it Cleveland and Baltimore were close to a deal. That speculation proved to be accurate.

2. A Slow Start

After using just three pitchers in the first three games, Lopez needed five pitchers in the fourth. The White Sox, still looking for their first victory of the young season, disposed of Tribe starter Art Houtteman in the first inning. Houtteman's third pitch of the game was bashed over Municipal Stadium's left field fence by light-hitting Chicago shortstop Chico Carrasquel, and before Lopez could get Dick Tomanek warmed up and into the game, the White Sox had scored five times. Tomanek, Jose Santiago (another spring training find, and not to be confused with the Jose Santiago who pitched for Kansas City and Boston in the 1960s), Ray Narleski and Don Mossi held Chicago to four hits over the final eight and one-third innings, but the damage had been done. Former Yankee Bob Keegan limited the Indians to four hits and the White Sox were in the win column, 8–1.

Tomanek had been forced from the mound in the second inning with an elbow injury. "At first I thought it would go away, but instead it kept hurting more. Now I can hardly lift my arm," the pitcher said.[13] Lopez was prepared to make a roster move as the Indians prepared for a lengthy road trip. "If his arm feels better, maybe he can rejoin us somewhere along the way. If not, he'll just have to stay here and work out as best he can."[14]

Tomanek stayed in Cleveland when the Indians hit the road. His injury was termed "curve ball pitcher's disease" by team physician Dr. Don Kelley, and it would sideline him for the rest of the season. Tomanek would be sent to the Tribe's Triple-A farm club in Indianapolis on April 26. Lopez called Tomanek "an outstanding prospect. I consider him a starter, not a relief pitcher. Otherwise, I would keep him with us."[15] Tomanek wouldn't pitch for the Indians again until 1957. He'd finish his career with a 10–10 record and 4.95 earned run average.

The negotiations with the Orioles produced a deal that was announced after the loss to the White Sox. The Indians sent outfielder Bob Kennedy to Baltimore for outfielder/third baseman Jim Dyck. "We hated to let Kennedy go, but maybe he will get the chance at Baltimore," said Lopez. "I know that's what he wants. When we went to spring training this year, he asked me where he stood on the club and I told him there was little chance for him to play every day. I told him if we kept

.721

him it would be for insurance sake. He said he didn't think he had many baseball years left and he hated to spend them sitting on the bench. I don't blame him. I hope he gets the break in Baltimore."[16]

Lopez said Dyck, who hit .213 with nine homers and 27 RBI for the Browns in 1953, would strengthen the Indians' bench. Since Dyck wasn't about to move Rosen off third base and wasn't needed in the outfield, it was immediately speculated that he'd been acquired only to be sent elsewhere in a deal that was still being negotiated. "We're still trying to strengthen the team, and if we can do it by trading Dyck, we will," was all Lopez said about the possibility that Dyck's stay in Cleveland would be brief.[17]

Former Indian Orestes "Minnie" Minoso, then with the White Sox, was among those surprised that Nelson had batted just once (and failed to get a hit) in the Tribe's first four games. "Rocky real good hitter in Cuba. Good fielder, good hustler, too. Sure is funny he don't hit up here," said Minoso.[18] The Indians didn't find it funny, although Glynn's quick start made Nelson's failure easier to swallow.

Lopez sent Wynn to the mound to try to win his second decision against Chicago in a week in what was supposed to be the first game of a doubleheader on Easter Sunday. Wynn and the Indians led, 2–1, in the fifth inning before the sky caved in both figuratively and literally. The White Sox plated five runs in the fifth, the big blow being Minoso's three-run homer. The Indians cut their deficit to 6–3 before it began to rain after the home half of the sixth inning. The game wasn't resumed, and the second game was postponed. The first home stand of 1954 was over.

White Sox manager Paul Richards offered an early assessment of the American League pennant race after his club had split its first four games with the Indians. "I definitely feel Cleveland has a very good chance to win the pennant, along with us. This year the Yanks aren't strong enough to say they've got it, by any means."[19]

Only five games had been played, and some Cleveland writers were already, if not reaching for the panic button, at least eyeing it warily. Harry Jones was concerned about the upcoming 18-game road trip. The good news was that after the trip was over, the Indians would already have played slightly more than a quarter of their road schedule for the

2. A Slow Start

entire season by early in May. The bad news was that the Indians, according to Jones, were a poor road club and could find themselves out of the race early with 20 of their first 23 games being played away from home. The trip was crucial, in Jones' estimation, and he thought a 10–8 record was a reasonable expectation.

"It's an important trip, all right. It might even be our most important trip of the year," admitted Lopez.[20] For the record, the Indians had posted road marks of 40–37, 44–33 and 39–38 in Lopez's three years as manager.

The trip opened with a 2–1 Tribe victory in Baltimore's Memorial Stadium on April 21, achieved in front of 43,383 disappointed fans who attended the first night game in the city's brief major league history. Baltimore's Bob Turley carried a no-hitter into the ninth inning, striking out 13. After he fanned the first batter in the ninth, the game turned quickly as Rosen singled and Doby smashed a two-run homer that held up as the game winner when Lemon kept the Birds off the scoreboard in the ninth. Lemon scattered eight hits in picking up his second victory.

After the game, Feller was asked if he feared Turley might break his major league record of 18 strikeouts in a game, set against Detroit in October of 1938. "I figured he'd have a chance to beat me if he had 15 at the end of seven innings," said Feller. "When he got only one in the sixth to raise his total to 11, I was sure my record wouldn't be broken."[21]

Baltimore earned a series split with a 4–1 win the following day. Orioles pitcher Duane Pillette dispatched the offensively challenged visitors with ease, allowing just five hits. Pillette forced in the Indians' only run with a first-inning, bases-loaded walk. Baltimore made quick work of Garcia, scoring three times on four hits in the first frame as the Big Bear departed without recording an out. Houtteman followed with eight innings of brilliant relief in a losing effort. There was one positive development: Dave Philley had one of the five hits allowed by Pillette, snapping an 0-for-25 slump. That was a rough way to debut with a new team, especially one expected to be a contender.

Rumor had it that the Indians would make another trade with Baltimore, either while they were in town or sometime during their eastern trip. If they did, Clint Courtney wouldn't be included. Asked about the Tribe's overtures—or lack of overtures—toward Art Ehlers during the off-season, Orioles manager Jimmy Dykes said "that was the best trade that Hank never made. It was a pleasure not doing business with him. Courtney has been going great and I wouldn't trade him now for the same players we wanted last winter."[22]

The Indians' usual early season slump, as Jones termed it, was extended with a 6–1 loss in Detroit on April 23. The game was delayed an hour because the trunks carrying the team's equipment had somehow been diverted to Pittsburgh. Once the equipment arrived, Detroit's Ned Garver rendered the bats practically useless, holding the Tribe to six hits. Seeking an offensive spark, Lopez benched two-thirds of his outfield, replacing Westlake and Philley with Mitchell and Dave Pope. The replacements produced one hit in seven at-bats between them. For the second straight game, Cleveland's starter failed to navigate through the first inning. The Tigers pounded Wynn for five runs in just two-thirds of an inning.

The Indians' third straight loss, 6–3 on April 24, left the club in critical condition in the opinion of Jones, despite the fact that 145 games were left on the schedule. Solo home runs by Doby, Avila and Glynn couldn't offset a three-run blast by Ray Boone which helped ruin Hal Newhouser's homecoming. The Tigers scored five times during their former ace's four and two-thirds innings of work. It was the only game Newhouser would start in 1954, and the last start of his Hall of Fame career. While Newhouser couldn't handle his former team, ex–Indian Steve Gromek had little trouble holding the Tribe in check.

Lopez engaged in more lineup tinkering before the final game in Detroit. He moved his MVP third baseman, Rosen, across the diamond to first and inserted the phenom of the Arizona desert, Regalado, at third. "Maybe Regalado can give us the lift we need," he explained. "The way we've been going we need a lift from somebody. I hope he can do it. Rosen has had some experience at first base and I know he can do the job. Maybe Rudy can do it, too. I know he played some first base in college, but Rosen has had actual pro experience at that position."[23]

The Indians needed five pitchers to subdue Detroit, 10–9, in the final game of the series. Regalado contributed three hits and Rosen drove in three runs, but the game-winning hit was Philley's tenth-inning, two-run homer off former Indian Dick Weik. The extra frame was needed because Garcia, working in relief, couldn't hold an 8–6 lead in the bottom of the ninth. Mossi, who took over for Garcia, almost blew the 10–8 advantage Philley's homer had given him, and Lopez summoned Wynn from the bullpen. Wynn retired Matt Batts on a fly ball to end the contest.

Lopez was pleased with the early returns of the Rosen-Regalado experiment. "I'll play Rosen at first and Regalado at third until I'm sure one way or the other," he said after the game.[24]

"It may take me a while, but you can rest assured I'll learn how to play first base as well as third," Rosen vowed. "I want to do what is best for the ball club and I've got no complaints at all. Lopez gave me a choice of staying at third or moving to first and I told him if he wanted me to move I would."[25] Though Rosen was a team player, he had another reason for gracefully accepting the change of positions.

"That was taken care of when he signed his contract for 1954," explained Greenberg. "We made him a generous offer — and he certainly had it coming — but one of the stipulations was that he'd change to another position if Al Lopez asked him to." As to why Lopez would've asked the league's MVP to move to another position, Greenberg said, "There were all sorts of possibilities. We wanted to see Al Smith at third. We were considering a trade in which we'd have gotten another third baseman. Rosen has improved remarkably, but he wasn't such a superstar at third that we felt we had to keep him there, whatever happened."[26]

The Tribe caught a break as it arrived in Boston for a three-game series. Cleveland pitching wouldn't have to deal with Ted Williams, who was recovering from surgery to remove a piece of metal protruding from the wire that had been inserted in the collarbone Williams fractured while diving for a ball during an exhibition game late in March. Many of the Indians, when informed of Williams' injury, didn't believe it at first. Williams was never known for his defense, and several Tribesmen couldn't believe that he'd dive in an attempt to make a catch, especially in an *exhibition* game. Williams wasn't expected to return to Boston's lineup until the second week of May.

.721

Not only did the Indians not have to deal with Williams, they barely had to deal with the Red Sox. Weather postponed the first two games of the series, and the Indians won the third, 6–3. It proved to be a costly victory as Regalado suffered a pulled leg muscle running to first base in the cold weather and was expected to miss at least ten days. Lopez opened himself to criticism by replacing Regalado with outfielder Al Smith and leaving Rosen at first.

Garcia's velocity continued to improve in the victory over Boston. Although Lopez didn't think Garcia's arm strength had reached 100 percent, Jim Hegan said his fastball was "really moving" against the Red Sox. Hegan acknowledged, however, that Garcia threw "twice as many curves and sliders as fastballs."[27]

The Indians had a lot of time to kill in Boston, and while relaxing in the lobby of the team's hotel, Lopez was called to the telephone. The caller identified himself as Arthur "Red" Patterson, the publicist of the Yankees, who were next on the Tribe's itinerary. Patterson asked Lopez who would be starting the two games at Yankee Stadium, and Lopez answered that he'd tell Patterson what he wanted to know if Patterson would reveal who Casey Stengel's two starters would be. Patterson complied, informing the Indians manager his club would be facing youngsters Tom Morgan and Bill Miller. Lopez was certain Patterson was pulling his leg and told him as much. But when the Yankees took the field for the opener of a brief two-game set on April 30, the 23-year-old Morgan was on the hill. Lopez, and his players, were surprised.

Before the first series between the teams most experts predicted to battle for the American League pennant got under way, the league's standings looked like this:

Chicago	8–5	.615	—
Detroit	6–4	.600	½
Washington	6–5	.545	1
Philadelphia	5–5	.500	1½
New York	6–6	.500	1½
Cleveland	5–6	.455	2
Baltimore	5–7	.417	2½
Boston	4–7	.364	3

2. A Slow Start

Morgan allowed four runs and six hits in two and two-thirds innings of work, but his teammates rallied against Lemon to tie the game at four apiece and send it into extra innings. With Whitey Ford on the mound in the tenth, the Indians exploded for five runs, two coming on Doby's bases-loaded single. The center fielder drove in four runs for the day and Cleveland captured the first of its 22 meetings against the team it had to beat in order to win the elusive pennant, 9–4. Lemon went all the way for the Indians, allowing six hits and notching his third win.

3

PICKING UP THE PACE

True to Red Patterson's word, the Yankees sent 26-year-old right-hander Bill Miller to the hill to start the second game of the series with the Tribe. Miller was given a 1–0 lead against Early Wynn in the first inning, but, like Morgan the previous day, he failed to make it out of the third. A five-run uprising gave the Indians a lead they never surrendered. Aided by errors by Yankees stalwarts Yogi Berra, Phil Rizzuto and Joe Collins, the Indians pounded their tormentors, 10–2, to sweep the short series. They left the Big Apple wondering what Casey Stengel, baseball's resident genius, had been thinking.

There was some justification for Stengel's decision to give Morgan the start in the first game. Morgan had compiled a 9–3 record for New York in 1951 and was 5–4 in 1952. Miller, however, had been 4–6 in 1952 and 2–1 in 1953. Both were unlikely candidates to start games in such an important series, even early in the season. Miller's start against the Indians was the only one Stengel would give him in 1954. He'd pitch in five games for Baltimore in 1955 and his career would be over.

Stengel explained the rationale for using two of his lesser pitchers (although Morgan would win 11 games in 1954) against his chief competitor. The Old Professor said he thought it was wise to save Jim McDonald and Harry Byrd for the Tigers, who visited Yankee Stadium after the Indians left town, because Detroit was ahead of Cleveland in the standings.

Bob Feller had waited since September of 1953 for the chance to win his 250th career game. Al Lopez gave him the opportunity in the first game of a doubleheader at Washington's Griffith Stadium on May

2, but a blister on the big toe of Feller's right foot forced him to leave the game after four and one-third innings. Bob Avila booted a potential double-play ball that would have gotten Feller out of the fifth inning with the lead, and the Tribe's 6–4 victory was credited to Ray Narleski, with an assist from Hal Newhouser. Art Houtteman pitched the nightcap, which the Indians won by rallying to tie the game at three apiece with a run in the ninth inning. A three-run tenth inning outburst gave Houtteman his first victory of the season. Wally Westlake paced the offense with four hits. The third game with the Senators was rained out.

Senators manager Bucky Harris, in his third tour of duty as Washington's bench boss, was asked about the Yankees, one of several teams he'd formerly managed. "They looked terrible against us. They don't look good in the field and that's where they're supposed to be strong."[1] Like the Indians, the Yankees had broken slowly from the starting gate. It wouldn't be long, however, before the other six American League teams would be looking up at Cleveland and New York in the standings.

The Indians led the Athletics, 2–0, at Connie Mack Stadium when Al Smith's wild throw of a bunt by Forrest "Spook" Jacobs skipped past Al Rosen and allowed Bob Trice to score his team's first run on May 4. Philadelphia would score twice more for a 3–2 victory, but Harry Jones felt Smith's error, and the subsequent unearned run it allowed to score, cost the Indians the game. It was Smith's sixth error in the six games he'd played at third base since Rudy Regalado had been sidelined by a leg injury. Harry Jones and Gordon Cobbledick couldn't understand why Lopez didn't return Rosen to his natural position. Cobbledick admitted that the Indians hadn't yet lost a game with Smith playing third base and noted that managers are always reluctant to tamper with a winning lineup. Cobbledick also conceded that Smith's bat and speed on the base paths were benefiting the Tribe.

Smith had the support of his teammates, particularly the man whose old position he was then playing. "Don't fool yourself about Smitty," said Rosen. "He's a pretty good ball player, and he'll be a good third baseman, too, when he gets his feet on the ground. The guy can hit and there aren't many who can run the bases the way he does."[2] One anonymous Indian criticized Regalado for leaving the lineup, pulled muscle

3. Picking Up the Pace

or no pulled muscle. "Any time they move the best player in baseball to another position to make room for you, you stay in the lineup no matter how badly you're hurt," said the unidentified Indian.[3]

Cleveland rebounded from the disappointing loss (any loss to the miserable Athletics was a disappointment in 1954) with a 7–2 trouncing of the home club on May 5. Lemon held the Athletics in check on a yield of nine hits, and Dave Philley celebrated his return to his old stomping grounds with a three-run homer that gave Lemon all the offense he needed. The Indians made it two-of-three the next night, 3–2, with the much-maligned Smith's home run being the decisive blow. Smith's blast gave Early Wynn his third victory of the year.

During a workout in Connie Mack Stadium on the Tribe's off-day, May 7, Rosen told the writers in attendance that "we're going to win. We'll win and without much trouble."[4] Rosen wasn't talking about the next day's game in Baltimore. He was referring to the American League pennant. Rosen's prediction wasn't the big story of the day, however. The headline belonged to the club's sale of Rocky Nelson back to the Montreal Royals of the International League. After hitting .308 for the Royals in 1953, with 34 homers and 136 RBI, Nelson, despite being virtually handed the Cleveland first base job on a silver platter, couldn't hold it. Nelson batted .163 in spring training and was hitless in four at-bats during the regular season.

Nelson left Cleveland singing the same tune he sang when he arrived. "I never got a chance!" he moaned. "I didn't get much of a chance the other times I came up in the National League but this time I had no chance at all. This is the first time I know of a guy had to make the team in spring training. I never played in a single game once the season started." Nelson said he'd been promised by both Lopez and Hank Greenberg that he'd see action at first base on the Tribe's lengthy road trip.

> "Both Hank and Al promised me I would. Even when they shifted Rosen to first I still thought I'd get my chance. I know I could have hit up here. Some of the same pitchers I hit in the minors, guys who couldn't get me out, are successful up here. I thought I rated a chance on the basis of what I did in the minors last year, not on spring training. I don't think I got a fair chance at all with Cleveland. I don't think they did right by me."[5]

Interestingly, Greenberg agreed. "He didn't have a fair trial. Once the season opened, he didn't start a single game."[6] Greenberg gave no indication, however, that he disapproved of the way Lopez handled Nelson.

"I still think he could be a good ballplayer, and he's a good fellow. This is one of the really tough things about baseball. This may be his last chance," said Lopez.[7]

Nelson was nothing if not persistent, and his major league career wasn't over. He'd be back in the majors in 1956, playing 69 games for the Dodgers and Cardinals, and would enjoy two productive seasons as a part-time player in Pittsburgh in 1959 and 1960, including batting .333 with two RBI for the 1960 World Series-winning Pirates.

Rosen, meanwhile, was rapidly becoming acclimated to first base. "It's so much easier over there. I'm much more relaxed. Let's face it. Every day I went out to play third it was a challenge to me. I did the job acceptably but it was a mighty battle. At first base, I don't feel that way at all. Frankly, I feel more natural over there."[8]

Lopez wasn't surprised. "Just the other day he told me he's liking it more every day. He says it's simple compared with playing third. This makes sense. At third you're playing close a lot of times and they're shooting cannons at you. Or if you're back they bunt on you. You have to throw a lot more, too, so it's just more ornery."[9]

The Indians concluded the longest road trip of the year by splitting two games in Baltimore. Hal Naragon's three-run double gave the Tribe a 5–0 cushion that Garcia, Narleski, Newhouser and Wynn managed to hang on to for a 5–3 victory on May 8, and Bob Turley, who'd come within two outs of a no-hitter before losing a 2–1 heartbreaker to the Indians in late April, had his revenge with a 2–1 victory, besting Houtteman and allowing just four hits in ten innings. The marathon journey ended with the Indians winning ten games. They lost five to their opponents and three to bad weather.

Next on the Tribe's agenda was winning a game at home. With the season nearly a month old, the Indians were 0–3 at Municipal Stadium as they awaited the arrival of the Yankees. It appeared they were headed for a fourth straight loss at home when New York reached Lemon for

3. Picking Up the Pace

three first-inning runs, but Cleveland responded with eight tallies against Yankees starter Whitey Ford and his replacements, Bob Kuzava and Bob Grim. Lemon yielded to Mossi after the Yankees cut the deficit to 8–5 in the second inning, and Mossi surrendered two more runs in the third before settling down and keeping the visitors off the scoreboard until the eighth. With one out, Garcia was summoned and pitched an inning and two-thirds of scoreless relief. The Indians were held at bay by New York's bullpen, but the first-inning barrage held up for an 8–7 victory witnessed by 22,456 fans.

Jones felt kudos were in order for the 15,581 who attended the May 11 game on a night when cold weather would've justified a postponement. After Rosen's eighth-inning single drove in two runs to tie the score at 3–3, pitcher Dave Hoskins failed to cover first base on a ground ball off the bat of Joe Collins that would've been the third out of the ninth inning. Yogi Berra made Hoskins pay for his mistake with a double that scored Bill "Moose" Skowron and Collins for a 5–3 Yankees victory.

Ed Lopat barely threw hard enough to shatter a pane of glass, but that didn't stop him from being a mainstay of the Yankees pitching staff and a winner of 166 games during his major league career. The Indians were Lopat's favorite victim, and he carried a lifetime record of 37–11 versus the Tribe into the rubber game of the series, which he improved to 38–11. Lopat had the Indians shut out until the eighth inning, when they drove him from the mound with a four-run rally. Johnny Sain, who had announced his retirement after the 1953 season and then changed his mind, trudged out of the bullpen to put out the fire and make a 5–4 loser of Garcia. The Yankees left town tied with the Indians for third place at 13–10.

Despite the pair of defeats, Lopez wasn't discouraged. "I'm more optimistic than I've ever been since I've been managing the Indians that we can take them," the manager said.[10]

In addition to dealing with their main rivals, the Indians had to reduce their roster from 32 players to 26 on May 12. They were permitted to keep one player more than the league's 25-man limit because Naragon had been in the service the previous year, and players returning from military service, with the war in Korea having just ended, were not counted on a team's 25-man roster. Lopez didn't anticipate making any trades to move players who didn't fit in the club's plan for the rest of the season and beyond. "The other clubs think they have us over a barrel, but we can cut down without being forced to make a bad deal," said the manager.[11]

Few were surprised when the Indians sent Luke Easter to Ottawa of the International League. The 38-year-old could no longer handle first base on a daily basis, and he'd been limited to 68 games in 1953, his home run total plunging from 31 in 1952 to a mere seven. Among Easter's accomplishments in Cleveland was the longest measured home run ever hit in Municipal Stadium, a 477-foot blast into the right field upper deck off Washington's Joe Haynes on June 23, 1950.

"Don't want to come back to this team, but I'll be back someplace else," Easter promised.[12] Easter played another ten seasons in the minor leagues, but never returned to the majors. He did return to make Cleveland his home.

To reach the roster limit, the Indians optioned pitchers Hoskins and Jose Santiago to Indianapolis of the American Association and Bill Wight to San Diego of the Pacific Coast League. Santiago refused to report and aroused the ire of club officials, but returned to Cleveland in 1955. As had been speculated, Jim Dyck's stay in Cleveland was brief. The Indians sent Dyck to Richmond of the International League. Jim Lemon was sold to the Senators.

"I just couldn't get going here, so maybe the change will do me good," Lemon said.[13] Lemon smacked 39 homers at Oklahoma City in 1950 but hit just .218 for the Tribe's top farm club, Indianapolis, in 1953.

"This is the toughest thing in baseball — when cutting time comes around," said Lopez.[14]

Regalado's pulled muscle had healed and Lopez put him back at third base when the Indians opened a series against Washington. "At the time Rudy got hurt I said I would put him back in when he recovered. Smith has been hitting so well, though, that I want to keep him in the line-up."[15] Smith batted .293 while filling in for Regalado and was moved to left field, replacing Wally Westlake, who was benched in the midst of a 2-for-19 slump. Lopez had been particularly impressed by the way

3. Picking Up the Pace

Smith battled Allie Reynolds in the recent series against the Yankees. "Other guys went up there and took their swings and got out, but Smith gave him a fight all the way," noted the skipper.[16] Smith had a hit and walked twice against Reynolds, but that wasn't enough to avoid a defeat.

The day after being blanked for the first seven innings by Lopat, the Indians were held in check through eight frames, their one hit being Regalado's first big league home run, by Washington's Mickey McDermott. Trailing 7–1 in the bottom of the ninth, Rosen led off with his third home run of the season, and before Bucky Harris knew what had hit him, his Senators had surrendered six runs. Philley tied the game with a two-out, bases-loaded double, sending it into extra innings. Washington reliever Johnny Schmitz walked Smith in the 11th, and Al scampered home with the winning run on Rosen's double. Newhouser earned his first win as an Indian with two scoreless innings of relief. It was Prince Hal's 201st career victory. "I waited two years for that baby," Newhouser noted after the game. "My 200th came on the last game of the 1952 season."[17]

"What a struggle. All I can say is we have won 14 ball games without being solid everywhere. If we ever get straightened out, we shouldn't lose at all," said Lopez.[18] He had no idea how accurate that statement would prove to be.

No late heroics were needed on May 15 as the Tribe plated five runs in the first inning, four scoring on a grand slam by George Strickland. Bob Lemon didn't get any additional run support, but he didn't need any. The 5–2 victory was Lemon's fifth without a loss. Cleveland completed the sweep with a 5–4 victory the next day, achieved thanks to a two-run eighth inning rally that wiped out Washington's 4–3 lead. Avila's solo home run, Philley's double, a bunt by Rosen that moved Philley to third, and Doby's single turned the trick. "I can't remember any team I've had pull games out of the fire like this one's been doing," said Lopez after the squeaker. "They're hard on the nerves, but I'm not complaining."[19]

With the season just over a month old, Cobbledick sized up the race to date, deciding that while the Indians were the contenders he and most everyone else expected them to be, they didn't look like pennant winners.

.721

Light-hitting shortstop George Strickland crosses home plate after a grand slam, and is congratulated by teammates Dave Philly (17), Larry Doby (14) and Rudy Regalado (8). It was one of just 36 homers Strickland hit in his 10-year career (Cleveland Public Library).

The Athletics may have begged to differ with Cobbledick after the Indians took both ends of a Sunday doubleheader from them on May 16, 12–7 and 6–0, in front of 21,713 spectators. Feller's second attempt of the season at his 250th victory was denied as Philadelphia scored five runs on seven hits before Bob Chakales relieved Feller with one out in the third inning. Chakales didn't give up a hit and picked up the victory when the Indians scored six times in the fifth.

Feller said he'd have to get accustomed to pitching on a less than regular basis. "I'll have to change my routine to get accustomed to less starts. Until now I've been training the way I did in the past. One thing

I'll have to do is get on the pitching mound more between starts."[20] Feller throughout his career and beyond was a firm believer that pitchers' arms didn't wear out, they rusted out.

Garcia was as effective in the nightcap as Feller had been ineffective. Philadelphia shortstop Joe DeMaestri's leadoff single in the fourth inning was the only safety Garcia allowed as he improved his record to 3–4. He walked a pair and struck out five. "Yeah, it was the best game I ever pitched, all right. I had a good fastball and my control was perfect. I was putting the ball just where I wanted it," he said in the clubhouse.[21] Garcia's one-hitter was the fourth pitched in the major leagues with the season just over a month old.

The sweep of the Athletics vaulted the Indians into a first place tie with the White Sox. Cleveland wasn't exactly in the grip of pennant fever, however, as attendance was running a disappointing 8,000 ahead of 1953s languid pace. First place in mid–May was no big deal. Tribe fans had seen that many times before.

The Red Sox, with Ted Williams back in harness, followed the Athletics into Cleveland, and the Tribe posted a 6–3 victory on May 18. The Red Sox made quick work of starter Houtteman, sending him to the showers after just an inning and two-thirds of pitching, and Chakales came out of the bullpen to earn his second victory in three days, keeping Boston scoreless until leaving in the eighth. Rosen's double and two homers paced the offense.

Asked about his quick hook of Houtteman, Lopez told reporters that he had less patience with his starters than in years past because "we've got a stronger bullpen now. When you have a few good men in the bullpen you can take your starters out earlier."[22] As for Chakales, he wasn't even supposed to be on the club. The Indians, on cut-down day, had planned to send him to Richmond, Virginia. "We would have preferred sending him out to Dave Hoskins," Lopez explained. "Chakales said he was willing to go to Richmond. Said he felt fine, didn't see much for him to do here, and it would be near home. It so happened he couldn't be optioned without waivers, and that's why Hoskins had to go."[23] Hoskins would return shortly when the Indians found a way to allow Chakales to pitch closer to home and get more than the waiver price in return.

.721

Rosen entered the game with six homers and on a pace to drive in 182 runs for the year, and Boston's manager (and former Rosen teammate) Lou Boudreau thought he knew why. After Rosen had swatted his seventh home run early in the game, Boudreau waited until his next trip to the plate and then signaled to catcher Sammy White to ask umpire Charley Berry to inspect Rosen's bat. Berry did, found it to be illegal, and ordered Rosen to find another stick. Rosen admitted after the game to having pounded several small nails into the business end of his bat, in violation of the rules. "I knew someone was going to catch up with this sooner or later, but I was going to keep it up as long as possible. I've used this one practically all season. The bat started to check [the grains had begun to separate] a while back and I began to put the nails in. It's frequently done."[24]

Lopez absolved his star player of any wrongdoing. "I've been around baseball quite a while, and it's been going on all the time."[25] Rosen was neither fined, suspended, nor even tossed out of the game for using the illegal bat.

The home stand concluded with a visit from the Orioles, the first appearance by a Baltimore team in Cleveland since the waning days of the 1902 season, when the Orioles, who had been gutted by their former manager, John McGraw, as a result of a blood feud with AL president Byron Bancroft "Ban" Johnson, were playing out the string before being transferred to New York to become the Highlanders, who would later be known as the Yankees. Although the new Orioles consisted mainly of the remnants of the pathetic St. Louis Browns, they'd given the Indians fits in four games in Baltimore earlier in the season, and they continued to play Cleveland tough in a 2–1 loss on May 21. The Tribe managed just three hits, but it was enough for Wynn, who shut out the Birds until Dick Kryhoski, his wrist healed after having been broken by a pitch in spring training, homered leading off the ninth inning.

The Indians struggled with Baltimore again the next day but prevailed, 4–3, in ten innings. Smith's two-out single off Don Larsen scored Regalado with the winning run. Garcia evened his record at 4–4 with a complete-game ten-hitter that was witnessed by only 6,933 fans. It was the Tribe's ninth straight win at home.

3. Picking Up the Pace

The Indians' surge may not have captured the fancy of the fans, but it got the attention of the other tenant of Municipal Stadium, the Cleveland Browns. With the Indians apparently in the pennant race to stay, the Browns were concerned about the availability of Municipal Stadium for their scheduled October 3 home game versus the Detroit Lions. The fifth game of the World Series, if a fifth game was necessary, would be played on October 3, and it would be played in the ball park of the American League champion. Cobbledick joked that NFL commissioner Bert Bell, who put the schedule together, gave the Browns a home game on October 3 based on the reasonable assumption that the Indians would finish second again and have no need for Municipal Stadium on that Sunday afternoon. The NFL would re-schedule the game for December.

Bob Feller waited a long time to post his 250th career victory. The Indians made sure that wait would end in the first game of a doubleheader on May 23. Scoring three times in the first inning and four times in the fourth off Baltimore starter Lou Kretlow, the Indians slammed the Birds, 14–3. Feller allowed eight hits, walked one and struck out two in notching the landmark triumph.

"It seemed to be a long time coming—one start last year and three this season," said Feller afterward. "I went back to my old training routine this week, plenty of calisthenics and as much throwing from the mound as possible. Maybe that's what did it. I have to have control and keep ahead of the batter. The only way to get it is by pitching."[26]

Gibbons noted that "Feller has given up on the notion of winning 300 games, but he thinks he still might get lucky and pitch a fourth no-hitter."[27] Feller admitted that "luck is the big thing in one of those."[28]

Pitching dominated the nightcap. Houtteman hooked up with Turley and the two hurlers battled into the 12th inning before the Indians plated the winning run, which Houtteman drove in himself with a double, scoring Strickland from first base. Turley had pitched three complete games against the Indians, and each had ended with a score of 2–1. Turley was on the short end of two of them. The sweep extended the Indians' string of victories to 11.

Shortly after deciding the Indians were contenders but not champions, Cobbledick changed his tune. The 11-game winning streak, six of the victories achieved by coming from behind, made him a believer, and he told his readers he no longer thought the Yankees had what it took to win the pennant, but the Indians did.

Frank Lane and Paul Richards thought their White Sox also had what it took to win a pennant. Lane did what he did best in late May, sending third baseman Grady Hatton and $100,000 of the Comiskey family's money to Boston for third baseman George Kell, the 1949 AL batting champion who brought a lifetime .311 average to the White Sox. Kell was hitting just .258 at the time of the deal, but had been struggling with a back injury. Kell was given permission to drive his family from Boston to their home in Arkansas, meaning he'd miss a two-game series with the Indians in Chicago on May 25 and 26.

Lane's acquisition of Kell didn't please Lopez. "Unless Kell is all through, there isn't much doubt he will help them. It's one of the funniest deals I've seen in a long time. Boston gets a benchwarmer and money. Boudreau doesn't need an extra hand and [Red Sox owner Tom] Yawkey doesn't need money."[29]

The White Sox swept their series with the Indians without Kell. In front of a Comiskey Park crowd of 43,039, Chicago took advantage of errors by Regalado and Lemon and snapped the Tribe's winning streak, 4–2. It was Lemon's first loss of the season. The next day, the White Sox ran wild on Garcia and Hal Naragon, stealing six bases, five of them during Garcia's four innings of work, and held off the Indians, 5–4. The Tribe's little-used third-string catcher, Joe Ginsberg, lashed a triple pinch-hitting for Hegan to tie the game in the ninth inning. Ginsberg quickly went from hero to goat by trying to score the winning run on Smith's short fly to center fielder Johnny Groth. Groth's throw to the plate arrived in plenty of time to nail the Tribe's back-up catcher, whose progress on the base paths could have been timed with a sundial. Chicago then tallied the game winner when Newhouser couldn't pitch out of a bases-loaded, none-out jam inherited from Houtteman in the bottom of the ninth. Cass Michaels' single over Doby's head scored Nellie Fox.

Lopez displayed his annoyance with Garcia when removing him from the game in the fifth inning. Instead of offering his pitcher the customary pat on the back, Lopez took the ball from Garcia, pointed to the

3. Picking Up the Pace

bullpen, and turned his back to his starting pitcher. Lopez had caught more than 1,900 games in the major leagues and knew stolen bases were usually the fault of the pitcher. Garcia hadn't given Naragon a chance.

Ginsberg's triple would be his last hit as an Indian. His contract would soon be sold to the Tribe's Indianapolis farm club.

The Indians left Comiskey Park with a half-game lead over the White Sox. "They'll win if they get the pitching," said Chicago manager Richards, meaning the Indians. "But I doubt whether their pitching will hold up."[30]

With his Yankees in the unaccustomed position of third place, Casey Stengel was in a foul mood. They weren't winning often enough, and they were being abused both on and off the field. "I've got to make my players meaner," Stengel grumbled a week before the Indians were scheduled to make their second trip to Yankee Stadium. "I had to appeal to the park police here [Griffith Stadium] to stop spectators in a box next to our dugout from leaning over and shouting obscenities into our bench. The names they called Mickey Mantle were particularly disgraceful. Pitchers have been throwing at Andy Carey. Gil McDougald and Phil Rizzuto have been getting a real going over around second base."[31]

Before visiting the Big Apple, the Indians returned home for a five-game stand against the Tigers and White Sox. As important as the Memorial Day doubleheader with Chicago would be, Lopez, convinced that New York and not the White Sox was the team the Indians absolutely had to beat, arranged his rotation so that Lemon, Wynn and Garcia would face the Yankees. No one other than the big three had started a game against the Yankees since June 14, 1953, and the Indians had won 14 of those 20 meetings. Lopez would use only his front-line pitchers against the defending champions.

Using the Tigers as a tune-up, Wynn prepared for his start versus the Bronx Bombers by tossing a two-hit, 3–0 shutout on May 28. Rosen's two-run homer off Steve Gromek gave Wynn all the runs he needed. The next night, Lemon authored a 12–0 victory over Detroit. Six Tiger errors sabotaged starter Ray Herbert and gave Lemon an eight-run cushion after just two innings. Doby provided the highlights of the night with a home run and a leaping catch of a smash by Walt Dropo against the center field fence in the fifth inning that preserved Lemon's shutout.

Detroit manager Fred Hutchinson, a pitcher during his playing days, knew what had happened to Garcia in Chicago and planned more of the same when he faced the Tigers in the series finale. "You can generally run on a pitcher as big as Garcia. Takes 'em a while to get the ball away,"[32] said Hutchinson, who promised his players would run on Garcia at every opportunity. The Bear had other ideas.

An unearned run due to an error by Rosen was all that separated Garcia from the Tribe's third straight shutout. He held the Tigers to a run on four hits as the Indians completed the sweep, 3–1. The series drew 51,042 fans, most of whom made the trip to downtown Cleveland from outlying areas.

> "We suspected this all along," said Nate Dolin, the Tribe's director of stadium operations and supervisor of box office program and policy, "but checking the parking lot the other night we found that three out of every four cars had out of town license plates. Actually, the out of town fans are keeping us in business. We are drawing as many from out of town as we did a few years ago when the season attendance was more than a million and a half. We're about 30,000 ahead of last year, but being in first place, we ought to do better than that. I wish I knew the answer. Why people in Cleveland aren't coming to the games I don't know."[33]

The Indians' 14-game home winning streak ended in the first game of a Memorial Day doubleheader as the White Sox handed Feller his first loss of the season, 6–4. Minnie Minoso's two-run homer off his former teammate snapped a 3–3 tie in the eighth inning, and Bob Keegan bobbed and weaved through a complete-game ten-hitter to win for the seventh time in eight decisions. Cleveland salvaged a split with a 6–3 victory in the second game as Houtteman outdid Keegan, pitching a complete game despite surrendering 13 hits. Admitting the effort had been a struggle, Houtteman said "I threw everything I had, but I didn't have much of anything."[34] He had enough to maintain the Indians' one-game lead over the White Sox, thanks to Hegan's game-winning solo home run off Harry Dorish, Chicago's third pitcher, in the eighth inning. The Tribe made Houtteman's job easier by adding two insurance runs after Hegan's blast. A crowd of 39,997, well below the club's expectations,

3. Picking Up the Pace

watched the holiday twin bill. There was no repeat of the track meet the White Sox had staged at Comiskey Park a few days earlier, in part because the Municipal Stadium grounds crew had thoroughly hosed down the infield following the final game of the series with Detroit. Particular attention was given to the area surrounding first base.

Before leaving Cleveland, Frank Lane took issue with Greenberg's many critics. "I've read that the Indians are the same old faces," said the White Sox general manager. "I wish they were. It's a new ball club and a much better club."[35]

With May in the books, the standings looked like this:

Cleveland	28–13	.683	—
Chicago	28–15	.651	1
New York	25–17	.595	3½
Detroit	20–17	.541	6
Washington	17–23	.425	10½
Boston	13–21	.382	11½
Baltimore	14–26	.350	13½
Philadelphia	14–27	.341	14

It was on to New York. Lopez would have his big three rested and ready. The Indians could only hope things would go as well as during their first visit to the House That Ruth Built.

4

AVOIDING THE SWOON

The Indians weren't the only team to fall victim — frequently — to the dreaded June swoon. It only seemed that way to Clevelanders. It had been a four-game sweep at Municipal Stadium, administered by the Yankees, June 12 through 14 of 1953 that had dropped the second-place Indians 10½ games behind and effectively ended their pennant aspirations well before the halfway point of the season. That may have explained why Clevelanders weren't stumbling over each other in their haste to reach the team's box office. Most Indians fans were taking a wait-and-see attitude toward the 1954 edition.

June started with a trade that Hank Greenberg and Al Lopez hoped would provide some badly needed offense. The on-again, off-again discussions with Baltimore produced another swap, this one hopefully more beneficial than the Bob Kennedy for Jim Dyck transaction. Greenberg dipped into the team's surplus of pitching and sent Bob Chakales, the 26-year-old right-hander long on potential but short on performance that the Indians had planned to demote to Richmond in mid–May, to the Birds in exchange for Vic Wertz. In 32 games with the Indians from 1951 through May of 1954, Chakales had won six and lost eight. He'd pitched well in three outings in 1954, but he wasn't about to crack the starting rotation of Bob Lemon, Early Wynn, Mike Garcia, Art Houtteman and occasionally Bob Feller, and Greenberg felt his bullpen was well fortified with the additions of Hal Newhouser, Don Mossi and Ray Narleski. The Indians needed a bat, and Wertz was a career .285 hitter who had struggled through the first six weeks of 1954, bringing a .202 average to Cleveland. Lopez and Greenberg were banking on Wertz

.721

returning to at least some semblance of the form he'd shown with Detroit from 1949–1951, when he slammed 74 homers and drove in 350 runs. "I finally got him," said Greenberg. "This deal ends five years of trying."[1]

"I think Vic can do us a lot of good," Lopez said. "He's going to be good insurance in case anything happens to our other outfielders. He hits a long ball and may give us some added scoring punch. This fellow has been a real good ball player and we're hoping that, once he gets over here with us, he'll start to go again and help us a lot."[2]

Wertz was happy to escape Baltimore and gain six places in the standings. "I can't complain about a chance at some World Series money. I've still got a lot of baseball left and I know I can hit as well as I ever did. All I ask is the opportunity to prove it."[3] Wertz would pocket some World Series cash and, in four months, hit one of the most famous fly balls in baseball history at New York's Polo Grounds.

The Indians opened their second eastern trip with yet another come-from-behind victory, made all the more impressive because it was achieved at the expense of the Yankees and their ace pitcher, Allie Reynolds. New York sent Wynn to a quick shower, scoring seven first-inning runs off him and his replacement, Mossi. Then the Indians' bullpen and offense went to work. Mossi, Narleski, Bob Hooper, Garcia and Newhouser held the Yankees scoreless without a hit after the first inning, while the Indians tied the game on a home run by George Strickland in the top of the ninth off Johnny Sain and won it in the tenth when Al Smith homered, also off Sain. The 8–7 triumph inspired Harry Jones to suggest the Indians were a team of destiny in his account of the game.

Lopez wasn't fazed by the early deficit. "I had the feeling. It's because I've seen the way we keep coming back game after game."[4]

Even a team of destiny couldn't handle Ed Lopat, who improved his career records versus Cleveland to 39–11 with a 2–1 win in the second game of the series on June 2. Joe Collins' eighth inning homer made a loser of Lemon (7–2), who permitted just four hits. Lopat surrendered 11 safeties but was bailed out frequently by his defense, including Irv Noren's diving catch of a drive by Strickland in the ninth inning with Rudy Regalado on first base, representing the tying run.

Jones may have wondered if his euphoria after the unlikely victory

4. Avoiding the Swoon

in the first game of the series had been misplaced when the Yankees won the rubber game, roughing up Wynn for the second time in three days. Yogi Berra's three-run homer in the first inning gave New York a quick lead, and after the Indians had sliced their deficit to 3–2 against Whitey Ford in the sixth, single Yankees runs in the sixth and seventh chased Wynn and saddled him with his third loss against six victories, 8–3. The Indians left New York in a virtual first place tie with Chicago.

Not satisfied with taking the series from the Indians, Casey Stengel rubbed salt in the wound by accusing Cleveland's base runners of dirty tactics. "We play hard but fair," he told writers, "you don't see our guys goin' in with their spikes high. If that's the way they want it, we will, too."[5] The Indians were quick to respond to Stengel's accusation that they played too rough by claiming Yankees outfielder Hank Bauer had slid hard into second base and jammed Bob Avila's thumb, but the Indians didn't whine about it. "We don't complain. That's part of the game," said the Tribe's second baseman.[6]

"We never say a word as long as a runner doesn't go out of the base line," added Lopez. "The trouble is that [Gil] McDougald is new at second and he doesn't know how to avoid being hit. When [Jerry] Coleman plays second, he never gets touched. He knows how to get out of the way."[7]

In addition to losing a game, the Indians prepared to lose the league's leading hitter, Avila, for ten games after Avila bumped umpire Bill Grieve while arguing a called third strike. Earlier in the season, AL president Will Harridge had informed each team that any player making physical contact with an umpire would be automatically suspended for ten games. There was no appeal. But there was no suspension, either. The league office notified the Indians the day after the incident that Avila would be fined $100 for bumping Grieve, but the "automatic" suspension would be waived. Harridge warned, however, that the rule calling for an automatic suspension "would be strictly enforced" from that point forward.[8]

Despite losing two of three to the Yankees, Lopez's players shared their manager's optimism that 1954 was going to be their year. "We know it's going to be a tough fight," said Jim Hegan. "But we believe we can do it this year."[9]

.721

From New York, the Indians journeyed south to Philadelphia and topped the Athletics, 4–1, on June 5. Garcia limited the home team to a pair of hits, but trailed until Dave Philley's seventh-inning homer tied the game. It remained tied until the 11th when, with the bases loaded, Philley's 400-foot fly to center field scored both Smith and Avila. The deciding runs were surrendered by reliever Alex Kellner.

The Indians had caught a break when Harridge decided not to enforce the ten- game suspension mandated by league rules against Avila. They wouldn't be as fortunate with Al Rosen. Rosen had been playing despite a painful index finger on his right hand since he'd injured the digit fielding a hot grounder hit by Jim Rivera at Comiskey Park on May 25. X-rays taken when the Indians reached Philadelphia revealed a chip fracture, and Rosen was sent back to Cleveland. Dr. Don Kelley, the Indians' team physician, described the injury as "a torn capsule at the joint of the index finger."[10] Kelley speculated that Rosen would be in pain at least three to four weeks and more likely six. Kelley didn't, however, suggest resting Rosen while the finger healed. He would intervene in Avila's case.

Tribe trainer Wally Bock told the *Press* that "I would say Bob Avila's thumb is not hurt as badly as Al Rosen's finger was, and that Rosen's finger may be much better in a day or two. In fact, both should be much better by then."[11] Bock's assessment of both injuries proved to be far off base.

Avila had his thumb examined by the Athletics' team doctor when the club arrived in Philadelphia. Another chip fracture was the diagnosis. "[The doctor] says if I rest a week now I will be all right," said Avila. "If I go on playing, I will not be right for a month. It is best for the team and for me that I do not play."[12]

Lopez didn't see it that way. "He has played and hit well since he got hurt in New York and I'm going to ask him to go right on playing. First we lose Rosen and now this. I'm going to ask Avila to stick it out."[13] Lopez changed his mind after Kelley told him it would be advisable for Avila to sit out at least a few games, and possibly more, to allow the thumb to heal.

As for Bock's diagnosis of Rosen's injury, Rosen admitted that "I

4. Avoiding the Swoon

suppose I should have had the thing X-rayed the day after it happened, but I thought the swelling would go down and it would be all right." The night after sustaining the injury, May 26, Rosen ignored the pain and swatted a pair of home runs and a double, but

> "Later on, I was convinced that something was broken. We had important games with the White Sox, Tigers and Yankees coming up, so I asked Lopez to let me stick it out. I know I wasn't helping the team much, but I don't think I was hurting it, either. I wanted to play through the Yankee series so the team wouldn't have a letdown. Any time you lose a key man there's some reaction. I know I'd feel let down if we'd lose Strickland or Avila before a big series."[14]

"He promised me he'd have the finger X-rayed if I let him play the last game in New York, so I let him play,"[15] said Lopez. The manager, however, didn't seem overly concerned by the injury. "I'd like to play him. He's had the injury since our first game in New York and it doesn't seem to have bothered his play. I know it hurts. I've played with broken fingers. So have hundreds of ball players."[16] Rosen wouldn't hit as he had in 1953, or as he had in April and May of 1954, when his batting average peaked at .375, for the rest of the season, or the rest of his career, which ended in 1956 at age 32.

A few days after Frank Gibbons broke the story in the *Press*, both Lopez and Bock admitted they were concerned about how Tribe fans would react to their insistence that neither Rosen nor Avila was hurt badly enough to leave the lineup. "I told both of them at the start there was the chance of a fracture," said Bock. "I didn't think, and I still don't, that it was dangerous for either to play. The term 'chip fracture' probably sounds uglier than it is. The chip [in Avila's case] isn't detached from the second thumb joint and it is a long shot that this would happen. My job is to keep men in the line-up as long as I don't think it's dangerous for them. I wouldn't ask any player to do what I wouldn't ask my children to do."[17] Bock continued to serve as Cleveland's trainer into the 1970s.

"I didn't intend to order Avila to play," said Lopez. "I just intended to ask him."[18]

Philadelphia pitching held the Indians, minus Rosen and Avila, to 11 hits in a June 6 doubleheader, but the lack of offense didn't stop the

.721

Tribe from winning both games, 2–1 and 7–5. Feller pitched an eight-hitter in the opener, needing help from Newhouser for only the final out. A home run by the opposing pitcher, rookie Arnold Portocarrero, deprived Rapid Robert of a shutout as he won his second game of the season. Houtteman won his fifth game in the nightcap, with relief help from Hooper, Newhouser and Lemon. The sweep improved the Indians' record against the league's second division clubs to 21–3. Against New York, Chicago and Detroit, they were a significantly less imposing 11–12. They were following the recipe practiced by their former manager, Lou Boudreau, who often talked of "beating up on the bums and breaking even with the contenders."

Half of the Indians' infield was laid up with injuries. The absences of Rosen and Avila continued to be keenly felt during the opener of a series in Washington. Mickey McDermott, who'd carried a one-hitter against the Indians into the ninth inning the last time he'd faced them before being driven from the mound, suffered no such fate in a 5–2 Senators victory. Without their first and second basemen, the Indians managed just two hits. The defeat, charged to Wynn, a former Senator, dropped his record to 6–4 and dropped the Tribe out of first place.

Washington's Bob Porterfield was almost as good as McDermott the next day, limiting the Indians to a run on four hits. Having to pitch a shutout to win, Garcia did, allowing only five hits. The game's only run was unearned, when Philley scored on an error by third baseman Eddie Yost. The Senators took the series with an 8–4 victory in the rubber match as Lemon suffered his third loss of the year and second in succession. A week after dubbing the Indians a team of destiny, Jones described the Tribe, minus Rosen and Avila, as a club that had suddenly lost confidence in itself.

Lopez announced that he'd bench Regalado when the Indians began a marathon five-game series at Fenway Park on June 10. The "red-hot rapper" had stopped rapping, and though he'd played an adequate third base with only one error in 31 games, he lacked range and allowed too many balls to shoot past him. In addition to Regalado's problems, Philley, despite nine homers and 34 RBI, couldn't lift his average over the .200 mark, and Strickland, after committing 17 errors in 122 games in 1953,

4. Avoiding the Swoon

had already made 13 miscues in 1954. Sam Dente, who took Avila's place at second, wasn't expected to hit much and lived up to that modest expectation. Somehow, the Indians managed to cling tenaciously to second place.

As the Indians were struggling in the east, the White Sox hoped to strengthen their hold on first place with the acquisition of pitcher Morrie Martin from the Athletics on June 10. Frank Lane swapped pitcher Johnny Dixon (whom he'd obtained just hours earlier from Washington), pitcher Al Sima and outfielder Bill Wilson plus $20,000 the cash-strapped Athletics desperately needed, to Philadelphia for Martin. Lane's manager, Paul Richards, praised the deal. "If he pitches the way we know he can," Richards said of Martin, "he could mean the pennant for us. He's the extra pitcher we need."[19] Martin had won 10 games and lost 12 for the Athletics in 1953 and sported a 2–4 record at the time of the trade. As the Yankees had with former Athletic Harry Byrd, the White Sox banked on Martin's numbers improving with a much stronger team behind him.

The Tribe's rugged tour through the east made an abrupt about-face when they arrived in Boston for a five-game series. Although The Plain Dealer offered the opinion that Boudreau still had a bitter taste in his mouth over his dismissal by Hank Greenberg after the 1950 season and relished the opportunity to at least temporarily, and possibly permanently, derail the Indians' suddenly wheezing pennant express, revenge for the former Cleveland shortstop and manager wasn't in the cards. Houtteman benefited from homers by Doby, Strickland and Westlake in a 6–2 victory on June 11th, and Feller notched his third win of the season, 4–3, the next day. The game produced the second milestone achievement of the year for Feller, whose eight strikeouts enabled him to exceed the 2,500 mark for his career. Victim number 2,500 was Boston second baseman Ted Lepcio. Feller's 2,502 strikeouts at game's end moved him past New York Giants' legend Christy Mathewson into fourth place on the all-time whiff list. Feller trailed Tim Keefe, Cy Young and Walter Johnson. Keefe won 342 games and fanned 2,564 batters from 1881 to 1893; Young struck out 2,803 between 1890 and 1911 (including 906 strikeouts for the Cleveland Spiders of the National League, 1890–98 and 167 for the Cleveland Naps, the forerunners of the Indians, 1909–1911); and

Johnson whiffed 3,509 from 1907 through 1927. Johnson missed by just one year the chance to manage the young phenom many compared to him. Johnson served as Cleveland's manager from June 1933 until August of 1935. Feller joined the Indians in July of 1936. Feller joined the Indians in July of 1936. One can only imagine the advice the old strikeout king would've had for the next strikeout king. Feller's victory also pitched the Indians back into the American League's driver's seat by a half-game, thanks to New York's 2–0 win over Chicago.

The Indians completed the demolition of Boudreau's boys with a Sunday doubleheader sweep, 4–1 and 8–1, and a 13–5 trouncing in the series finale. Wynn and Garcia posted the victories in the doubleheader and Lemon won the concluding game. After losing the season series to the Red Sox in 1953, the Indians were enjoying some sweet revenge.

When a team puts together the kind of season the Indians fashioned in 1954, contributions often come from unexpected sources. The Tribe could've, and probably should've, been staring disaster in the face after Avila went down with an injury and was soon joined on the bench by his injured replacement, Sam Dente. Lopez, in desperation, turned to veteran journeyman Hank Majeski, who stroked eight hits in 14 at-bats in Boston. And Majeski didn't stop hitting when the Indians returned home.

Cleveland stretched its winning streak to eight in a row with a three-game sweep of the Senators. Rosen was the hero of the first contest, a 9–3 victory, making his first appearance since being sidelined June 5 by the fractured finger a memorable one with a pinch-hit double off Chuck Stobbs with the bases loaded. Rosen's blow was part of a six-run eighth inning that broke open a 3–2 game and made a winner of Houtteman, with ninth-inning relief help from Newhouser.

The June 15 trading deadline passed without the Indians making any deals. The acquisition of Wertz had set the roster they'd do battle with for the rest of the season. "We used to get a lot of calls on the day of the deadline. I guess no one wants to deal with us now," said Lopez.[20]

No one wanted to deal with the Indians on the field, either, although, for the second time, Mickey McDermott seemed to have their number. Earlier in the season, McDermott had baffled the Tribe through eight innings on one hit before weakening. On June 16, McDermott was working on a two-hitter and held a 1–0 lead in the seventh before being driven from the mound, literally. Rosen, again pinch-hitting, smacked a hot grounder that clipped him on the leg. McDermott's successors, Connie Marrero and Bunky Stewart, surrendered five runs and Mossi won his first career start, 5–1. The Indians finished off the sweep with a 6–4 victory credited to Wynn, his eighth, with relief aid from Bob Hooper.

"It all adds up to us being the best ball club with something to spare," crowed Rosen. "When we don't hit, our pitchers hold 'em and we win a low score, tight one. When our pitching isn't so good we make a lot of runs and win that one, too. We're going to take it all and we know it. Not just me and a couple of other guys, but everybody."[21]

Wertz paid immediate dividends, taking over at first base when Rosen was sidelined and batting .350 in his first two weeks in a Cleveland uniform. "Coming to the Indians has been a real tonic for me. I was pretty much resigned to spending some time on the bench, but I made up my mind to be ready when the chance came. It was sooner than I expected and at a position I never even thought about."[22]

Having veterans like Wertz and Majeski available, plus a three-game lead over the White Sox, was making Lopez's job easier and had an effect on the intense manager's disposition. Jones told his readers that it was a more relaxed Lopez who presided over the Cleveland dugout in 1954, with the stomach trouble and sleepless nights that had plagued him in 1952 and 1953, as the Indians struggled to keep up with the Yankees, becoming a thing of the past.

Just three days after finishing a five-game sweep in Boston, the Indians faced the Red Sox in a four-game series at Municipal Stadium beginning June 18, and they stretched their winning streak to nine with a 2–0 victory authored by Garcia. The four-hit shutout lowered the Big Bear's earned run average to a sparkling 2.09, lowest among the "Big Three."

"Spring training was pretty much a nightmare, not being able to get anybody out," Garcia said, looking back three months. "I remember going to Al Lopez's hotel room and asking him what to do. Al just told me to keep throwing and I'd be all right and that seemed to be the right advice."²³ Few people knew more about pitchers and pitching than Lopez, who realized Garcia hadn't mysteriously lost his ability to get batters out over the winter.

A pair of nine-game streaks ended the next day. The Indians' nine-game victory skein was snapped by the Red Sox, who had lost nine in a row to Cleveland in 1954. Boston reached Lemon for 11 hits and five runs en route to the 6–3 triumph. Ellis Kinder, making his first start for Boston since 1952, earned the victory. Boston's one-game winning streak and Cleveland's one-game losing streak didn't last long. The Indians swept a twin bill from the Red Sox on June 20, 3–1 and 9–2. Feller improved his record to 4–1 in the first game. Houtteman notched his seventh victory in the nightcap.

"My control was really good, I thought," Feller said afterward, "and that was probably my biggest advantage. I think I've had better stuff this year but I was really getting it where I wanted it." As to whether, at that stage of his illustrious career, Feller had been relegated to the status of a "doubleheader pitcher," the right-hander responded, "I'd like all the work I can get, but when the team's winning, of course, you're happy to do whatever they want you to do."²⁴

Rosen returned to the Indians' starting lineup for the first time in two weeks and went 2-for-6. Despite the fact that Regalado's average had dropped to .267 and Wertz had apparently found his batting eye, Lopez insisted he wouldn't return Rosen to his natural position and leave Wertz at first base. Avila was ready to reclaim second base, which meant Majeski would go back to the bench, taking the .432 average he'd posted (16-for-37) while substituting for Avila and Dente with him.

The Sunday doubleheader versus the Red Sox had drawn 35,698 fans, but Jones wasn't satisfied. Jones pointed out that the four games the Indians played in Boston the previous weekend had attracted 74,166 fans to Fenway Park, while the four games the Red Sox played in Cleveland drew just 71,284 to Municipal Stadium. Many of those fans had come by special trains from such faraway places as Buffalo, New York, and Columbus and Wapakoneta, Ohio. Jones, and Indians officials, continued to wonder why Clevelanders weren't turning out in larger numbers to cheer their league leaders.

4. Avoiding the Swoon

With the Indians maintaining their slim lead over the White Sox and Yankees as the final ten days of June arrived, Cobbledick offered a reason for the team's improved performance. He credited the stellar play of Philley (despite his anemic .195 batting average), Doby, Smith (a player he'd maligned earlier in the season), Wertz and Majeski. He believed, however, that the club's attitude had also benefited from a case of addition by subtraction. Cobbledick suggested that the departures of Luke Easter and Harry Simpson, an outfielder the Indians had high hopes for who never became the player they thought he'd be, made the Tribe's dugout and clubhouse more pleasant and positive places.

Philley had impressed not only Cobbledick. Much more significantly, he'd impressed his manager, too. "If you look at his .200 average you'd say he was killing us," said Lopez. "Yet, if you saw him play day after day, you'd have to admit he's been a big help. His catches have saved us plenty of games. In fact, I put him back in the line-up to give us a better defense. I'm not one who goes in much for statistics. I go by what I see a man do."[25]

Whitey Lewis, who predicted before the season began that the Indians would slip to third place, had, like Cobbledick, changed his tune. On June 20, Lewis informed his readers that the Indians were clearly the class of the American League, and that a long Tribe losing streak was virtually impossible since there were so many patsies to feast on.

The Indians continued to hammer the league's second division clubs. By winning three of four from Boston, the Tribe improved its record against the Red Sox to a gaudy 11–1. The Indians were 7–1 against Philadelphia, 9–2 versus Washington and 6–2 against Baltimore, for a record against the bottom half of the league of 33–6. A chance to keep fattening up on the have-nots presented itself when the Athletics followed the Red Sox into Cleveland, but the Indians couldn't capitalize.

Rookie manager Eddie Joost's Athletics had won six of their previous eight contests before arriving in Cleveland, where Joost was asked about the Indians' pennant chances. "I won't say the Indians will win the pennant, but right now I'd say you have the best chance. As I see it, it all depends on what you do against the contenders, the Sox and the

Shortstop George Strickland (left) and pitchers Hal Newhouser (center) and Bob Lemon. Cleveland pitchers, especially the sinkerballer Lemon, appreciated Strickland's work with the glove (Cleveland State University, *Cleveland Press* collection).

Yanks. You don't seem to have much trouble with the other clubs. To stay on top, you've got to beat the contenders."[26]

With a weekend series against the Yankees, which was expected to draw the largest crowds of the season to Municipal Stadium, on the horizon, the Indians dropped two of three to Philadelphia. Wynn lost the first contest, 4–1. Lemon helped his own cause with a home run and won the middle game, 5–2. Houtteman lost the rubber match, 5–1. The defeat sliced the Tribe's lead over Chicago to two games. The White Sox beat Washington, 5–2, and the Yankees would arrive in Cleveland four games out of first after whacking Detroit, 11–2. The fans were apparently

4. Avoiding the Swoon

as unenthused about the series with Philadelphia as the players seemed to be. The three games drew 22,083 customers to Municipal Stadium.

First place wasn't at stake, at least as far as the Yankees were concerned, as the two antagonists squared off in the first game of a weekend series on June 24. As a Friday night crowd of 49,808 groaned, New York drove Garcia from the mound with a seven-run third inning uprising and waltzed to an 11–0 victory. The Yankees hit parade continued against relievers Mossi, Narleski, Hoskins and Hooper. Allie Reynolds was generous with the base hits, allowing nine of them, but kept the Indians off the scoreboard. One of the Cleveland safeties was a smash back to the mound off the bat of Dave Pope in third inning. Reynolds said the glancing blow numbed the fingers on his pitching hand briefly and left him with a swollen thumb after the game, but he wasn't expected to miss his next turn. The victory improved Reynolds' record to 9–1 while Garcia absorbed his fifth defeat against nine wins.

"Honestly, a beating like that doesn't hurt as much as a close one," said Lopez. "After a close one you eat your heart out, playing it over and over. It's not any fun, though, to get beat so badly in front of our biggest crowd of the season. We're in better position now than the past four years at this time. Usually June is our bad month. In other years the Yanks were on top and we were trying to knock them off. Now it's the reverse. They've got to catch us, and even though it didn't look it on the field tonight, we're much improved and I don't think they're as good as they were."[27]

The White Sox topped Boston, 6–4, to reduce their first place deficit to one game. The Yankees were three back. In his notes column of June 25, Jones pointed out that New York was having no problems winning games against the league's first division, having compiled a record of 21–11 versus the Indians, White Sox and Tigers (whose record had dropped below the .500 mark.) The Indians, meanwhile, had lost 13 of the 24 games they'd played against the same three teams.

Following their victory over the Indians, the Yankees were established by Las Vegas odds makers as 7–5 favorites to win their sixth straight pennant. Odds on the Indians were 5–2, and 3–1 on the White Sox. In the National League, the Giants were 7–5 favorites to dethrone their bitter rivals, the Dodgers, as pennant winners.

The Yankees torched Tribe pitching for 11 more runs in the second game of the series, sending Wynn to the showers and erasing a 4–2 deficit with a four-run fourth inning. Cleveland enjoyed more success than usual against Lopat, driving him from the game with two outs in the fifth inning after scoring four times on eight hits, but the Tribe bullpen couldn't contain the rampaging New York bats. Smith's three-run seventh inning homer off Bob Grim sliced the Yankees' lead to 9–8, but that was as close as the Indians could come. Sain relieved Grim and held the Tribe in check the rest of the way, allowing a harmless ninth-inning run that made the final score 11–9, sending 46,192 patrons home both unhappy and concerned that the Indians were about to be overtaken by the dreaded Bronx Bombers yet again. The loss shaved Cleveland's lead over New York to two games. The White Sox lost to Boston and missed an opportunity to forge a tie for first place.

The final game, with a paid attendance of 47,782, began less than promisingly for the home team. Lemon had to leave the game after pulling a muscle while popping up a Whitey Ford pitch in the second inning. Lopez called on Newhouser, who pitched four scoreless innings before tiring and allowing single runs in the seventh and eighth. By that time, Wally Westlake's sixth inning two-run homer had broken a 1–1 tie and given the Indians a lead they didn't relinquish. Six-innings, was Newhouser's longest outing of the season, and he told Lopez he was out of gas after the Yankees closed to within 4–3 in the eighth. Lopez sent Garcia to the mound in the ninth. Garcia closed it out and the Indians had salvaged one game.

"Afternoons like this make me glad I stuck with baseball," Newhouser said in the Tribe clubhouse after notching his third win in four decisions. "I didn't have much on the ball and had to be very careful where I put it. That's why I was behind the batters so much."[28]

The Indians' lead over the Yankees grew to three games. They picked up a half-game on Chicago, which split a doubleheader with the cellar-dwelling Red Sox. The Tribe concluded its home stand with an 8–5 record. The Yankees returned to New York having won nine of 13 games on their trip. Stengel had something to say about the last one. "Two games it means to you guys, winning that one. We'll be waitin' for you in New York, though."[29]

4. Avoiding the Swoon

"We're going to be all right," Lopez assured those worried about dropping two of three to their arch-nemesis. "They got a lot of breaks in those first two games, even as we had been getting them for a long time."[30]

Of more immediate concern to the Indians was a visit from the second-place White Sox, which would follow a brief two-game trip to Baltimore and a stop in Pittsburgh for an exhibition against the Pirates to benefit a local charity. The Indians won, 10–2, as 13,581 watched in Forbes Field. Among them was Branch Rickey, who was trying to achieve in Pittsburgh the success he'd enjoyed as general manager of the Cardinals and Dodgers. Rickey was particularly interested in Strickland, who was property of the Pirates when Rickey came to town. In August of 1952, Rickey sent Strickland to Cleveland along with pitcher Ted Wilks for utility player Johnny Berardino, minor league hurler Charlie Sipple, and cash. "I don't see how I could have been so wrong about that boy," Rickey confided to Lopez before the game.[31]

Rudy Regalado collected five hits in five at-bats in the exhibition victory, but Lopez wasn't impressed. While still the darling of the writers, Regalado was rapidly falling out of favor with the people whose opinions really mattered. Lopez thought Regalado was concentrating too much on hitting, to the detriment of the rest of his game. "It is characteristic of all young players to think this game begins and ends with the bat. There is more to it than that, and this I have told Regalado," said the manager, who left unsaid his belief that Regalado hadn't gotten the message.[32]

Said one unidentified Indians coach, "Regalado looks like a .270 hitter with the reactions of a guy about 40. Either he hasn't got the right slant on this game, or he hasn't got what it takes."[33] It was rumored that the red-hot rapper of spring training would be demoted to Triple-A when catcher Mickey Grasso was activated after the All-Star break. Grasso's broken ankle didn't heal quickly enough for that to happen, so Regalado remained in Cleveland, but was used sparingly.

When the Indians beat Baltimore, 5–1, in Memorial Stadium on June 29, Orioles fans saw a familiar face at third base for the visitors. Saying the move was "experimental," Lopez returned Rosen to his natural position and stationed former Oriole Wertz at first. "Rosen says his finger feels all right, so this is as good a time as any to make the move," the manager explained. "I'd have switched him in the Yankee series last weekend if he had been able to throw. I thought Vic did a pretty good job [at first base] so I want to take another look at him. This is a good time to do it, before the White Sox series. If he does as well as he did before, I'll let him stay there."[34]

Garcia rebounded from his miserable outing against the Yankees to whitewash Baltimore on four hits, 2–0, on June 30, shaking off three errors by his teammates to become the first member of the Big Three to reach double figures in victories. As the sun set on the final day of the month, the American League standings looked like this:

Cleveland	48–22	.686	—
Chicago	46–26	.639	3
New York	45–27	.625	4
Detroit	31–37	.456	16
Washington	29–40	.420	18½
Philadelphia	28–41	.406	19½
Baltimore	27–44	.380	21½
Boston	25–42	.373	21½

The Indians had avoided the dreaded "June swoon," which Lopez admitted had been the team's downfall during his first three years as manager, going 20–9 for the month. In most seasons, by winning 69 percent of their games, they'd have lapped the field. But 1954 wasn't most seasons. The Yankees had already lost more than half of the games they'd lose the entire year. The Indians would need an effort of historic proportions to outlast them.

5

SEEING STARS

Vic Wertz had swung a hot bat since joining the Indians in early June. But that wouldn't be enough to keep him in the lineup for an important four-game series at Municipal Stadium against the second-place White Sox. Al Lopez announced on July 1 that Bill Glynn, the defensive half of the offense/defense first base platoon the Tribe planned to use for the remainder of the season, would get the nod against Chicago.

"We'll need all the defense we can get against the White Sox," Lopez explained. "They like to run and bunt."[1] The style Lopez used when he managed Chicago to the 1959 American League pennant had been introduced by his predecessor, Paul Richards, and Richards' style kept the White Sox nipping at the Indians' heels as July began.

July opened with a pair of strong denials. One was issued by Bob Feller, who refuted the claim of a Baltimore newspaper that a rift had developed between himself and Al Lopez due to Feller's lack of work. During the Indians' visit to Baltimore, Feller had spoken to a press luncheon and admitted he wanted to pitch more. That was hardly news to anyone in Cleveland, but a Baltimore writer chose to make a story from Feller's statements. When the team returned home, Feller denied claims that there was bad blood between him and his manager. "A manager does what he thinks is best," said Feller. "That's what he gets paid for. Sure, I think I could pitch and win oftener. I suppose most pitchers feel the same way. I'll pitch whenever I'm called upon and as long as they pay me on the first and fifteenth."[2] Maybe that wasn't such a strong denial after all.

Responded Lopez, "in my opinion, we're getting the most out of our staff the way it is now. I certainly don't blame Bob for wanting more work. In fact, I like to have players feel that way."[3] Lopez's use, or misuse, of Feller would be a favorite topic of Cleveland scribes throughout the season.

Before the series with Chicago began, Al Rosen vehemently denied a report in a New York newspaper that, due to his injured finger, he had decided not to play in the All-Star game, which would be held in Cleveland. "That is completely untrue. I hope I get enough votes to make the team and would be very proud to play. I would consider it a great honor." Rosen admitted his finger was still swollen and painful. "The other day in diving for a ball I landed right on it and made it worse. The doctor tells me the pain will remain for some time. I suppose the only real cure is rest and I'm torn between wanting to play in an effort to help the team as much as I can or sit on the sidelines and help myself." Rosen revealed that Hank Greenberg had offered him a two-year contract at $40,000 per season in 1953, and he had declined. "Why should I limit my earning power?" the slugger asked. "I expect to prove I'm worth more." Now that Rosen's injury had essentially ended his chance for a raise in 1955, Rosen pondered, "I wonder, when we talk salary next year, if he'll take into consideration that I'm not letting this finger keep me on the bench?"[4]

It hadn't been lost on the Yankees that the Indians were maintaining their lead by laying waste to Philadelphia, Washington, Boston and Baltimore while struggling against the contenders. New York's players didn't think the Indians' domination of the tail-enders could continue. They also thought Richards' White Sox showed more spark than the Tribe after playing both clubs in late June.

The Yankees may have been impressed with the White Sox, but the Tigers, who played them before Chicago visited Cleveland for the Independence Day holiday weekend, were not. "The Sox don't seem to have the same spark as before," said one unidentified Tiger. "They look a little tired," said another.[5] Lopez thought he knew why. "They know they've got to beat us or fall back in the race," said the senor. "Maybe they were thinking about us while playing the Tigers. They'll be charged up for us. They always are. We'll do what we've done all season—play each game as it comes up and give it our best shot."[6]

5. Seeing Stars

Fears that Clevelanders weren't interested in the pennant race were assuaged somewhat when 48,331 descended on Municipal Stadium for the Friday night doubleheader that opened the showdown with the White Sox. They watched the Tribe sweep their closest pursuers, 3–2 and 5–4. Bob Feller improved his record to 5–1 with a four-hit, complete-game victory in the opener, a game he said afterward that he'd been lucky to win. "I might have gotten a pasting except for a couple of good breaks. I didn't have much of anything except pretty fair control [four walks]. I felt weak and not right in a pitching sense before the game. I couldn't overpower anybody [just one strikeout]. Had to outsmart them." Feller expressed the hope that he'd be back on the mound soon. "With no open dates and a couple of doubleheaders coming up, maybe it won't be so long."[7] Feller's last start had been June 20 in Boston. Eleven days' rest between appearances was more than he felt he required, but he was the fifth starter in an era of four-man rotations.

Wynn's complete-game eight-hitter won the nightcap, his ninth against six losses. Four Cleveland runs in the fifth inning gave Wynn a lead he managed to hang onto, and together Feller and Wynn gave the Tribe bullpen the evening off. That development proved to beneficial the next day.

A Saturday crowd of 27,704 got its money's worth and then some as the Indians and White Sox battled for 15 innings before the Tribe prevailed, 5–4, rendering Lopez's protest of a stratagem by Richards moot. With the White Sox ahead, 3–2, in the home half of the eighth inning, Richards shifted pitcher Sandy Consuegra to third base and summoned Morrie Martin to pitch to Larry Doby, who was leading off the inning. After Martin retired Doby, Richards waved Consuegra back to the mound and the umpiring crew permitted him to toss the customary eight warmup pitches, much to Lopez's consternation. Consuegra couldn't hold the lead, as a solo home run by Wally Westlake tied the contest and set up the marathon that ended when Hank Majeski's pinch single off Jack Harshman plated Doby and Al Rosen with the tying and winning runs. Chicago's Johnny Groth had given his team the lead in the top of the 15th with a single that scored Phil Cavarretta and appeared to give the White Sox the victory. Hal Newhouser earned his fourth win in five decisions with six innings of three-hit, one-run relief pitching.

Flouting tradition, the schedule maker gave the Indians a single game against the White Sox on the Fourth of July. With the holiday falling on a Sunday, the traditional doubleheaders had been scheduled for the following day, when the Tribe would be in Detroit. The 26,842 who celebrated Independence Day by visiting Municipal Stadium were almost treated to a piece of history, as Mike Garcia, Ray Narleski, and Early Wynn came within one out of tossing the first combined no-hitter in major league history. Minnie Minoso spoiled the fun with a two-out single in the ninth inning, but the Indians won the game, 2–1, to finish off the sweep. Garcia had to leave the game in the second inning when a blood vessel in the middle finger of his pitching hand ruptured. Narleski got the win with five and two-thirds innings of scoreless and hitless relief, and Wynn would've earned a save had saves been a statistic in 1954. The White Sox scored an unearned run in the eighth inning on a walk, a wild pitch, a ground out and an error.

"I seem to pitch better in relief and I suppose that's why I'm not doing any worrying about starting," said Narleski.[8] The four nail-biting, one-run victories improved the Indians' record in games decided by a single run to 18–6. According to baseball tradition, the team in first place on the Fourth of July was supposed to win the pennant. That bromide had held true since 1948 in the American League, which boded well for the Indians, who enjoyed a 4½-game advantage on Independence Day. The White Sox left Cleveland licking their wounds and anxious for another shot at the Tribe, which they'd get the next weekend in Comiskey Park.

Hal Lebovitz, in the *News,* wrote the next day that had Wynn retired Minoso and completed the no-hitter, it would not have been recognized by *The Little Red Book* of major league baseball, which conferred official status only on no-hitters pitched by a single pitcher.

"I'm home again. Mentally, I feel 100 percent better,"[9] said Rosen of his return to third base, only weeks after claiming that first base was much easier to play and felt completely natural. Rosen had asked Lopez to return to his accustomed position before the series against the Yankees, but Lopez kept him at first, fearing his injured finger wouldn't allow him to throw

5. Seeing Stars

the ball across the diamond. Asked if the move was permanent, Lopez answered, "I think so. Of course, if we can't find an answer at first base we'll move him back, but now that he's expressed himself as wanting to play third I'll try to keep him there."[10] As to the possibility of Wertz being the answer at first, Lopez said, "he's the first baseman as long as he hits. That's what his job depends on. If he doesn't hit, he won't be much help."[11]

The results of fan voting for the All-Star Game were announced during the holiday weekend, and the American League's starting lineup would feature two Indians, both on the right side of the infield. Despite playing only two weeks at first base, and ignoring the fact that he'd been permanently returned to the other side of the diamond, fans made Rosen the league's All-Star first baseman, and Bob Avila won the nod as the starter at second. Rosen was batting .337 with 14 homers and 58 RBI, and Avila was assaulting American League pitching at a .359 clip. All-Star manager Casey Stengel added Doby as a backup outfielder and selected Garcia and Bob Lemon as pitchers.

Glynn, the defensive half of the Glynn/Wertz first base platoon, enjoyed a career day at the plate with three homers and eight runs batted in as the Indians trounced the Tigers, 13–6, in the first game of the July 5 twin bill at Briggs Stadium. Houtteman picked up the victory in relief of Dave Hoskins, who failed to make it through the fourth inning. The nightcap was a pitchers' duel between Don Mossi and former Indian George Zuverink, who combined to permit just seven hits and one run, that run provided by Detroit's Harvey Kuenn, whose solo homer in the 11th inning gave the Tigers a 1–0 victory.

The Tribe's visit to Detroit was brief. The Indians returned home for a three-game series with Baltimore, the last games they'd play in Cleveland until July 27. Waiting for them after they concluded matters with the Orioles was a 16-game road trip, interrupted by the three-day All-Star break and starting with a four-game series in Chicago.

By this point in the season, no visiting manager could escape Cleveland without being asked to size up the Indians' pennant chances. In the opinion of Orioles boss Jimmy Dykes, "you ought to win it. You've got the pitching, the power and the bench. Now or never."[12]

The Indians barely broke a sweat sweeping the Orioles. Their 11–3

.721

victory on July 6, in which Cleveland put up 11 first-inning runs and Wynn held the visitors without a hit until Jim Brideweser tripled with one out in the eighth inning, gave them a record of 54–23 after 77 games, the halfway point of the 154-game season. They led the Yankees by 3½ games, and were on a pace to win 108 games. Harry Jones wrote that the players were confident 98 victories would win the pennant, meaning they needed to go 44–33 the rest of the way.

"You don't want to use up all your luck in one night," Wynn said of his foiled bid for a no-hitter. "I would have liked a shutout, but I'm satisfied. Sure, I'd like to get a no-hitter in the record book before I'm through, but I figure I've got some time left."[13]

Garcia pitched eight innings in the Indians' 6–1 victory in the second game, giving way to Narleski after the finger in which the blood vessel had ruptured in his previous start became sensitive. "It began to swell up some in the eighth inning and I decided I'd better get out of there. I couldn't grip the ball too well and didn't throw too hard. Guess I didn't use anything but a fastball."[14] A fastball was more than enough to shackle the woeful Orioles.

A brisk wind held up two balls Rosen was sure he'd powered over the fence. It was a problem he'd encountered frequently since incurring his nagging finger injury. "Sometimes I'm afraid this finger just won't be right until next year. I just can't get any right hand in my swing. I'm afraid I'm about 20 feet short of my full power since I hurt the finger," lamented the discouraged slugger.[15]

Feller finished off the sweep with a complete-game, 4–1 win on July 8. The victory was achieved almost 18 years to the day after he'd made his Cleveland debut in an exhibition game at League Park on July 6, 1936. The 17-year-old Iowa farm boy fanned eight stunned St. Louis Cardinals in three innings. The fastball Feller used to set the American League on its ear during the latter years of the Great Depression was just a fading memory by 1954. "I fired the ball by a couple of them," said Feller of his sixth win of the campaign. "That doesn't happen too often anymore. I figure I'll get about ten more starts this season. Sure 15 victories would be a nice total, but it'll take a lot of pitching to make it. I'm not setting any target of victories, just trying to win one at a time."[16]

5. Seeing Stars

After disposing of another also-ran, Lopez commented on the lack of competitive balance in the American League. Five of the circuit's eight clubs had lost more games than they'd won. Lopez believed that would change. "It looks that way right now, I'll grant you. But you watch. I'm positive those other five clubs will wake up and cause plenty of trouble. They're all better than the standings would indicate. It's just that right now there are three hot clubs, the Yanks, the White Sox, and us."[17]

Lopez also answered those who wondered how long the Indians could stand the pressure of the Yankees continuing to win. "People keep saying to me that no matter how much we win, the Yankees are always right there, waiting for us to slip. They say this puts the pressure on us. Well, I happen to know Casey Stengel is very upset that he can't get closer no matter how much they win. That's pressure too, isn't it? Frustration can wreck you."[18]

As the Indians prepared for a lengthy road trip that would take them first to Chicago and then east, pundits looked for the reasons the club was hanging on to first place, unlike previous editions which had, by early July, fallen behind the Yankees, destined never to catch up. The answer could be found in the team's second-line pitching. The Big Three was holding up its end, with a combined record of 30–15 as compared to 29–17 at the same point in 1953. But the contributions of Houtteman, Feller and the bullpen of Mossi, Narleski and Newhouser far surpassed those of their 1953 counterparts. The Indians' spot starters and relievers had a sparkling record of 25–8, compared to 17–18 in 1953. The additions of Mossi, Narleski and Newhouser, plus the return to form of Feller and Houtteman, were proving to be crucial.

Houtteman, in particular, was an intriguing case. Lopez, who knew a thing or two about the science of pitching, said, "Houtteman has everything needed to be a great pitcher, but he can't seem to find the right combination."[19] Houtteman found the right combination in 1954, but couldn't sustain it. He would never again be consistently effective.

Hank Greenberg knew why the Indians were leading the league.

> "Seems that whomever [sic] we call on comes through. That's how Stengel has been winning for five years. He points his finger to somebody on the bench, the player goes in and produces. Until now it has been the other

way with us. We brought up [Harry] Simpson. He didn't help. We brought up Al Smith last year. He didn't come through. There were so many others. No matter whom we tried it was the same story. But this year every time we make a line up change the new player rises to the occasion."[20]

Still stinging from being swept in Cleveland the previous weekend, the White Sox opened the final series before the All-Star break with an 8–3 victory on July 9. Houtteman was driven from the mound during a four-run seventh inning which wiped out a 3–2 Tribe lead. Newhouser, Mossi and Hooper couldn't quiet the Chicago bats, with the loss charged to Newhouser. Richards, who'd been one of Newhouser's catchers in Detroit, thought he'd figured out his old teammate after Hal had stymied the White Sox during the 15-inning marathon in Cleveland the week before. "We were swinging at bad balls," said the White Sox skipper. "He didn't throw a strike the whole night."[21] Richards instructed his players to lay off Newhouser's offerings out of the strike zone, and two bases on balls proved to be his downfall.

Jack Harshman enjoyed a measure of revenge for suffering the loss in that 15-inning game when he and Sandy Consuegra blanked the Tribe, 3–0, in the second game of the series. Chicago extended the Indians' losing streak to four with a Sunday doubleheader sweep, 3–0 and 8–2. Chicago pitchers Bob Keegan, Harshman, Billy Pierce and Virgil Trucks kept the Indians from denting home plate for 28 consecutive innings before the Tribe pushed across two runs against Trucks in the ninth inning of the second game of the doubleheader. The Indians had squeezed out four hard-fought, one-run victories over the White Sox in Cleveland. The Sox had thoroughly dominated the first-place Tribe in Comiskey Park, outscoring them 22–5 in the four games. Cleveland's lead over New York was reduced to a half-game. The Indians had arrived in Chicago leading the White Sox by a comfortable seven games. They departed with a not-so-comfy three-game advantage.

Things got so bad during the second game of the doubleheader that scholarly Tribe pitching coach Mel Harder, who authored 223 victories while wearing a Cleveland uniform from 1928–1947, was given the heave-ho by umpire Ed Hurley. Harder had questioned Hurley's strike zone after Hurley called Lemon's 2-and-1 pitch to rookie first baseman Ron

5. Seeing Stars

Jackson a ball. Lemon made the 3-and-1 pitch too good and Jackson slammed a three-run homer.

"All I said to Hurley was 'that kid's got a big strike zone,'" Harder insisted.[22] For good measure, Hurley ended Lemon's day early by ejecting him in the fifth inning. Lemon had to be physically restrained by Lopez from going after Hurley. "The Indians have had trouble all season with this umpiring crew," noted the *News*.

Richards summed up the difference a week made. "You were hot then and we were cold. This time you got cold and we heated up."[23]

The debacle in Comiskey Park was enough to sour Hall of Fame second baseman Rogers Hornsby on the Tribe's chances. Hornsby, whose managerial resume included stints with the Cardinals, Braves, Cubs, Browns and Reds, in addition to an interim appointment with the Giants in 1927 while John McGraw was ailing, declared the Indians dead. Never one to mince words, Hornsby, despite the fact that the Indians were still clinging to first place, declared, "the Indians had their chance and blew it."[24] A lot of Indians fans, fearing the "June swoon" had been delayed until July, probably agreed with the Rajah.

The sweep at the hands of the White Sox cost the Indians more than several games in the standings. They lost the honor of carrying the best record in major league baseball into the All-Star break. The Indians were 56–27. The Giants were 57–27. Far more importantly to Lopez and his charges, the Yankees were 56–28.

Cleveland hosted its second All-Star Game in 1954, and the American League out-slugged the Nationals, 11–9, as 69,751 fans looked on and cheered for the game's reluctant hero, Cleveland's own Rosen. Dean Stone of Washington earned the victory while throwing just three pitches and not retiring a batter — Red Schoendienst was caught trying to steal home — simply because he got somebody out, which nobody on either team (except Whitey Ford, who started and pitched three scoreless innings) seemed to be capable of doing. Rosen, required to start at first base after having been voted on to the team by the fans, told Stengel he'd hold no grudge if the manager chose to remove him after one at-bat, even though starters were supposed to play at least three innings. Rosen was in the throes of a slump that had seen his batting average plunge

.721

from .382 prior to his finger injury to .313, and he'd hit just one home run since May 28. Knowing Stengel was anxious to win his first All-Star Game (he was 0–4 as the American League pilot), Rosen told Casey, "I probably won't do your club any good because I haven't helped my own club lately."[25]

Rosen's attitude changed after he was fanned by Philadelphia Phillies ace Robin Roberts with two runners on base to end the first inning.

> "The fans voted me into the game and I wanted to start, but I figured I'd be out of there after one time at bat. Probably would have been, too, if it hadn't been for that strikeout. I couldn't leave after that. I wanted at least one more crack at it. With this bum finger and being in a slump, I was scared to death about being the All-Star Game goat. But that strikeout made me mad and I forgot about the finger. Yeah, the finger is painful, but I know that wasn't causing all my trouble. I was doing everything wrong up there. The way I feel now, this has snapped me out of it."[26]

Perhaps inspired by the fear of failing in front of his home fans, Rosen slammed a three-run homer off Roberts with Minoso and Avila on base in the third inning, and added a two-run shot off Johnny Antonelli of the Giants, scoring Yogi Berra ahead of him, in the fifth. Rosen played the entire game and contributed three hits to the American League's first victory since 1949. His two homers and five runs batted in tied Ted Williams' record for the midsummer classic. But the AL still needed a two-run bloop single by Chicago second baseman Nellie Fox in the eighth inning to nail down the win.

After the game, Stengel chatted with writers about the contributions made by Cleveland's Rosen and Avila (six hits, seven runs batted in between them) and Chicago's Minoso and Fox, who added three hits and a pair of runs batted in. Virgil Trucks worked a scoreless ninth. "Now they see what I'm up against in this American League,"[27] cracked Stengel, who could, for one day, appreciate the talents of the star players of the two clubs fighting his Yankees for the pennant.

Lopez had no doubt that his team would shake off its miserable weekend in Chicago as it continued its lengthy road trip on the east coast. "We ought to start rolling again now. Rosen and Avila look as though they're ready to go again. And there shouldn't be any more talk

5. Seeing Stars

of benching Rosen. I knew his finger was bothering him, but I felt all along that Rosen was simply in a slump. He wasn't swinging right and it wasn't only because of his finger. That two weeks rest just set him back."[28]

An Indian who needed a rest, apparently, was George Strickland. "I want Strickland to get a good rest before starting the second half. He's had three days off now, so two or three more ought to do the trick,"[29] said Lopez. Strickland would get a much longer rest than Lopez, or anyone else, wanted, thanks to a serious injury sustained in Yankee Stadium at the end of the road trip.

Lopez's confidence was justified. Not only did he believe in his team, but the Indians opened the post–All Star break portion of the season with series against also-rans Philadelphia, Washington and Boston, each of which they had dominated up to that point. Lopez was certain the Tribe's mastery over the second division of the American League would continue.

In Philadelphia, which had been put on notice by Earle and Roy Mack, feuding sons of the club's former manager and founder, 91-year old Connie Mack, that attendance would have to increase dramatically in July, August and September or the Athletics would be sold to out-of-town buyers, the Indians started the unofficial second half of the campaign with a 4–0 victory. The shutout was authored by Wynn, who retired the last 13 batters he faced. The Indians managed only five hits off Alex Kellner and Mario Fricano, bunched in the fourth and fifth innings. The offense came to life the next day, slamming 18 hits in a 9–3 rout. Garcia won his 12th game but left early again in deference to his fragile middle finger. Narleski came out of the bullpen and pitched three perfect innings. While this was going on, the Yankees were extending a winning streak that began on July 3 to 11 straight games. Nonetheless, Lopez thought the streak had exposed a weakness, as neither Allie Reynolds nor Ed Lopat were responsible for any of the victories. "They've managed to get along lately without Reynolds and Lopat, but I doubt they can go very far without them," the Tribe skipper said.[30] All 11 of New York's victories had come against second division clubs, the same clubs the Indians had been fattening up on and would could continue to feast on for the rest of the year. They finished their stay in Philadelphia with a 6–0 victory on July 17. Feller faced just 29 Athletics, walking none and allowing two hits, both to Don Bollweg. Feller needed only 97 pitches to subdue the dreadful Athletics. Seventy-five of the pitches were strikes. "I seem to recall pitching to 29 batters in a game a few years ago," Feller said. "Just when it was I don't remember. I had pretty good stuff, but control was the thing. I could throw the ball just about where I wanted to."[31] The shutout improved Feller's record to 7–1.

The Indians dropped out of first place, but just briefly, on July 18. Losing the first game of a doubleheader to the Senators at Griffith Stadium, 8–3, sank them a half-game behind the Yankees, who shut out the Tigers in the first game of a twin bill, 6–0, behind the five-hit pitching of Harry Byrd. Within hours, the Tribe was back on top, as it captured the nightcap, 7–4, while Detroit was outscoring New York in the second game of their doubleheader, 8–6. Cleveland scored twice in the seventh and eighth innings to overcome a 4–3 deficit and make a winner of Mossi, in relief of Lemon, who continued to exhibit the effects of the pulled muscle he sustained before the All-Star break. The loss in the opener marked the first time the Indians had been out of first place since June 11.

Dale Mitchell's pinch-hit single the next day scored Doby and produced a 4–3 victory that Lopez needed three pitchers to preserve in the ninth inning. Houtteman, Mossi and Narleski tamed the Nats in the ninth and saved the victory for Wynn. Rosen drove in three of the Indians' four runs, giving him 71 for the season and 12 since the All-Star break. It appeared the Tribe third baseman really had conquered his prolonged slump. Senators fans who took in the game from the bleachers on a hot July afternoon probably didn't even notice Lemon sitting among them, soaking up the sun. Lopez suggested his ace pitcher watch the proceedings from the stands, minus a shirt. "Let the sun bake your side," said Dr. Lopez. "Might do it some good."[32]

From Washington, it was on to Boston, where the Indians and Red Sox battled through 16 innings before the league's 12:59 A.M. curfew forced the umpires to declare the game a 5–5 tie. With the Red Sox one out from a win, Avila's two-run homer off Willard Nixon in the ninth inning drove in Al Smith ahead of him and ended the scoring for the evening.

5. Seeing Stars

Twelve hours later, the two teams went at it again and slugged their way to a 7–7 deadlock that ended when rain descended on Fenway Park in the ninth inning. The Indians had fought back from a six-run deficit to take a 7–6 lead that reliever Hoskins couldn't hold. The umpires waited 41 minutes before declaring the game a tie. The rain stopped minutes later, but the umpires' decision couldn't be reversed. The statistics from both games went into the record books, but the games had to be replayed.

An afternoon baking his ailing side in the blazing Washington sun was apparently just what Lemon needed. After Feller stopped the Red Sox in the first game of a Thursday doubleheader, 6–3, with a complete-game seven-hitter, Lemon duplicated the feat and finished the sweep with a 5–2 victory, the 150th of his career. The double victory kept the Tribe in first place by a half-game as the Yankees took two from the White Sox, 4–3 and 11–1.

Lopez joked about how his fan mail had changed recently. The manager said he was accustomed to getting letters urging him to not use Feller since, in the opinion of the writers, the one-time ace was now obviously washed-up. In 1954, however, Lopez got letters from fans begging him to let Feller pitch more often. There was nothing derogatory about the term "doubleheader pitcher" as it applied to Feller, whose record stood at 8–1 after his victory over the Red Sox. Lopez also said he wasn't interested in Detroit coach Lynwood "Schoolboy" Rowe's opinion of the pennant race. That was after Rowe claimed that "the Yankees will win the pennant because Cleveland will fold up like an accordion."[33]

Stengel had promised that the Yankees would be waiting for the Indians when they arrived in New York to wrap up their 16-game journey, and he greeted the visitors by sending to the mound their chief nemesis, Lopat, seeking his 40th career victory over the Tribe. Lopat's assortment of junk, which usually totally flummoxed the Clevelanders, was no mystery to them on the 23rd of July. Doby homered twice, Smith went deep and drove in five runs, and the Indians bagged an 8–2 victory, scoring all of their runs after the fifth inning. A crowd of 61,446 watched Wynn scatter 14 Yankees safeties to notch his 13th win in 20 decisions. The Indians increased their lead to 1½ games. "I liked him better than in many of the games where he gave up less hits," said Lopez of Wynn's

.721

outing. "At least ... he wasn't running the count to three-and-two on every hitter. When he does that it kills me. I'd rather see them hit."[34]

The win came with a price. Strickland suffered a fractured jaw when hit by a throw while sliding into third base. New York team physician Dr. Sidney Gaynor examined the Indians shortstop and urged him to return to Cleveland immediately to have the jaw wired, rather than waiting for his teammates to finish the series in two days. Gaynor thought Strickland would miss at least a month of action. He'd be replaced by light-hitting (even lighter than Strickland, who was batting .231 at the time) Sam Dente, who'd be expected to hold the fort at the infield's most difficult position until at least Labor Day. WIN PLENTY WITH DENTE

Al Smith (left), Larry Doby, Hal Newhouser and Bobby Avila. Doby led the American League with 126 RBI in 1954, and Avila led in batting average at .341 (Cleveland State University, *Cleveland Press* collection).

5. Seeing Stars

became the club's rallying cry in the absence of their regular shortstop, and that was just what the Indians did.

The Tribe wasn't the only contender to suffer a serious loss due to injury. The third-place White Sox, who were still within striking distance, would have to do without the services of first baseman Ferris Fain for an indefinite period after Fain tore ligaments in his right knee. Speculation as to the length of time Fain would need to recover from surgery ranged from several weeks to the rest of the season.

Doby's third home run in two games, a two-run blast off reliever Johnny Sain in the tenth inning, proved to be a game-winner after Narleski fell behind Gil McDougald three balls and no strikes with the tying run on third in the home half of the inning, then rallied to fan the New York third baseman to end the second game of the set. The 5–4 victory stretched Cleveland's lead to 2½ games and guaranteed they'd leave New York in first place. It also ended a streak of 15 consecutive appearances by Sain in Yankees victories.

"After games like these, they ought to take the manager and walk him around the field three times to cool him off and then put him under blankets the way they do race horses," said Lopez of the nail-biter. "My stomach is all tied up. I'd rather be playing. When you play you can get rid of your nervous energy." Told that, in the Yankees clubhouse, Stengel had called his team's close defeat "a great game," Lopez responded, "I'd take it in stride, too, I think, if I had won five pennants in a row."[35]

The Yankees needed 11 innings to salvage the final game of the series. The Indians couldn't hold a 3–1 lead before 57,259 fans, and a bases-loaded single by Andy Carey off Houtteman scored Mickey Mantle with the winning run in a 4–3 game. The Yankees hadn't lost more than two straight games all season, and they kept that record intact. The Indians nonetheless had no complaints about a swing through the east that saw them win nine of 11 and add a game to their margin over the Yankees.

It wasn't often that a coach would take an exhibition game seriously enough to get himself tossed over a play that didn't go his way, but it happened in the annual match-up between the Indians and a National League visitor on July 26, for the benefit of the Cleveland Baseball Federation. St. Louis Cardinals first base coach Bill Posedel got the thumb

.721

from umpire Ed Hurley in the first inning for arguing too strenuously over a call Hurley made in a game that didn't count. Manager Eddie Stanky, who probably wanted to be somewhere else to begin with, had to take Posedel's place in the coach's box. Then again, maybe Posedel wanted the night off himself and goaded Hurley into accommodating him. The game, won by the Cardinals, 2–1, drew 33,775 fans on a Monday evening and raised $34,000 for sandlot baseball in Cleveland.

The exhibition with the Cardinals marked the Cleveland debut of catcher Mickey Grasso, who was still recovering from the severely broken ankle he'd suffered in spring training. Grasso played briefly, stroking a single and gunning down a runner attempting to steal. He could barely run, however, and was a long way from being activated.

July 26 was a memorable day for Garcia, for reasons both good and bad. Garcia's wife gave birth to a son, Michael Martin Garcia, after a difficult pregnancy. But the Big Bear's joy at becoming a father was dampened by the death of his father, Merced Garcia, in Visalia, California, on the same day. Garcia's mother-in-law had passed away earlier in the season. Garcia left immediately to attend his father's funeral.

The Indians opened a home stand against the Red Sox on July 27 with a 6–3 victory, highlighted when Doby somersaulted over the center field fence trying to catch a home run off the bat of Jackie Jensen, spraining his neck in the effort. Doby was replaced by Westlake, but his injury wasn't considered serious and proved not to be. Lemon spaced ten hits while pitching a complete game for his 12th win.

It has often been said that people should be careful what they wish for since those wishes might come true. Hal Lebovitz wrote in the *News* on July 28 that while most of the Indians believed the Dodgers would defend their National League pennant, they hoped their spring training antagonists, the Giants, would win the NL flag. The Polo Grounds could accommodate more paying customers than Ebbets Field, Brooklyn's tiny home park, and that would mean larger World Series shares for the participating clubs, of which the Indians were confident they'd be one. Lebovitz added that the Indians had no doubts they'd beat whoever represented the NL in the Series.

Cleveland took the second game of the series from Boston, 2–1,

5. Seeing Stars

despite being limited to five hits by Russ Kemmerer. A two-run, sixth-inning rally, with Rosen doubling in Avila and then scoring on Wertz's single, gave Wynn his 14th victory. The Red Sox out-hit the Tribe, 11–5. Wynn had coughed up 25 hits over his last 18 innings but only three runs.

The fans who'd written to Lopez urging him to use Feller more often may have had second thoughts after the Red Sox routed the Tribe's fifth starter, 10–2, to salvage the final game of the series. Feller failed to survive the second inning as Boston beat Cleveland for just the second time in 17 tries.

Houtteman halted the one-game losing streak with an 8–3 victory over Washington on July 30, keeping the visitors off the scoreboard after Roy Sievers clouted a first-inning homer with a teammate aboard. Houtteman got a large assist from Doby who, after almost stealing a home run from Boston's Jensen a few games earlier, committed highway robbery against the Senators' Tom Umphlett. Doby leapt over the five-foot fence in center field, caught the ball while bouncing off the awning covering the Indians' bullpen, and returned to Earth within the confines of the playing field, clutching the ball. Dizzy Dean, who was in the broadcast booth for the national television broadcast, called Doby's grab the greatest he'd ever seen. "I seen them all," said Diz, "[Terry] Moore, [Joe] DiMaggio, and this here fellow named Mays. But I never seen a catch as good as this one and that pitcher ought to pay that Doby a month's salary."[36]

"Larry really took off and most of him was over the fence when he back-handed that ball," said umpire John Flaherty, who watched the play to make sure Doby held on to the ball. "He bounced off that awning like a rubber ball. I thought he broke his back until he held up his glove with the ball in it."[37] "I just went for the ball," said Doby modestly. "The fellows in our bullpen told me my right hand went through the awning before I bounced off. If it did, I didn't notice. I didn't get hurt much. Knocked the wind out of me. And my left shoulder gave me a little jolt, where I hurt it before. Maybe it hit a nerve."[38]

Dean Stone, the winning pitcher in the All-Star Game the last time he took the mound in Municipal Stadium, didn't fare as well this time, although his appearance was almost as brief. Stone's record fell to 8–4 as the Indians touched him up for six hits and five runs in two innings. In Baltimore, the Orioles spoiled Stengel's 64th birthday by routing the Yankees, 10–0. Cleveland's lead increased to 2½ games, but Stengel wasn't concerned. "It'll take 100 games to win it," the Yankee boss told reporters. "We'll win it because I got the money players."[39]

Lemon barely broke a sweat as he closed out July by pitching the Indians to a 6–0 victory over the Senators. Lemon faced just 30 batters and allowed only three harmless hits. Doby and Rosen slammed first-inning homers off Frank "Spec" Shea and Lemon coasted to his 13th victory. The loss was Shea's ninth in ten decisions.

At the conclusion of business on July 31, the American League standings showed little change from the final day of June.

Cleveland	69–30	.697	—
New York	68–34	.667	2½
Chicago	64–39	.621	7
Detroit	45–55	.450	24½
Washington	42–54	.438	25½
Boston	40–58	.408	28½
Baltimore	36–65	.356	34
Philadelphia	35–64	.354	34

In an ordinary season, the Yankees and White Sox records would have put them in first place, in the Yankees' case by a substantial margin. But 1954 was no ordinary season. If New York continued to win at its current pace, the 98 victories the Indians thought would be enough to nose out the defending champions would earn them the ignominy of a fourth consecutive second-place finish. No one in Cleveland was willing to settle for that.

6

CAN'T SHAKE THE YANKS

There aren't many better ways for a pennant contender to start a month than with a doubleheader sweep, and that's how the Indians ushered in August. They needed a solid effort from Early Wynn in the first game as Washington's Johnny Schmitz held them to five hits. A three-run seventh-inning rally gave Wynn all the support he needed as he posted his 15th victory, 3–1. The Senators put up more of a fight in the nightcap, knocking Mike Garcia out of the game with four fifth-inning runs. That was all the scoring Washington would do, and Hal Newhouser picked up not only a victory with a strong relief effort, but also his first hit of the season, off Bob Porterfield, scoring Sam Dente with the winning run in the seventh inning. The Indians prevailed, 5–4.

Newhouser conceded after the game that he no longer had the kind of stuff that enabled him to win 80 games while losing just 27 for Detroit from 1944–1946. But he hadn't forgotten how to pitch. "I'm certainly glad I can do a little to help this ball club," he said, after helping with both his arm and his bat.[1]

While the Indians were sweeping the Senators, the Yankees were winning two from Baltimore. New York would come to Cleveland for a three-game series trailing the Tribe by 2½ games. The two contenders couldn't have been much more evenly matched. They'd split the 14 games they'd played so far. Each team had scored 74 runs. The Indians had compiled 140 hits off Yankees pitchers. New York had reached Cleveland pitching for 130 hits. Both teams had played 29 games since the second of July. The Yankees had won 23 and lost only six. The Indians had won 21 and dropped eight.

.721

Even though they boasted of the strongest pitching staff in baseball, the Indians were always looking to fortify it. With that in mind, they auditioned former St. Louis Brown and Detroit pitcher Bob Cain before the August 3 game with New York. Cain, who lived in the Cleveland suburb of Euclid and worked in the Indians' ticket office in the off-season, will forever be remembered as the pitcher who delivered a base on balls to Eddie Gaedel, the midget Bill Veeck sent to bat for the Browns in 1951. With the rosters expanding to 40 players on September 1, the Indians thought Cain's experience might help them as Newhouser, Don Mossi, Ray Narleski, and the rest of the bullpen figured to be weary after a long summer of pitching in tight, pressure-packed games (even though Indians starters would lead the league with 77 complete games.) Cain didn't show enough to Al Lopez or pitching coach Mel Harder to warrant the offer of a contract.

Speaking of pressure, the pressure of starting the first game of the crucial series against New York may have been more than Mossi's nerves could handle. Mossi complained of an upset stomach before taking the mound, but Lopez attributed it to a case of jitters that would disappear once he'd thrown a few pitches and the competitive juices started flowing. When Mossi didn't feel any better after retiring the Yankees in the first inning, Lopez replaced him with Art Houtteman. Larry Doby's first-inning homer off Whitey Ford gave the Indians a 1–0 lead and finished their scoring for the evening. Yogi Berra's two-run single in the third finished the scoring for the game. As 60,643 watched, the Yankees sliced the Tribe's lead to a game and a half.

George Strickland looked on from the bench, wearing a uniform for the first time since his injury. He wasn't expected to be ready to play for at least a week, and then only as a late-inning substitute. His jaw ached when he ran. There was no need to rush Strickland back. Dente was filling in capably.

The Indians evened the series with a 5–2 victory on August 5. Bob Avila's three-run homer off Allie Reynolds in the third inning landed just two rows deep in the left field stands, fair by inches, and wiped out New York's 2–0 lead. It was all the offense Bob Lemon and Garcia would need. Garcia pitched the eighth and ninth innings after Lemon ran out

6. Can't Shake the Yanks

of gas. "I'd had it," Lemon said in the clubhouse. "I was really worn. I guess I must have thrown a lot of pitches, because my arm really got tired. I had good stuff, but I was wild. Couldn't put it just where I wanted it. They had all those good left-handed batters coming up, and we just couldn't take a chance on walking some of 'em."[2]

Reynolds allowed the Indians seven hits, none of them by Al Rosen, whose hitless streak reached 15 at-bats. Despite his offensive display in the All-Star game and shortly afterward, Rosen's batting average had been falling steadily since his finger injury, and his home runs were fewer and increasingly further between.

Home runs flew in the final game of the series in Municipal Stadium. Mickey Mantle slugged two, Joe Collins added one, and Doby swatted one for the Indians. Unfortunately, Doby's two-run blast off Johnny Sain in the eighth inning came with the Tribe trailing, 5–0, and merely made the final a more respectable 5–2. There was a glimmer of hope as Rosen doubled in his first at-bat, but it was his only safety, and his slump reached one hit in 19 times up. Dave Philley was having an even harder time than Rosen. Philley's last 19 trips to the plate hadn't produced any hits. The loss once again cut the Indians' lead over the Yankees to 1½ games. The White Sox topped Boston and moved to within five games of the front-runners.

The loss of the series to the Indians' closest pursuers didn't shake Lopez's confidence in his team. "I'm more optimistic than ever about the race. Here's why: we've been a good ball club and we're going to get better. Secondly, if Lopat and Reynolds don't snap out of it for the Yanks, they're in trouble."[3] Lopez also hadn't lost confidence in Rosen, in spite of the reigning MVP's prolonged slump. "Mark my words, Rosen's bat will get hot when we need it ... in the stretch. His hitting will carry us down the wire. He's still our big man."[4]

Lopez didn't think the Yankees' 13 remaining games against the lowly Athletics gave them an advantage over the Indians, as Casey Stengel did. "I hope they get that feeling. That's just when you get knocked off. We don't take anybody lightly. The last place club can be just as tough as the first place club. I've seen it happen many times."[5]

Eddie Joost relished the chance for his sad-sacks to play spoilers.

"If [the Yankees] expect us to be a soft touch, maybe we can fool 'em," the Philadelphia manager said when his club arrived in Cleveland to open a series with the Indians. "We can score runs against them. All we need are some well pitched games."[6] Joost also weighed in on the Tribe's pennant chances. "You've got the best chance you've had since 1948 to win the pennant. The Yanks are a fine club, strong at bat and on defense, but your pitching is so much deeper. I like your chances."[7]

As the patriarch of the Mack family and the founder of the Athletics, Connie Mack, watched from a box seat near his team's dugout, the A's startled Garcia by scoring twice in the first inning and then reverted to form. The Indians responded with a five-run second inning and cruised to a 7–3 victory, Garcia's 13th. Feller's ninth victory, a complete-game four-hitter, tamed the visitors the next day, and Lemon and Houtteman completed the sweep, 7–2 and 5–2, on a Sunday afternoon. The Indians didn't need the services of their bullpen during the entire series. Harry Jones referred to the A's as a Yankees farm club since six of Philadelphia's starters in the game Feller pitched had come from New York in the trade for pitcher Harry Byrd. Interestingly, Stengel hadn't started Byrd in any of his team's 17 games against the Indians.

The sweep of the A's improved the Indians' record against second division clubs to an astounding 56–10. And it increased their lead over the Yankees, who dropped two of three in Detroit, to four games. That was the good news. The bad news was that Philadelphia pitching had held Rosen without a hit in the doubleheader, and his average dropped to .299, the first time it had been below .300 all season.

A team with a winning percentage in the neighborhood of .700, such as the Indians, could beat their opponents a number of ways. Cleveland defeated other teams with its bats, its pitching, and its defense. Not, however, with its speed, a commodity sorely lacking on the 1954 squad. The stolen base had long since fallen out of favor in the American League (with the exception of Chicago), but the Indians took station-to-station, swing-for-the-fences offense to the extreme. Rosen's six stolen bases were high on the team. No one else had more than two.

Having just hosted the Yankees while the Indians were feasting on the Athletics, Detroit manager Fred Hutchinson was in a good position

6. Can't Shake the Yanks

to offer an opinion on the two top contenders in the American League when the Indians opened a three-game series at Briggs Stadium.

> "I said all along it would be a two club race and I expect it to be very close. Your club has the edge. If Reynolds and Lopat don't improve, your pitching is far superior. You have just as much power hitting and your defense is almost as good. You've been able to overcome injuries to your key players. I wonder if the Yanks could. But right now, even though we play you 12 more games, I'd have to give you the edge."[8]

Former Indians pitcher Al Aber, who was enduring a 5–11 season for the Tigers, was asked his opinion. "If the Indians don't win this year, they'll never win. I can't see the Yankees this year. They don't impress me as much as Cleveland does. You should have seen Stengel here over the weekend. He was jittery as all get out. Going crazy on the bench."[9]

After winning two of three from New York, the Tigers added another victory at the Indians' expense on August 10. Wily veteran Ned Garver blanked the Tribe on five hits, 4–0, before a weekday crowd of 53,778, the largest at Briggs Stadium since 1952. Wynn allowed 11 hits in taking his ninth loss. The Yankees beat Philadelphia and moved to within three games of first place.

Garcia out-dueled Steve Gromek, a key contributor to the Indians' 1948 World Series victory, in the second game. Two unearned runs, thanks to errors by first baseman Wayne Belardi and shortstop Harvey Kuenn, were all Garcia needed to notch a 2–0 victory. Garcia allowed only four hits and Gromek surrendered only three in his eight innings of work. Lopez dropped Rosen from fourth to fifth in the batting order, putting Vic Wertz in the clean-up spot, but Rosen's slump continued, his average falling to .294 as he had just two hits in his last 30 at-bats. "The Yanks and Indians are both evenly matched," Gromek said after his hard-luck defeat. "But the Indians should win because I'm rooting for them — except against us."[10]

"I'll bet when you fill out the line-up you hate to write my name down,"[11] Rosen said to Lopez after he'd contributed nothing offensively to the victory over Gromek. Lopez begged to differ. "You're our guy. You'll hit. I'm not worried," Lopez assured Rosen. "Look, I just went over the figures. Do you know the first five hitters in the batting order have averaged only .207 in our last eight games? And that includes Bobby Avila's two hits today. Nobody's hitting, and then, suddenly, we'll all start hitting again. That's the game."[12]

To reporters, however, Lopez admitted that "if it were anybody else, I probably would have him out of there. But how can you take the most valuable player in your league out of there? Wouldn't it do something to our morale? Wouldn't it do something to us around the league? I'm not sure. Maybe a day or two on the bench would help. But maybe that day or two would be when he would get started. Right now, I've just got to go on hoping."[13]

The last time George Zuverink, like Gromek a former Indian, faced his ex-team, he pitched 11 scoreless innings and yielded only three hits. Zuverink didn't fare nearly as well on August 12, surrendering nine hits and seven runs in six innings, including home runs by Rosen (his first since July 31) and Wertz. Dente, whose offense had been a pleasant surprise since taking over for the injured Strickland, boosted his average to .280 with three hits. Lemon toyed with the Tigers, allowing seven hits in eight innings. Mossi pitched the ninth inning of the 10–1 drubbing, preserving Lemon's 16th win against five losses. Lopez, for one day at least, looked like a prophet.

While the Indians were trashing the Tigers, the Yankees were sweeping a doubleheader from the Athletics, after which Stengel met with "my writers" and talked about the upcoming schedule. "We've got a break in the schedule in that we play Philadelphia nine more games while Cleveland plays them only four more. Also, we've got only three more with Chicago and five with Detroit while them other fellas have six with Chicago and 10 with Detroit. Of course, the whole thing may backfire on us, who knows? But I'd rather have it this way."[14] Stengel didn't mention that his Yankees had five more head-to-head encounters with the league leaders.

Back at Municipal Stadium after their brief visit to Detroit, the Indians removed the suspense early, plating five runs in the first inning and allowing Feller to coast to a 9–4 victory over Baltimore, his tenth. Feller weakened in the ninth, giving up four hits and two runs and giving way to Narleski, who recorded the final out. The crowd of 19,323 pushed the season's attendance above the one million mark at 1,012,653. The club figured to exceed its 1953 attendance during its current home stand.

Wynn and Don Larsen, who entered the game as the losingest pitcher in the league with a record of 3–15, exchanged zeroes through seven innings in the second game of the series. Oddly, both clubs broke through for three runs in the eighth, and the Indians won in the 11th on Hal Naragon's single that scored Dave Pope for the 4–3 victory. Mossi was the winner in relief, and Naragon's heroics hung the loss on former Indian Bob Chakales, who'd been banished to Baltimore in the June deal that brought Wertz to Cleveland.

The Indians completed the series sweep by taking both ends of a Sunday doubleheader on August 15, barely putting forth the minimum effort needed to cast aside an inferior opponent in the opinion of Jones, while chalking up 5–2 and 3–1 victories. The visitors out-hit the Tribe overall, 14–13, but the Indians, again in Jones's opinion, swaggered like a team that could score at will but preferred to score only enough to win the game. Houtteman held the Birds to six hits and two runs over six innings to win his 12th game in the opener, with an assist from Narleski. Garcia limited Baltimore to a run on six hits in eight innings to pick up his 15th victory in the nightcap. Mossi pitched a scoreless ninth.

"I don't see how you can miss winning the pennant," said former Tribe outfielder Bob Kennedy after his team's twin bill loss. "Here we are going along [with a 2–0 lead in the sixth inning of the first game] and it looks as though we've got the game won. Then all of a sudden a bloop, a walk and somebody hits the ball out and you've got the game. With your club every batter up there is dangerous."[15]

Baltimore skipper Jimmy Dykes was so bored coaching at third base that he spent some of his time scratching notes in the dirt with his spikes for his Cleveland counterpart, Tony Cuccinello. Cuccinello, who wasn't overly busy himself with the Indians scoring only eight runs on the afternoon, used his spikes to scratch out responses. Dykes must have been happy to get out of town. The Orioles lost all 11 games they played in Cleveland in 1954, and the franchise hadn't tasted victory in Municipal Stadium since August 13, 1952, when it was based in St. Louis. The combined Browns/Orioles had lost 27 straight contests against the Indians in Cleveland. "How can the Indians lose?" Dykes asked. "They've got the equivalent of four 20-game winners and any time Lopez puts anybody new in the line-up he catches on fire."[16]

There was a downside to the double victory. Rosen's average fell to .288 as he managed just one hit in the two games. "I thought when he got a hit in the first game and drove in those runs that it might give him a lift," Lopez told reporters afterward. "I hoped he'd have a big game in the second. The guy is still swinging good and he's kept his spirits up. He'll just have to keep swinging. I'm sure he'll start hitting."[17]

The Indians picked up a half-game on the Yankees, who beat Boston, 14–9. Jones pointed out in his game notes that the Tribe had 17 home games remaining and, by winning them all, could remove New York from the American League record books as holders of the mark for most victories on one's home field. The 1927 Yankees, who rarely lost anywhere, won 62 of their 77 games at Yankee Stadium.

In the National League, the onrushing Dodgers had reduced the Giants' once substantial lead to a mere half-game, with the Braves only 3½ back. After posting major league baseball's best record at the All-Star break, the Giants had won just 13 of 30 games since then.

> "We're absolutely going to win 105 games," Cuccinello promised. "That's the least amount we'll win. If that's enough, we've got it. We're a cinch to win 105. I've been saying right along we're going to win the pennant. Look at our record. We're playing .713 ball in spite of all the bad breaks. We've had Rosen hurt, Avila hurt, Lemon hurt, Strickland hurt. We've taken all the bumps and still won. Now we're due for our share of the good breaks."[18]

George Zuverink, who'd been either very good or horrid when pitching against his former team, was very good on August 17, holding the Indians to three hits over eight innings. The Tribe managed four hits in the ninth, with a single by Avila the game-winner. The win was achieved without Rosen, who was suffering from bursitis of the left shoulder and had been ordered by team doctor Don Kelley to take three days off. Rosen had aggravated the condition when he landed on the shoulder while making a diving catch of a line drive in the doubleheader against Baltimore.

"I had an idea it might be bursitis because I had it in the same

6. Can't Shake the Yanks

shoulder a couple years ago. I don't feel right sitting on the bench like this, but as Dr. Kelley explained, there is no use taking chances. In a day or two it'll be all right,"[19] Rosen said. Rosen supplied moral support to his teammates, earning a warning from umpire Ed Runge to "shut up or get out" for excessive bench jockeying. Rosen needed the time off. He'd had just five hits in his last 55 times at bat.

Among those in the Municipal Stadium stands were comedians Bud Abbott and Lou Costello of "Who's On First" fame. According to Jones, Abbott and Costello were genuine baseball fans who'd rooted for the Indians back in 1948 and traveled with the team to Boston for its historic one-game pennant playoff with the Red Sox.

When Avila smashed a home run in the sixth inning of the Tribe's August 18th game against Detroit, it was only the fourth run the club had scored with Wynn on the mound in 30 innings. Wynn had allowed only six runs during that span but had nothing but defeat to show for his sterling pitching. Wynn knew exactly what to do with the prosperity, blanking the Tigers, 4–0. Avila wasn't a power hitter but had developed a knack for connecting for a long ball when the Indians needed it most. Of the second baseman's 13 home runs, six had tied the game, four had broken ties, and two had brought the Indians within a run of their opponent. Wynn was grateful for Avila's 13th blast of the season. "I was afraid for awhile we weren't going to get any runs," he said in the clubhouse. "I didn't feel too strong, either, but I got a lot better when I got a lead."[20] Wynn felt even better when Al Smith gave him some breathing room with a three-run, eighth-inning round-tripper.

"That guy [Detroit starter Billy Hoeft] had been pitching me inside and low — right across the knees — all afternoon and I just couldn't get the wood on it," Smith explained. "So the last time I came up, I decided I was gonna give him six inches of that plate and get around on that inside one. I moved back in the box just a little and he gave me the same pitch again. I'm mostly a poke hitter and I don't try for long ones very much. When I can get some pitcher in the right spot, though, I'll go for it." Smith lamented his inability to be consistent. "I drop down to .260 and then I go back up to about .290 — then I drop down again. I just can't seem to get over the hump to .300."[21]

.721

After walking Avila following Smith's home run, Hoeft sailed a pitch high and behind Doby, who took a few steps toward the mound before being restrained by home plate umpire Bill Summers. "Summers told me that if he threw another one like that he would warn Hoeft," Doby said after the game. "I don't want to be a target. I've been a target too long. I want to finish out the season and help win the pennant. I'm getting tired of this kind of stuff."[22]

Hoeft, according to Lebovitz, was seething because he was convinced Cuccinello and Indians first base coach Red Kress were tipping his pitches off to Tribe batters using "vocal signals." Hoeft had warned both Cleveland coaches that "if you keep it up, somebody's going to get hurt."[23] Afterward, both Cuccinello and Kress refused to confirm or deny that they'd been telling Tribe batters what pitch Hoeft was going to throw, and if they were providing that information, it didn't help much as the Indians managed just five hits. When asked if Avila's and Smith's homers were the result of tipped pitches, both coaches answered "no comment." There was no doubt in Hutchinson's mind that Cuccinello and Kress were engaged in skullduggery. "They were calling our pitches," said the Tigers manager succinctly.[24]

The Indians finished their home stand by splitting a doubleheader with Detroit. Feller won the opener, 4–3, for his 11th victory in 13 decisions. Narleski put the icing on the cake by striking out the side in the ninth inning. Garcia lasted just four innings in the nightcap, allowing four runs and nine hits in an 8–2 defeat. The Tigers were the first team other than the Yankees to pin a loss on Garcia since May 4th. The Big Bear was booed lustily when Lopez sent him to the dugout and didn't like it. "You'd never think I had won six in a row and 13 of my last 14 games to listen to those fans," moaned Garcia. "What do they want, blood?"[25]

His bursitis cured, Rosen returned to the lineup only to sustain another injury. Detroit's Al Kaline hurt Rosen's finger (not the finger that had been injured earlier) sliding into third base in the second inning of the second game. Rosen was removed from the game and sent to a hospital for X-rays which indicated the finger wasn't broken. Rosen had stroked consecutive hits in the first game, the first time he'd achieved that minor feat since July 31.

6. Can't Shake the Yanks

The Yankees picked up a half-game on the Indians and stretched their winning streak to ten with an 8–5 victory over Philadelphia. Cleveland's second-game loss to Detroit meant the Indians wouldn't break New York's record of 62 home victories in a season. But Jones optimistically noted that they could still tie the mark by winning all of their remaining home games. They wouldn't play at home again for quite a while, however, leaving for Baltimore after the double bill to open a 19-game road trip.

The road trip began promisingly with a 7–2 victory on August 20. The Tribe settled matters quickly by scoring four runs in the first inning and two more in the second. Houtteman won his 13th game, coasting for six innings before giving way to Newhouser. The Yankees had their winning streak snapped by the Red Sox, dropping them 3½ games behind the Indians. Cleveland's victory and New York's loss were the perfect gifts for Lopez's 46th birthday.

Cleveland's 4–1 victory in the second game of the series was highlighted by a fourth-inning triple play. Vern Stephens led off against Lemon with a single and moved to second when Clint Courtney beat out a bunt. Lemon worked his way out of the jam by snatching Jim Fridley's smash back to the mound and throwing to second to double up Stephens. Avila's throw to Wertz wasn't in time to retire Courtney at first, but Courtney's momentum took him past the bag and Wertz applied the tag for the third out. Lemon wasn't seriously threatened the rest of the way and won his 18th game. Lou Boudreau's Red Sox stunned the Yankees for the second straight day, 10–9, and New York's first place deficit was 4½ games.

The 1954 Indians didn't overpower many opponents, but they enjoyed a laugher at the Orioles' expense on August 22, strafing Baltimore's pitching staff for 20 hits in a 12–1 victory. Despite the much-appreciated offensive outburst, Wynn pitched as if he were involved in a typical nail-biter, stopping the Birds on just three hits over seven innings before Lopez excused him for the day. Mossi finished up and kept Baltimore off the scoreboard. At Fenway Park, the Red Sox completed their improbable sweep of the Yankees, 8–2. The Indians' lead grew to 5½ games. The Yankees hadn't been that far from first place since

.721

May 13, 1952. On that date, they'd lost to the Indians at Municipal Stadium, 10–6, sinking their record to 11–12. The Indians held first place at 18–8. New York overcame that early deficit and won both the pennant and World Series. The Indians wanted to prevent another such comeback.

Were the Yankees folding, Lopez was asked? "Naw, I don't think so. That fold up line is overrated. Didn't they win ten straight before the Boston series?" Frank Gibbons, who posed the question, asked another. Was Lopez ready to declare the Yankees dead as pennant contenders? "Nobody's going to get me to say that until we've got it sewed up. They're dead when they stop breathing."[26]

The Yankees made a roster move on August 22, acquiring former National League Most Valuable Player Jim Konstanty from the Phillies via the waiver route. Konstanty had been part of the 1950 Whiz Kids pennant winners, winning 16 games (all in relief) and saving 22 more. After having made all 74 of his appearances in relief, Konstanty started the first game of the World Series against the Yankees and lost, 1–0. He had a 2–3 record for the Phillies when he was waived out of the National League and passed on by the six teams in the American League beneath New York in the standings. The Indians weren't impressed. "He's not as fast and isn't nearly as tricky as Johnny Sain," said Cuccinello.[27] "I guess the Yanks figure he can fool us with his freak pitches until we get wise to him," said Lopez.[28]

As they prepared to face another patsy, the woeful (and soon to be former) Philadelphia Athletics, Jones noted just how unimposing the Indians had been in constructing their commanding advantage over the Yankees, and even more commanding lead over the White Sox, who still harbored pennant hopes. Cleveland had been out-hit by its opponent in 24 of its victories. On 29 occasions the Indians had been held to seven hits or fewer but won the game anyway.

The Indians were limited to four hits in Connie Mack Stadium on August 24, and that wasn't enough to squeeze out another victory against a second division club. Johnny Gray, one of the boatload of players obtained by the A's from the Yankees in exchange for pitcher Harry Byrd, won just his second game of the year, out-dueling Garcia, 4–1. Six walks

6. Can't Shake the Yanks

by Gray enabled the Indians to bring the potential tying run to the plate in four of the last five innings, but they couldn't get the clutch hit they needed in a game watched by an unusually large crowd of 9,175. Philadelphians had been put on notice by the Mack family in June that the club would have to average 13,000 per home date in order to remain in the city it had called home since 1901, and by the time the Indians arrived it was a forgone conclusion the team would be moved. The only question was where, and the smart money was on Kansas City. Gray's victory over the Indians was one of the final times the wretched A's would give their few remaining fans something to cheer in the dreadful 1954 season. Gray, while glad to win, was pulling for the Indians to win the pennant. "I really want to see 'em beat those Yanks," he said, his bitterness over being traded to the moribund A's on display.[29] Thanks to Gray, the Tribe's lead was cut to 4½ games as New York defeated Baltimore, 9–2.

The Indians struggled to a 4–3 victory in the final game of the brief series. Naragon's tenth inning triple scored Bill Glynn with the go-ahead run, and Lemon and Garcia combined to make it stand up. The victory was Lemon's 19th. The run batted in was only Naragon's tenth of the campaign, but five of them had been game-winners. A crowd of 7,311 viewed the last game the Indians would ever play in Connie Mack Stadium, where they had been doing battle with the Athletics since 1910, when the state of the art facility was christened as Shibe Park. They won nine of their 11 match-ups with the A's in Philadelphia in 1954.

Paul Richards, who brought his White Sox into Philadelphia for their series with the Athletics early enough to witness the Indians-A's final match-up, admitted that his club's pennant chance was fading. "I had been hoping we might slip by the Yankees and then make a late charge on the Indians if they flopped. We have gone along at a steady pace, but you fellows just win too many."[30]

After giving Wynn an avalanche of runs to work with in Baltimore, the Indians returned to their stingy ways in Washington. They scored only twice off Mickey McDermott, but two runs were all Wynn needed. Smith's eighth-inning homer was the margin of victory as Wynn captured his 18th win, 2–1. It was Cleveland's 90th victory in 125 games, marking the fifth straight season and sixth time in seven years the Tribe had won 90 or more games. The bad news was that McDermott had held Rosen hitless, and the third baseman hadn't hit safely in his past 13 times at bat. The Indians kept on winning, but Rosen noted that "I could have made it a lot easier."[31]

The Yankees weren't making things easy on the Tribe, either. New York pounded Detroit, 11–2, to stay 4½ games back.

It doesn't take long for a professional athlete to go from the penthouse to the outhouse. The reigning league MVP, hailed as the best player in baseball by Hank Greenberg when he signed his 1954 contract, and the toast of Cleveland as recently as the All-Star Game in mid–July, Rosen's season hit bottom on August 27, as the Indians lost to the Senators, 3–2. Though the winning run was scored off Feller in the tenth inning when Philley bobbled Mickey Vernon's single, allowing Pete Runnels to gallop home from first, Jones told his readers that "the real goat of this affair was Al Rosen, who failed utterly in the role of clean-up man, leaving seven runners stranded in five chances to break the game apart. Rosen made the final out in five innings, stretching his streak of hitless at-bats to 18. He has failed to hit safely in the Indians' last four games, two of which they lost, costing them precious ground in their narrowing race with the Yankees."[32] Jones lamented the fact that Feller was charged with his third loss of the year when he should've been celebrating his 12th victory. New York shut out Detroit, 4–0, and suddenly the Yankees were only 3½ games out of first place.

Rosen admitted after the loss to Washington that he was "whipped." The reigning American League MVP had become his club's weakest link, hitting .136 thus far in August, with a puny 12 hits in 88 at-bats. Lopez had little choice but to bench him. When asked how long Rosen would sit, Lopez responded, "I don't know for how long. We'll see how Regalado does. Maybe a day or two is all Rosen needs." Lopez defended his decision to keep Rosen in the line-up. "I kept playing him because I hoped he would snap out of it. Besides, we were winning and his fielding has been very good."[33]

With Rosen watching from the bench, replaced by Rudy Regalado, the Indians finished the series in Griffith Stadium with a 5–2 victory, to which Rosen contributed by drawing a walk as a pinch-hitter during a

6. Can't Shake the Yanks

three-run, eighth-inning rally that wiped out the Senators' 2–1 lead. Regalado was hitless in three at-bats. Garcia won his 16th game against seven losses and Mossi pitched two scoreless innings in relief. The Tribe's late rally pinned the loss on Chuck Stobbs. The Indians improved their record in games Rosen didn't start to an impressive 17–3, and they stayed 3½ games in front of the Yankees, who finished off a three-game sweep of the Tigers.

George Strickland returned to Cleveland after playing one game in Washington. "He came home because he found himself weak due to lack of solid food and the heat and humidity of Washington,"[34] explained Dr. A. J. Tomaro, the physician who had wired Strickland's fractured jaw. Strickland had been on a liquid diet since July 23. The Indians hoped he could return to the shortstop position soon, although Sam Dente had been playing well in Strickland's absence. "I'm weak as a cat and I get spots before my eyes, but I'm glad to be able to do something," said Strickland.[35]

Senators manager Bucky Harris, who had piloted three pennant winners and two world champions in his long managerial career, but, according to Lebovitz, appeared to enjoy the lack of pressure on his sixth-place ball club, had a word of warning for the Indians. "The season is just starting for you fellows. The games that have been played up 'til now are nothing. Here's where you feel every one, where the money rides on every pitch. That month of September is a year in itself. It's where, to coin a phrase, the men are separated from the boys."[36]

Feller, undoubtedly speaking from frustration after his teammates had blown several scoring opportunities in what became his third and final defeat of the season, sounded an alarm as well. "If we don't start hitting in 48 hours, we could become the biggest sports joke of the season."[37] The Indians took Feller's words to heart. Although they were never an offensive juggernaut in 1954, they picked up the pace in the final game against Washington and kept it up as the trip continued.

While Strickland went west, his teammates headed north for a three game set against Boudreau's disappointing Red Sox in Fenway Park, the same Red Sox who'd swept the Yankees while the Indians were in Baltimore. The largest crowd to watch American League baseball in Boston

.721

in 12 years, 36,344, groaned as the Indians bounced the Red Sox twice on August 29, 6–2 and 8–1. The day off in Washington may have been just what the doctor ordered for Rosen, who had four hits in seven trips to the plate in the sweep, including a home run, triple and double. Lemon joined the 20-victory club with an eight-hit complete game in the opener, and Houtteman went the route in the nightcap for his 14th victory. The Indians gained a half-game on New York, which beat Chicago, 4–1. The Yankees would take the next day off to rest and prepare for the arrival of the Indians.

"I don't know if we can win the pennant with Rosen," said Feller after the double victory, "but I know darn well we can't win it without him."[38]

The Indians, meanwhile, had business to attend to in Boston and scored in just one of the game's nine innings on August 30. The five runs they plated in the seventh off starter Willard Nixon and reliever Ellis Kinder were just enough to eke out a 5–4 victory. Lopez used five pitchers to secure the win, starting with Narleski, who made only his second major league start and exited with two out in the third inning. Dave Hoskins, Bob Hooper, Newhouser and Garcia followed, with Newhouser getting the victory. Hank Majeski's three-run homer was the key blow as the Indians finished the campaign undefeated in Fenway Park. The Tribe gained a valuable half-game on the idle Yankees. They would invade Yankee Stadium the next night holding a 4½ game lead and were guaranteed to leave the Big Apple in first place, even if they were swept in the three-game showdown.

"If we take 'em three straight, we'll beat 'em out for the pennant," Yogi Berra promised. "If we take two we'll still be in pretty good position. If we take only one we'll be in sad shape. If we don't take any ... hey, what am I saying?"[39] The Indians wasted no time making sure the Yankees wouldn't take 'em three straight.

With Wynn pitching brilliantly again, the Indians scored four times in the eighth inning off Bob Grim to put what had been a 2–1 game out of reach. Philley, inserted by Lopez in right field for defensive purposes in the sixth, whacked a three-run homer to secure Wynn's 6–1 victory and shove New York 5½ games behind. Wynn's two-hitter was his 19th

6. Can't Shake the Yanks

victory of the season. A Yankee Stadium throng of 58,859 watched the Indians equal the one-month league record with their 26th win in August. The record had been set by the 1931 American League champion Athletics in July.

"I don't see how either ourselves or the Yankees can keep up this tremendous pace," said Mel Harder. "I look for both of us to lose our share of games down the stretch."[40] Harder proved not to be prescient — at least not as far as the Indians were concerned.

As the month of September dawned, the standings looked like this:

Cleveland	95–36	.725	—
New York	89–41	.685	5½
Chicago	85–47	.644	10½
Detroit	57–73	.438	37½
Boston	56–72	.438	37½
Washington	53–76	.411	41
Philadelphia	44–87	.336	51
Baltimore	43–90	.323	53

In a normal season, Chicago's record might have put it 10½ games in front instead of 10½ games behind. Had the White Sox been in the National League, their 85–47 record would've given them a 1½-game lead on the Giants. The Yankees would've led the Giants by a whopping 6½ lengths. But it bears repeating that 1954 was no average season, and the battle between the two top teams would extend well into the final month.

7

Magic Numbers

As usual, the Old Professor had it all figured out.

Casey Stengel, his Yankees trailing the Indians by 5½ games as September began, knew what his club had to do to regain its accustomed position at the top of the American League standings and claim its sixth consecutive pennant. "Lopez never loses a game and I can't do nothing about that. But I know what I got to do. I got to win every game from here in. I can't wait around for somebody else to beat him. If Lopez beats me this series, I'm hurting. I'm hurting real bad. If I win every day and Lopez wins every day he still wins the pennant. But if I win every day he can't win because he's got to beat me."[1] Stengel had four more shots at Lopez, starting on the first day of September, and winning all of them would've greatly enhanced New York's chances of erasing its deficit and coming from behind to play in yet another World Series.

The surest way for Stengel to notch one of the victories he needed was to send Ed Lopat to the mound. Lopat's turn in the rotation came in the second game of the early September showdown, and Lopat didn't disappoint, racking up his 40th career win over the Tribe in 51 decisions. With the Yankees up, 2–1, in the sixth inning, the Indians loaded the bases against their ancient antagonist with no one out. Lopat calmly retired the heart of the Cleveland batting order, Larry Doby, Al Rosen and Vic Wertz, without allowing a runner to move off his base. Cleveland threatened again in the seventh when the first two batters reached, but Lopat bore down and disposed of Jim Hegan, Rudy Regalado and Al Smith. The Yankees tacked on a pair of insurance runs off Mike Garcia and won, 4–1. The Indians' lead was reduced to 4½ games.

.721

"It was a game we had to win, and just as we've been doing for six years, we won it," chortled Stengel afterward. "That's why you can't count us out yet. Never sell the Yankees short until they are mathematically eliminated. The other guys don't have it wrapped up yet. They just think they have. Don't forget, they haven't had a slump all season. But if we can beat them again today and keep the pressure on them, we might scare them into one. I'm not saying they'll choke. They never have. I know one thing. We better not choke. We can't afford to lose any more."[2]

A pair of errors by Wertz, who was still getting the hang of playing first base after having spent his entire career in the outfield, on sixth-inning ground balls by Joe Collins and Eddie Robinson gave New York two unearned runs that were just enough to enable Whitey Ford to beat Bob Lemon, 3–2, in the series finale. Each pitcher allowed only three hits. One of the hits the Tribe managed off Ford was a home run by Sam Dente, only his fourth in 2,204 major league at-bats. Hank Majeski tried to duplicate Dente's blast with Regalado on base in the eighth inning but was robbed by left fielder Irv Noren's sensational, leaping catch. The Indian's lead was shaved to 3½ games. The Yankees would come to Cleveland for a Sunday doubleheader on September 12, the last time the two teams would meet … in the regular season. "I should have had both of them. That's all there is to it. I should have had them," said a disconsolate Wertz of the ground balls he failed to field.[3]

"It's not his fault," said Al Lopez of Wertz's errors. "He's doing the best he can at a strange position. For one who never played the infield before he's doing darn well. Naturally, he doesn't have the reflexes of an infielder."[4] As to whether he considered replacing Wertz with Bill Glynn for defensive purposes with the Indians up, 1–0, in the fifth inning, Lopez responded "that's not much of a lead, and my policy has been to put Glynn in late when we're ahead enough to need defense."[5]

The series in Yankee Stadium opened a closing stretch during which the Indians would play 17 of their final 24 games against the American League's first division. Included were six against Detroit, which, despite holding fifth place, had lost 18 more games than it had won. Eleven of those 17 games were against the Yankees and White Sox. Three of the contests versus New York were in the books, and two of those games had been lost.

7. Magic Numbers

"We're in fine position. The loss didn't do much damage," Lopez insisted.[6]

Doby's seventh-inning solo home run broke a 2–2 tie and the Indians bullpen preserved a 3–2 victory in Comiskey Park on September 3. Bob Feller exited with one out in the seventh, clinging to the one-run lead Doby's blast had given him, and Don Mossi and Garcia managed to keep the White Sox off the scoreboard the rest of the way. The Yankees hammered Washington, 9–2, to stay 3½ games behind.

The Indians sustained another injury to a key player in the victory over the White Sox. Doby pulled a hamstring in his left leg running out a double in the third inning. Though he stayed in the game and clouted the game-winning home run four innings later, the leg would impair his play for the rest of the season.

Defensive problems handed the White Sox an 8–5 victory in the second game of the series. Bill Glynn, inserted by Lopez to give the Tribe a more steady glove than Wertz's at first base, and Avila, who was playing shortstop for the first time that season, uncorked wild throws, and the five unearned runs the miscues allowed to score in the sixth inning proved to be Wynn's undoing. Wynn allowed just four hits before being relieved with two out in the sixth, but his record dropped to 19–10. New York was beaten by Washington and stayed 3½ games behind.

Cleveland's 8–2 triumph in the final game of the series didn't clinch the pennant. In fact, it only reduced the Tribe's magic number to 15. But as far as Harry Jones was concerned, it concluded the 1954 American League pennant race. A Cleveland pennant, in the opinion of The *Plain Dealer's* baseball scribe, was a foregone conclusion.

Houtteman lost his chance at an easy victory when he wilted early in Chicago's unseasonable 97-degree heat. Houtteman couldn't finished the required five innings to pick up the win, which went to Narleski, his third against two losses. New York lost to Washington, 5–4, dropping it 4½ games behind the Indians. In spite of his declaration that a Tribe pennant was a lead pipe cinch, Jones did sound a cautionary note. The following day was Labor Day, and Jones recalled that in 1948, the Indians had trailed by 4½ games on the traditional end of summer holiday before rallying to force a one-game playoff with the Red Sox, which

Cleveland won. Jones wondered if the Yankees could pull off a similar miracle.

Ed McAuley agreed with Jones. The headline over McAuley's September 7 column in the *News* read: PENNANT RACE IS A SIMPLE STORY: INDIANS TOO GOOD TO LOSE.

Paul Richards wasn't convinced. Richards told Cleveland writers the Indians had to at least split their upcoming doubleheader with New York at Municipal Stadium. Losing both games, in Richards' opinion, would cost the Tribe the pennant. In Stengel's words, "there's no use kidding anyone. I have to win every day."[7]

Lopez had to win every day, too, in order to hold off Stengel's relentless bunch, and, while Cleveland writers mentioned how much more relaxed the Tribe skipper was in 1954 compared to his first three seasons at the helm, the pressure may have been getting to him. Lopez said he planned to retire after his contract expired following the 1955 campaign. "Don't let anybody tell you this isn't hard work. It's no fun sitting on that bench trying to figure out things before they happen. Paul Richards of the White Sox told me the same thing. He admitted if it wasn't for the money in it, he would quit. Casey Stengel is different. It's fun for him and I was certain he would be back in 1955."

Lopez was asked if he would retire after the 1954 season, even if the Indians failed to maintain their lead and win the pennant. "I wouldn't say that. All I know is that this isn't the easiest way to make a living and I wouldn't stick with it too long."[8]

Because the American League schedule maker considered Baltimore, having replaced St. Louis, as a "western" city despite the fact it sat on the banks of the Chesapeake Bay, which empties into the Atlantic Ocean, the Indians, after having played in Philadelphia, Washington, Boston and New York on their trip before going to Chicago, had to go east once again for a holiday doubleheader in Memorial Stadium. The Indians banged out 14 hits to capture the opener, 6–1, their 17th straight victory over the Birds. Don Larsen blanked the Indians for eight innings in the nightcap before they rallied to tie the game at 2–2 in the ninth before Baltimore pushed across the winning run in the tenth. Cleveland's magic number was shaved to 13 as the Yankees split their doubleheader

7. Magic Numbers

with Boston, blowing a 7–0 lead in the second game to lose, 8–7, and stay 4½ games behind the front-runners.

The Indians completed their trip, which took them to every city in the league except Detroit, with a 13–6 record, falling short of their manager's stated goal of 15 wins. "Deep down, I didn't think we could do it," Lopez confessed. "I thought we'd be doing pretty good to come home with 98."[9] At the All-Star break, Jones had written that the Indians were convinced 98 victories would mean the pennant. All it meant was a precarious lead over the Yankees.

A large crowd was anticipated at Cleveland Hopkins International Airport to welcome the Indians home from Baltimore. Club officials, fearing a mob scene, expressed the hope that no more than 200,000 rooters would venture to the city's western edge to greet their returning heroes. They got their wish. About 10,000 Tribe supporters were on hand when the team's plane touched down. Wertz was impressed with the display of affection. "Lucky me," said the Tribe first baseman. "To think I started the season with the last place Orioles. Baltimore was never like this."[10]

Upon their return to Cleveland, Gordon Cobbledick anointed the Indians the league champions, despite the fact the upcoming home stand afforded the Yankees one final chance to cut into their deficit in a head-to-head match-up. "Leave us waste no more precious minutes in speculation about the Indians chances to win the pennant," Cobbledick wrote. "The Indians have won the pennant. Not because they're 4½ in front, although it helps, but simply because they're too good for the competition."[11]

A cold front blew through Cleveland before the Indians met the Athletics on September 8, sweeping away the late summer heat wave that had baked the city in 98-degree temperatures over the Labor Day weekend and replacing it with a cold, biting wind off Lake Erie. The conditions made it difficult for Wynn to control his bread-and-butter pitch, the knuckleball. Had the opponent been someone other than the pathetic visitors from Philadelphia, Wynn might have been in trouble. Regardless of the change in the weather, Wynn managed to vanquish the Athletics, 5–2, for his 20th victory.

.721

"That cold and wind was really rough," Wynn remarked. "I knew it was going to bother me before the game, when I tried to warm up. I just couldn't loosen up. After all the hot weather, the temperature change hurt."[12]

The Tribe's magic number was an even dozen. New York topped Baltimore, 8–2, to remain within 4½ games of the lead. Cleveland's 99th victory was a franchise record, breaking the mark of 98 set during the 1920 pennant-winning season.

As he felt a sixth consecutive pennant slipping away, Stengel groped for reasons (excuses?) why his Yankees couldn't catch the rampaging Indians. His contention that New York's opponents saved their best pitchers for the defending champions, even though the Indians were in first place, irritated Lopez. "What does he want them to do, lay down?" Lopez asked.

> "If the Yanks think we're getting any soft touches, they're crazy. He should know that baseball isn't played that way. The team in first place always faces the best. "If Jimmy Dykes had been trying to play favorites he would have saved Larsen for the Yanks. Larsen owns a shutout over the Yanks this year. But it was Larsen's turn to face us, so we got him. We expect to face the toughest pitchers all the way in. That's what we'll get — and that's the way we want it. Anybody who studies the box scores — and you can bet I know the Yanks do — knows darn well that we have faced only the best pitchers all season. We're on top because we've beaten the best. All this crying about clubs laying for the Yanks is a joke."[13]

Hal Lebovitz revealed before the Indians' final meeting with Philadelphia that substitute infielder "Win Plenty" Dente had been playing with a broken right index finger since August 12. Lopez knew of the injury, as did Dr. Don Kelley. Dente managed to keep the media and most of his teammates from finding out. "The finger hurt for about a week. It's still swollen," said Dente.[14] Fortunately for the Indians, George Strickland was ready to return to the lineup, his broken jaw having healed.

The Indians needed 11 innings to beat the Athletics, 5–4, in the final meeting between the two clubs on September 9. The Tribe trailed, 4–1, when the Yankees' 1–0 loss to Baltimore was flashed on the scoreboard. With a chance to lop two games off their magic number and drop New

7. Magic Numbers

York a game further behind in the standings, the Indians rallied to send the game into extra innings and won it when reliever Ed Burtschy walked Hal Naragon with the bases loaded, forcing in Dave Hoskins with the winning run. Hoskins was pinch-running for Rosen, who pulled his right thigh muscle running the bases during the ninth-inning rally that tied the game. Said Rosen,

> "It just seems that one thing leads to another. I guess when you start getting hurt, you favor the injury, and that leads to something else. When I broke my finger I changed my swing and it made my arms and wrists sore. Later on I got something wrong with my foot and I started to favor it. My leg had begun to hurt a little, but today this cold weather aggravated the injury and when I had to run hard in the ninth inning to score the tying run, the strain became too much. I tried to stick it out, but when I got in scoring position in the 11th, I figured we'd better get someone who was able to run. I'm still not hitting the way I should. Now I have to come down with something else — and I don't know how long this will knock me out. Right now, the leg hurts too much to run on it."[15]

Lopez was grateful to escape with the victory. "You know, that's the first bad game Philadelphia has played against us this year — in spite of the number of times we've beaten them. They couldn't do right today."[16] The record would show that, in their final season in Philadelphia, the Athletics won four games against the Indians. They lost 18.

Among the witnesses as the Indians reduced their magic number to ten was former Cleveland center fielder and manager Tris Speaker. The man who guided the Indians to their first World Series title in 1920 was impressed with Lopez's squad. "This is a better ball club than most people think," Speaker said. "In some ways it's a great club."[17] Speaker wasn't asked if he thought the 1954 edition of the Indians was as great as his 1920 world champions.

The other player-manager to bring a World Series triumph to Cleveland was in Municipal Stadium the next night. Lou Boudreau, whose MVP season led the Indians to the 1948 world championship, was inducted into the team's hall-of-fame before Boston's game with the Tribe. "This is one of the greatest honors of my life," Boudreau told the crowd of 34,561 that turned out to pay homage to him. "It will go down in my memory along with all the wonderful years I spent here and at old

.721

League Park."[18] Steve O'Neill, Boudreau's minor league manager at Buffalo, and former Tribe pitcher Mel Harder, Boudreau's teammate from 1938–1947 and the Indians' pitching coach in 1954, were present at the ceremony.

The 1954 season would not provide many fond memories for Boudreau. He was finishing his third season at the helm in Boston, and with his team floundering in fourth place after having been expected to contend with Cleveland, New York and Chicago, he'd be fired at year's end. The Indians pounded another nail into Boudreau's coffin with a 4–2 victory. A three-run third inning was all Garcia needed to post his 17th win, tossing a complete-game eight-hitter at the Red Sox. The magic number fell to nine. The Yankees beat the White Sox, 6–3, to stay within 5½ games.

It would have been easy for the Indians to look past their final game against Boston to the one-day, two-game showdown with the Yankees that was on the horizon, but Houtteman stayed focused on the business at hand and twirled a neat, five-hit, 3–0 shutout for his 15th victory of the season. "I got along pretty well, all right," said Houtteman in the clubhouse, "but I think I pitched a better game against the Red Sox the last time we were in Boston. The situation today was different. I had that wind blowing in all afternoon, and in Boston I had the short fence to worry about."[19] The White Sox knocked off New York, 6–5, increasing the Yankees' almost insurmountable deficit to 6½ games and helping the Indians reduce their magic number to seven. Cleveland couldn't clinch the pennant the next day, but it could shove New York to the brink of elimination.

And that was precisely what a record crowd poured into Municipal Stadium to witness. The overflow mob of 86,563 (84,587 paid) wasn't disappointed. The Tribe's 4–1 and 3–2 victories reduced their magic number to a mere three. The proud, haughty Yankees left town 8½ games out of first place and needing a miracle to win consecutive pennant number six.

Offensively, Avila, the American League's leading batter, contributed five hits in eight trips to the plate, improving his average to .340, 13 points ahead of Chicago's Minnie Minoso. "What a day, what a

7. Magic Numbers

day!" Avila exulted. "Two things I always wanted to do when I started playing baseball. One was to play in an All-Star Game, another to be in World Series. I been in two All-Star Games, now I'm gonna be in a World Series. Maybe I've had better hitting days, but never one that meant as much as this."[20]

Hegan praised Lemon and Wynn, who held the Bronx Bombers to a paltry nine hits and three runs in 18 innings (Wynn fanned 12 Yankees.) "We had two real pitchers today, didn't we? Lem goes out and throws a great game, and then Gus tosses a better one. That Wynn pitched a terrific game. He only threw one bad pitch all afternoon. When he had two balls on Berra he tried to get a fastball past him on the outside. But he had to bring it in close enough for a strike, and he threw it too close."[21] Wynn suffered the fate many pitchers suffered when trying to sneak a fastball past Berra: a two-run homer that was all the offense the Yankees could muster in the second game. It wasn't quite enough.

"I'll take that game I won even over my no-hitter," Lemon said. "I never saw a game I wanted more or one that meant more. Getting a big lead now means we can relax during these last two weeks. I went through one of those hectic finishes in 1948, and I don't want any more of that."[22]

"Now maybe they'll call the Yanks a choke up club," exulted Newhouser. "You couldn't say they responded well to the pressure, could you, losing six of their last eight?"[23]

"I said after we left Yankee Stadium that we wanted to knock off the Yanks ourselves," said Lopez. "Now we've done it. Now nobody can make cracks about how we were able to knock off the second division clubs but not the Yankees. We beat 'em ourselves—and that's the way we wanted it."[24] The cautious Lopez, who reminded everyone that the Indians hadn't yet clinched anything, did allow himself the luxury of looking ahead to the World Series it was all but guaranteed his team would participate in. "Naturally, we want the Giants. It would be a great series."[25]

Stengel conceded that if his Yankees couldn't win a sixth straight pennant, he was glad Lopez would break the streak. "This fellow played for me and they don't come any better. If I was thinking of investing any money, he'd be the man."[26]

.721

But could the Indians, as Lemon suggested, relax? Even though any combination of Cleveland victories and/or New York losses equaling three would remove the pressure of clinching the pennant, there was still the matter of breaking the 1927 Yankees' record for most wins in a season. Lopez wanted that record. So did his players, so did the fans, and so did management. Club president Myron "Mike" Wilson sent Lopez a note after the doubleheader sweep that was tacked to the clubhouse bulletin board: CONGRATULATIONS. NOW LET'S WIN 111.

Winning 111 would prove to be both a blessing and a curse for the Indians.

With the sad-sack Senators following the Yankees into town, Lopez saw an opportunity to rest Doby, Rosen and Dave Philley, each of whom was nursing a leg injury. The Indians managed to nose out the Senators without them, 4–2. Wally Westlake, Hank Majeski and Dave Pope, subbing for the injured trio, each drove in runs. The Tribe scored four times off Washington starter Chuck Stobbs in the first inning and didn't find home plate again. Stobbs' replacement, Camilo Pascual, whose curveball would baffle American League hitters for years to come, held the Tribe to one hit over seven innings and retired the last 17 batters he faced.

The victory, Garcia's 18th, gave the Indians a record of 40 wins and only four defeats against the league's second division teams at home. Philadelphia and Boston had beaten the Indians twice at Municipal Stadium. Against Washington and Baltimore, the Tribe was a perfect 22–0. Cleveland's record overall against the second division was an astonishing 75–13.

The Yankees, angered over the loss of a pennant they considered to be their property by divine right, did the Indians no favors after leaving Cleveland. While the Tribe was idle on consecutive days, New York defeated Detroit, 4–2. The magic number remained two as the Indians packed for a weekend series at Briggs Stadium, from which they hoped to return as American League champions. "We'll go all out to end it here," said Lopez. "We'd like to get it over with as soon as we can."[27]

Avila went from goat to hero between the sixth and seventh innings of the first game of the series on September 17. The second baseman's error in the sixth helped Detroit to score a pair of unearned runs, tying

7. Magic Numbers

the game at 2–2. Rosen had given the Indians a 2–0 lead with a first-inning home run, and Lemon made it stand up until his defense betrayed him in the sixth. Avila quickly atoned for his miscues by depositing a pitch from Tigers starter Ned Garver into the lower deck in left field with the bases loaded in the seventh, and the Indians were on their way to a 6–3 victory that clinched a tie for the pennant. Lemon posted his 23rd victory with a six-hit complete game. New York kept its extremely faint hopes alive with a 10–3 trouncing of Philadelphia.

The Indians extinguished those faint hopes the next day. On a Saturday afternoon, in a game twice delayed by rain, the Tribe sloshed its way past Detroit, 3–2, to win the third pennant in the franchise's history. It was the second time the Indians had clinched a pennant in Detroit. The 1920 team wrapped up its pennant in the same stadium, then known as Navin Field, on October 2.

The Indians' offense consisted of Mitchell's two-run homer and Hegan's solo shot. Narleski saved the victory for Wynn, who may have been distracted by the rain and was removed by Lopez after walking Jim Delsing on four pitches with the bases loaded and two out in the seventh, cutting the Cleveland advantage to 3–2. Narleski induced Ray Boone to ground out to Rosen, and held the Tigers at bay in the eighth and ninth.

As the giddy Tribe players chanted "speech, speech, speech!" in Lopez's direction in the beer-soaked clubhouse during the clinching celebration, Lopez, cunningly, simply introduced Hank Greenberg, who'd made the trip to Briggs Stadium, his old stomping grounds as a player, to watch his handiwork result in the franchise's third league title. "I guess the best thing I did for this team was stay away from it all year," cracked the general manager. "I didn't tell one fellow how to hit or one pitcher how to pitch and I didn't tell Lopez how to manage. You seem to have done pretty well. Looks like you'll get a record of winning more ball games than any team in history. I hope you do and I hope you win the World Series in four games."[28]

"It's been a great season," Lopez understated in the happy clubhouse. "This is a great team. It is a greater team than anyone knows."[29] Unlike most pennant winners, the 1954 Indians couldn't bask in the glory of their triumph and club-record 107 victories and plan for the

.721

upcoming World Series. The league championship secured and the hated Yankees vanquished (for one season, anyway), the Indians faced the task of winning 111 games and wiping the 1927 Yankees out of the record books. They had seven chances left in which to win the four games needed to accomplish that feat.

The day after the pennant was clinched, Hank Greenberg talked about how close he came to having to hire a new manager following the disappointing 1953 season, when most people assumed Lopez had grown weary of Cleveland (and of finishing second) and, his contract having expired, would sign with another club. "Al did have an offer from another team," Greenberg revealed.

> "In fact, officials of the club contacted me and I presented the proposal to Lopez. We talked over the proposition and discussed the Cleveland situation. He was discouraged about the second place finish and couldn't sleep after the losses. I reminded him of the 90-plus Cleveland victories and the additional sleepless nights he'd have with any other team. Just the two of us were together when Al said, 'if you want me back, I'll be back.'"[30]

It was later revealed that the team hoping to lure Lopez away from the Indians was the Reds, as the newspapers had speculated. It will never be known if the 1954 Indians could have accomplished what they did for another manager.

Greenberg also wasted no time putting additional pressure on his manager. Barely giving Lopez a chance to savor the sweetness of his first pennant, Greenberg spoke to the Cleveland chapter of the National Journalism Fraternity on September 20 and declared that the Indians would repeat as American League champions in 1955, "but won't win as many games."[31]

The quest to become the winningest team in American League history began with a 4–2 victory in Briggs Stadium on September 19, the Indians' 52nd win on the road against just 25 losses. Cleveland earned the victory despite being out-hit by the Tigers, 13–5. The Tribe scored three first-inning runs off Ted Gray and, while neither pitcher was particularly sharp, Garcia and Mossi made them stand up. The victory was Garcia's 19th, leaving him with one more start in which to join Lemon and Wynn as a 20-game winner. The Indians headed home needing three wins in their remaining six games to set a record.

7. Magic Numbers

"I hope we can do it. This club deserves to go in the record books as the winningest of all time," said Lopez.[32] Setting a new record wasn't the senor's top priority, however. "We want to keep on winning, not because of the record, but because we want to be in a winning frame of mind for the World Series."[33]

The Indians stretched their winning streak to 11 with a 7–4 victory over the White Sox to open the final home stand of the season. It was another occasion on which the Indians were out-hit by their opponents but managed to pull out a win — a common occurrence in 1954. The Tribe struck early, reaching Chicago's 16-game winner, Bob Keegan, for five runs in the first two innings. Feller struggled through six innings before giving way to Narleski with one out in the seventh. Narleski and Newhouser combined to save Feller's 13th and last win of the season. Cleveland's 109th victory was in the books.

In the National League, the Giants dethroned the defending champion Dodgers with a 7–1 win in Ebbets Field. New York had finished 35 games behind Brooklyn in 1953. The Indians and Giants, long-time spring training antagonists, would meet in the World Series.

Lemon said the Giants would be a tougher match-up for the Indians than the Dodgers would've been. "They beat us 13 times this spring, didn't they? They've got more good left-handed hitters like Don Mueller, Whitey Lockman and Henry Thompson. That Willie Mays is right-handed, but he applies plenty of wood to the ball. He's a hard man to pitch for he hits bad balls good."[34] Lemon's reference to the spring barnstorming tour was significant. Although exhibition games generally aren't a reliable barometer of a team's strength (remember the Yankees won just eight of their 27 exhibitions in 1954), it was emphasized in the spring and throughout the season by Cleveland writers that the Indians-Giants spring series was different. It was noted that Leo Durocher played his regular line-up against the Indians, and Lopez, for the most part, reciprocated, although Lopez did some experimenting as he tried to find a first baseman and used Rudy Regalado at second in an effort to find a position for the "red-hot rapper." When the Indians played the Giants in the spring, it wasn't simply for fun and exercise. Thus, the results of the 1954 spring series couldn't be tossed aside as "just exhibition games."

.721

"You know, I can't tell you how glad I am we're in this thing with the Indians. They're our friends," said Durocher during the Giants' victory celebration.[35]

Tris Speaker picked his old team to win the world championship, because of its pitching. "The '48 team probably had a better infield and perhaps three pitchers as good as the Big Three but it didn't have the depth behind the starters. You'd have to go a long way to beat that '48 infield, though. How it could knock in those runs!" The Tribe's 1948 infield of first baseman Eddie Robinson, second baseman Joe Gordon, shortstop Boudreau and third baseman Ken Keltner accounted for 432 runs batted in. The Tribe's 1954 infield of Wertz, Avila, Strickland/Dente and Rosen drove home 276 runs. Adding Glynn's 18 RBI in limited duty at first base swells the total to 294.

Speaker was also impressed with the Indians' bench strength. "I've known of many good benches in my time in baseball but never one like this. Some looked better on paper but I don't think any ever produced like this one. New men consistently came in and did as good or even better a job."[36]

Rosen didn't play in Cleveland's 11th consecutive win, Lopez choosing to rest his star third baseman's sore leg. "I just want to be in number one shape for that series," Rosen commented. "Sure, my leg's been bothering me some and I've had a sore back, but you can bet I'd be in there if the pennant wasn't wrapped up. Then with our kind of bench anyone can lay off for a couple of days without being missed."[37]

For the second time in 1954, the White Sox snapped a Cleveland 11-game winning streak on September 21, edging the Tribe, 9–7, in a contest low-lighted by five Indians errors, a wild pitch, and a passed ball. The Indians could hardly be blamed if their heads weren't completely in the game. Being guests of honor at an 18-mile parade from Cleveland's far east side to its far west side, witnessed by an estimated half a million fans, to celebrate the American League pennant can distract a club from the business at hand, and that was how the players spent their late morning and early afternoon hours. Starting (and losing) pitcher Houtteman couldn't use the parade as an excuse for a poor outing in his last start of the season, as Lopez hadn't required him to attend the festivities, feeling

7. Magic Numbers

it unfair to ask his pitcher to spend hours waving at cheering fans and then use the same weary arm to propel baseballs at enemy batters. Why the parade wasn't scheduled for the team's September 23 off-day wasn't explained.

The Indians entered the record books on September 22, their 3–1 victory over Chicago tying the Yankees for the most victories by an American League club in the circuit's 54-year history. Mossi started and dodged bullets all day, allowing only five hits but walking six. Cleveland generated just enough offense to pin the loss on Jack Harshman who, like Mossi, hurled a complete game. The Indians' quest for immortality hadn't caused the fans to beat a path to the Municipal Stadium ticket windows. A slim crowd of 4,662 attended the history-making game.

During New York's futile attempt to overhaul the Indians in September, Stengel had said that if he couldn't guide his club to a sixth consecutive pennant, he deserved to be fired. Yankees co-owners Dan Topping and Del Webb wanted Stengel to return, however, and he did. On September 22, Stengel signed a two-year contract to manage the Yankees through 1956, for a base salary of $75,000, considerably more than Lopez was earning.

"We've got to fix our pitching and our hitting," Stengel said after signing the new pact. "When you get a setback you have to rebuild. After five years, I found out I forgot to win 140 games. I've got to find a way to catch Cleveland and so do six other clubs." It isn't often that a club which wins 103 games, as the Yankees did in 1954, needs much rebuilding. Asked about his remark that he should be fired if he didn't win the pennant, Stengel responded "by God, I'm surprised I lost it. I didn't expect to lose it until we left Cleveland."[38] Stengel often referred to the Yankees as "I" rather than "we."

The 1954 Yankees were the only team in Stengel's illustrious career as a player and manager to win 100 or more games. And their 103 victories earned them only second place.

The early betting line established the Indians as 8½-to-5 favorites to polish off the Giants. For those National League fans who claimed the Indians were champions of a much weaker league, former Cub Phil Cavarretta disagreed. Cavarretta, fired as Cubs manager in spring training,

.721

spent his first year in the American League in 1954 strengthening the White Sox bench after 20 seasons in the National, which included the 1945 pennant and batting title. "I don't see where they can say [that the National League is stronger.] They have less weakness at the bottom, yes, but I don't think they have as much strength at the top. I'll admit that even the tail-enders over there can give you trouble. In a short series like the World Series I've got to go with that pitching. I've liked the Indians all year and I think they should be able to stop the Giants. It won't be easy though."[39] Cavarretta had liked the Indians enough to seek employment with them after being dismissed as both a player and manager by the Cubs, only to be told by Lopez that he had virtually no chance of earning a roster spot. He hit .316 in 71 games for the White Sox.

The Indians pounded the stuffing out of the American League's bums, and needed to beat one of those bums, Detroit, at least once in Municipal Stadium to set the league record for victories they wanted so badly. The Tigers took the first game, 6–4, having little trouble with Lemon, who failed in his bid for his 24th victory. Lemon hadn't pitched in a week, and the rust showed. "I can work after three or four and feel right, but a longer layoff than that and I sometimes get wild. That was the trouble this afternoon. I was getting behind on the batters and had to come in with the ball."[40] Again the chance to witness history didn't entice Clevelanders to flock to the ballpark. Only 3,788 played hooky from work or school to watch the Friday afternoon contest.

The record for most victories in an American League season, held by the Yankees since 1927, was transferred to Cleveland on September 25, and the Indians established the new standard in style, thrashing the Tigers, 11-1, with Wynn holding the visitors hitless until Fred Hatfield led off the ninth inning with a single. The Tribe scored four runs in the fifth and four more in the eighth to make Wynn's 23rd victory a laugher. Pundits noted how appropriate the score, 11-1, was for the Tribe's record 111th victory.

The Indians played their only meaningless game of the 1954 season on September 26th, and no one could have blamed them for mailing it in to get the season over with and get on to the World Series. Instead, with Lopez using most of his regulars, Cleveland battled Detroit through

7. Magic Numbers

Three Tribe pitchers who helped the club achieve a 2.78 team ERA: Mike Garcia (left), Ray Narleski, and Early Wynn (Cleveland State University, *Cleveland Press* collection).

13 innings before losing, 8–7. Garcia started, seeking his 20th victory, which may explain why Lopez let the Big Bear, in his last tune-up before the World Series, struggle through 12 innings (surrendering six runs on a staggering 16 hits) before lifting him for a pinch-hitter. Narleski was touched up for a pair of runs in the 13th to suffer the loss, his third in six decisions. A final-game crowd of 17,225 brought the club's season attendance total to 1,335,472. While an increase of 266,000 over 1953, it was a disappointing turnout for a pennant winning, record-setting club. It had taken Clevelanders a long time to warm up to the 1954 Indians, thanks to three consecutive runner-up finishes that left fans fearing an inevitable collapse that never came.

7. Magic Numbers

There were some individual honors for the Indians. Avila won the league batting title with a .341 average, and Doby was pleased to learn after the season's final game that his 126 runs batted in had paced the circuit. Berra had driven in 125 for the Yankees. "I'm sure Berra must have knocked in at least a couple," Doby said when the topic was brought up in the Tribe's clubhouse. Informed that Berra went hitless in five at-bats and didn't drive in a run in New York's final game, Doby responded, "I backed in. Can you imagine that? I never thought I'd win it. This is my year."[41]

And that it had been. Many Indians, Rosen the most noteworthy, said in March that the Indians' pennant hopes depended on Doby bouncing back from a disappointing 1953 season, and Doby didn't let his team down. He batted a modest .272, but his 32 homers were tops in the American League, and he fielded flawlessly, committing just two errors in 411 chances for a .995 percentage and bailing Tribe pitchers out of numerous jams with circus catches.

When the sun set on the night of Sunday, September 26, the final American League standings showed a champion other than New York for the first time in six seasons.

Cleveland	111–43	.721	—
New York	103–51	.669	8
Chicago	94–60	.610	17
Boston	69–85	.448	42
Detroit	68–86	.442	43
Washington	66–88	.429	45
Baltimore	54–100	.351	57
Philadelphia	51–103	.331	60

New York's 103 wins were easily the most ever for an American League runner-up. In only seven of the league's first 53 seasons would 103 victories have failed to capture a pennant. In 17 of those same 53 seasons, including the war-shortened season of 1918, Chicago's 94 victories would have won the pennant. But 1954 was no ordinary season in the American League.

Opposite: **The 1954 American League champions. Their winning percentage of .721 is still the best in American League history (Cleveland Public Library).**

.721

The Indians had triumphed by following the Boudreau formula of breaking even with the contenders and beating the living snot out of the bums. The Indians split their 44 games with the Yankees and White Sox, and posted an amazing 89–21 record versus the rest of the league. Only Detroit came close to giving the Indians any trouble, winning eight of the 22 games between the two clubs. As noted earlier, the Tribe's mark against the Red Sox, Athletics, Orioles and Senators was a mind-boggling 75–13. The Indians had come from behind in 52 of their wins, including 22 such victories achieved in the seventh, eighth or ninth innings. Thirty times the Indians were out-hit by their opponents but still won the game. It all added up to the team's third pennant, a league-record 111 victories, and a date with an old friend in the World Series.

8

THE CATCH, THE HOMER AND OTHER CALAMITIES

The question on the minds of the overwhelming majority of Cleveland's baseball fans as the World Series approached wasn't who would win. An Indians victory was a foregone conclusion. The oddsmakers had established the Tribe as a prohibitive favorite to run the American League's streak of consecutive World Series victories to eight. The National League hadn't produced a world champion since the Cardinals had defeated the Red Sox in 1946. The Indians had already done the heavy lifting by dethroning the defending champion Yankees. The Giants didn't figure to be much of an obstacle to the Indians' winning their third World Series title. Few, if any, remembered that it was the Giants, not the Indians or Yankees, who had claimed the best record in baseball at the All-Star break. Since then, the Giants had coasted, playing just well enough (40–30) to outdistance the Dodgers by five games, while the Indians had played at a scorching (55–16) pace. True, the Giants had won 13 of their 21 exhibition meetings in the spring, but the key word was "exhibition." Those games hadn't counted.

The question most frequently posed to Al Lopez during the two-day layoff between the end of the season and the opening of the World Series was how many games the Indians would need to polish off the Giants. Could they sweep Leo Durocher's club? "I'd like to see us win in four or five games because it would be nice to wind it up here in Cleveland," Lopez answered. "But just so we win. That's the important thing. I don't care if it is four straight or if it runs the full seven."[1]

.721

For the superstitious, and those who believed in omens, the postseason didn't start well for the Indians. The club departed Cleveland's Union Terminal via train for New York on track 13. It was the only track the railroad had available for the Indians' "World Series Express." They left for the Big Apple as overwhelming 9–5 favorites.

Harry Jones picked the Indians to win the Series in six games. He admitted the Giants had better position players, but felt Cleveland's pitching would be the difference. Jones's boss, Gordon Cobbledick, agreed, also picking the Tribe in six. Frank Gibbons and his boss at the *Press,* Whitey Lewis, also forecast a Cleveland victory. Lewis said the Indians would need six games to do the job. Gibbons, who had correctly predicted Cleveland's pennant, said the Indians might need as few as five or as many as seven games to finish off the Giants. Ed McAuley of the *News* also thought the Tribe would capture the World Series in six games.

There were two contrary opinions. Geoffrey Fisher had been assigned by the *News* to follow the Giants once it became obvious they'd win the National League championship. Fisher was so impressed by Durocher's club he infuriated most of his readers by picking the Giants to vanquish the Indians in six games. Lou Darvas, the sports cartoonist for the *Press,* also picked the Giants. Nationally, 102 writers liked the Indians, while only 46 favored the Giants.

Tribe third base coach Tony Cuccinello, Lopez's right-hand man, was given the assignment of scouting the Giants once the Indians had clinched the pennant. "We'll win it all right. In five, maybe six games," said Cuccinello on the eve of the World Series. "I don't mean that it's going to be easy. No, it'll probably be a hard fought series. But I know what they've got and what we have, and I can't see them taking more than a couple games.

"The one really tough hitter is Al Dark. He's smart, has a good eye, and will fight you all the way. Now Willie Mays [the NL batting champion at .345] and Jim Rhodes are swingers. They can be pitched to, I think. In on the fists, especially."

Asked for his assessment of New York's pitching, Cuccinello said, "well, I don't see any reason why we shouldn't hit them. We've seen their

8. The Catch, the Homer and Other Calamities

pitchers and we know what they throw. I've been watching them and they all did well enough but nothing to scare you to death. The best looking one of the bunch, and the one that I think might give us trouble, is Don Liddle — and he's probably one guy who won't go against us."[2] Liddle, a left-hander, was 9–4 with a 3.06 earned run average in 1954, starting 19 games and pitching three shutouts. The Indians would face Liddle in the World Series (he'd start the fourth game) and he would give them trouble as Cuccinello warned.

Pitching coach Mel Harder was certain the Indians would win. "We have the better team as I see it. There is no comparison between the pitching staffs. They have only Sal Maglie, Johnny Antonelli and Ruben Gomez. On the basis of what they did against us this spring, only Antonelli might be real wicked. Our pitching staff is better all the way down the line."[3] The Giants had allowed only 550 runs and their team earned run average of 3.09 was the NL's lowest. The Tribe's staff, which Harder believed was much stronger than New York's, had surrendered 504 runs.

White Sox general manager Frank Lane, disappointed that his Pale Hose weren't in the World Series, didn't think the Giants would put up much of a fight against the Tribe. "The Indians are a cinch to knock off the Giants in the World Series. You'll win in five games. Antonelli might beat you once, that's all. All the Giants have is Antonelli and Mays. Maglie can give you a good game, if you give him plenty of rest. He's an old pro. But their infield is bad. The Indians are a much better club."[4]

Former Tribe owner Bill Veeck, whose current task was laying the groundwork for the relocation of a major league team to the west coast, planned to attend the Series and made no bones about which team he'd be rooting for. "Well, I may be prejudiced just a bit in favor of my boys, but I have to pick the Indians. They have everything."[5]

For the first time since 1948, Casey Stengel wouldn't be in a dugout directing his Yankees in a World Series. He was asked for his take on the Indians and Giants.

> "They played the best in our league and they won it clearly. But I don't think those Giants are going to be pushed around. Remember, they won in a tough league. What did Cleveland do with the teams in our league which

were just as good? They broke even. They won by beating the bad clubs. I haven't seen the Giants in a couple of years and I'm not saying that Cleveland isn't a good team. What I mean is that I'm not picking either one. But I don't see how any club can sweep the Giants."

Stengel should've known that a pledge of neutrality wouldn't satisfy the writers. So he confessed, "if I had to make a pick, I'd have to take the Indians."[6]

If the Indians were going to beat the Giants, they'd have to do it without Al Rosen at full strength. Rosen hadn't been healthy since late in May, and he'd been forced to leave the club's pennant clinching celebration in Detroit on September 18 with pain in his side and back. He was taking orthopedic treatments but wouldn't be near 100 percent when the Series began.

"Other players might be satisfied with the year I've had, but I'm not," said Rosen. "Ever since I broke my finger I've been plagued by injuries. I don't recall a day when I've felt right. I'm so anxious to have a good World Series to have something pleasant to remember all winter."[7] By the standards of most players, Rosen had enjoyed a productive season in 1954. But his home run total had dropped from 43 to 24 and his RBI plunged from 145 to 102. Rosen did manage to get his batting average back to the .300 mark with a late-season surge.

The *News* hired Jim Hegan and Early Wynn to compose daily commentaries about the clash with the Giants, and before the first game both, understandably, predicted their team would win. After saying the 1954 Indians were a stronger team than the 1948 world champions (whose starting catcher was a guy named Hegan), Hegan wrote that "if Rosen's leg is better, the Series will be a lot easier. If not, it will be a struggle. But pitching will win it for us regardless."[8] Wynn, who would supply some of that vaunted starting pitching, wrote, "this World Series will never go the limit of seven games if we get the pitching we should. I say we can win it in five or six games if our throwers are right."[9]

The first game of the World Series produced one of baseball's enduring images: that of Mays, the number 24 on the back of his uniform turned to home plate, reaching out to catch a 450-foot cannon shot off the bat of Vic Wertz as he raced toward the center field wall in the Polo

8. The Catch, the Homer and Other Calamities

Grounds in the eighth inning. Had Mays not caught the ball, which would have been a home run far beyond the center field fence in Municipal Stadium, two runners would have scored, Wertz may have motored all the way around the bases for an inside-the-park home run, the Indians would have broken a 2–2 tie and, in all likelihood, won the all-important opener for Bob Lemon. Mays's catch preserved the tie, the game went into extra innings, and the Giants won it in the tenth on a pop fly home run off the bat of Rhodes, the part-time "swinger" that Cuccinello was confident the Indians would be able to pitch to. Instead, Rhodes, pinch-hitting for Monte Irvin, lofted a pitch from Lemon just beyond the 257-foot right field wall, which would have been a routine fly ball in every other park in the major leagues, including Municipal Stadium. Mays's miracle catch and Rhodes' "Chinese" home run, to use the vernacular of the era, were too much for the Indians to recover from, and the Giants had a 5–2 victory and a one-game lead in the Series.

The Indians had several opportunities to win the game in regulation. They stranded four runners at third base, including Wertz, whose first-inning triple off Giants starter Sal Maglie gave Cleveland a quick 2–0 lead. The Indians stranded Wertz at third again in the sixth and Larry Doby in the eighth. Rudy Regalado, running for Wertz, reached third base in the tenth but didn't score. The Indians left 13 runners on base against Maglie, Liddle and Marv Grissom, who earned the victory. Lemon went all the way for the Tribe, heaving his glove high in the air in disgust when Rhodes' homer reached the stands. The glove landed behind home plate and didn't disrupt the jubilant Giants celebration.

"It was a curve ball and a good one, too," Lemon explained. "He didn't hit it well. Dark hit his ball earlier a lot harder than Rhodes."[10]

"The guy just got a piece of the ball," said Tribe catcher Mickey Grasso. Grasso had returned in September from the broken ankle sustained in spring training and went behind the plate after Lopez had pulled Hegan for a pinch-hitter. "He whacked it right on the trademark of the bat, and it just popped out toward right. Bobby Avila started back when he hit it. That's an idea how long it was."[11]

"The ball started out more toward center field and I was sure that I could catch it," said right fielder Dave Pope. "It was nothing but a

.721

routine fly ball. Then the wind got it and blew it nearer the foul line, where the distance is shorter. Some fellow stuck up his hands and caught it before it came down. The darn thing barely made it, even with the wind helping it."[12]

Wertz contributed four hits to the Indians' attack, but it was the ball that was caught that everyone was talking about afterward. "I never hit a ball harder in my life. I know this sounds funny, but I actually thought the thing was going to carry into the bleachers. When I smacked the ball it felt so good and I was so sure of how I tagged it that all the details were erased from my mind. I can't even tell you what I hit. They were throwing me a lot of stuff and I was hitting all of it. It doesn't mean a thing though —-we lost the game."[13]

"Wertz hits that ball as far as anybody ever will, and it's just an out," Lopez lamented. "We don't even get a run out of it. If [Mays] hadn't caught that ball, we never would have gone into extra innings. Vic played a great game, but that catch topped everything."[14]

The deflated Indians were defeated. The World Series was as good as over. "Today I'll be firing them at the Giants," wrote Wynn in his column. "All I can say is that if we don't win, my story tomorrow should be run on the obituary page."[15]

Game Two started promisingly enough as Al Smith poked 21-game-winner Johnny Antonelli's first pitch over the Polo Grounds' left field roof, but the Indians didn't score again, and the slim 1–0 lead wasn't enough for Wynn. The Giants managed just four hits off Wynn and Don Mossi, while the Tribe collected eight hits off Antonelli (and stranded 13 more base runners) in the 3–1 New York victory. A walk to Mays, singles by Hank Thompson and Rhodes (again pinch-hitting for Irvin), and a fielder's choice by Antonelli plated a pair for the Giants in the fifth, and Rhodes hit his second home run in as many games in the seventh.

"I know after I hit that first ball over the roof, I was aiming for home runs," Smith said. "But I didn't see another one over the plate all day."[16]

"I thought Antonelli was excellent, but Early was better," Lopez said. "I can't recall a time since I've been manager that we've left that

8. The Catch, the Homer and Other Calamities

many men on base two days in a row. I'm not disappointed in anyone or anything — except that we don't get a hit now and then when it counts. We have to figure some way to get some runs and we'll need all the speed we can get."[17]

"I know what you're thinking," acknowledged Hegan in his column after game two. "What about Rhodes? He beat us with a three-run homer in the opener Wednesday, and yesterday he knocked in two of the Giants' runs as they took us again. What are we going to do about him? Actually, I still think we have the right dope on him. I still feel his power is against the high fastball. We haven't given him one yet. He's hit other pitches."[18]

There was no whining from Wynn, who took the hard-luck loss in the second game. "I want to make it clear we weren't cheated, lied to or stolen from," he wrote, "we just got beat, that's all. I think it will be different now that we are going home to our own backyard. I, for one, think it will be a different story the next three days."[19]

A disgusted Lewis resurrected an old criticism as the World Series headed for Cleveland. Watching the Indians stumble through the first two games, the columnist suggested maybe the Tribe just didn't want to win as badly as the Giants did.

"We're not that bad and they're not that good," said Lopez, possibly trying to convince himself and his ball club of that fact as much as he was trying to convince reporters and Tribe fans. "I've seen this happen before. You lose a couple of close ones where a fly ball would have won for you, then you get your brains knocked out."[20]

As the Indians and Giants headed for Cleveland for Games Three, Four and (the Indians hoped) Five, Cleveland fans were reminded by the media that the 1920 Tribe had dropped two of the first three games of the best-of-nine World Series in Brooklyn and then rallied to win the next four, and the championship, at League Park. The Indians had won 59 of their 77 home games during the regular season, but the Giants wasted little time dashing any hope that history would repeat itself in 1954.

As a disappointed crowd of 71,555 —15,000 shy of attendance in Game Five of the 48 Series— looked on and groaned, New York jumped to a fast 4–0 lead against Mike Garcia in the third game, scoring a run in the first on a single by Whitey Lockman, a wild throw by George Strickland, and a single by Mays. New York added three more in the third when Dark and Don Mueller singled, Hank Thompson was intentionally walked, Rhodes (batting again for Irvin) singled in two runs, and Thompson scored on an error by Garcia. The Giants scored their fifth run in the fifth inning when Thompson doubled and Wes Westrum singled off Art Houtteman, and Ray Narleski surrendered a run in the sixth when he walked Lockman, who was sacrificed to second by Dark and scored on Mays's single.

The Indians didn't score until the seventh, when Wertz connected for a solo home run off New York starter Ruben Gomez. Bill Glynn's double off Gomez, who gave way to Hoyt Wilhelm, and Dark's error gave the Tribe its second run in the eighth. The 6–2 defeat shoved the Indians to the brink of elimination.

"So nobody's won the series after losing the first three," Wertz growled defiantly after the game. "Well, nobody in the American League ever won 111 games, either. Maybe we're due for another first."[21]

In his office, Lopez faced reporters asking what he could do to avoid the humiliation of being swept. It was a given that the Giants had won the Series. Lopez re-iterated that the Indians' lack of offense was the main culprit in their three defeats, although the pitching had also faltered in the third game. "We're still a good ball club, but we can't win without hitting and we're not getting it. Maybe we'll snap out of it. We have to. Rosen's injury has made a big difference in the series. If he can go, he'll be back in there," explained the suddenly beleaguered manager.[22]

In an effort to spark the offense, Lopez had benched Rosen in the third game, replacing him with Hank Majeski, who was hitless in four at-bats. The thigh injury Rosen had aggravated late in the season severely limited his mobility, but he insisted it didn't bother him at the plate. "Sure, the leg is still tender, but I can still swing a bat and hitting's what we need. I guess Al was thinking of using me as a pinch-hitter today, but the right opportunity never came along."[23] Rosen would be back at third base for the fourth game.

"The Yankees are a better ball club than the Giants," snarled Avila. "Sure, Gomez pitched a good game, but Bob Grim is a better pitcher.

8. The Catch, the Homer and Other Calamities

Whitey Ford is a better pitcher than Antonelli. This is just one of those things."[24]

With the Series all but lost, Lopez was under pressure from fans and the media to send Bob Feller to the mound to start the fourth game. Although six years had passed, Indian fans hadn't forgotten Feller's heartbreaking 1–0 loss to the Boston Braves in the first game of the 1948 Series, when second base umpire Bill Stewart was badly fooled by the Tribe's pick-off play and ruled Boston's Phil Masi had beaten Lou Boudreau's tag. The next day, photographs from all angles proved Masi had been picked off. Tommy Holmes followed with a single, one of just two hits Feller allowed, and the Braves won the game. With a chance to wrap up the Series before a mob of 86,288 fans at Municipal Stadium in the fifth game, Feller was driven from the mound in the seventh inning and the Indians lost, 11–5. With the Tribe on the brink of elimination, Game Four of the 1954 Series would probably be Feller's last chance to win a game in the fall classic, and sentimental fans (and writers, and probably some of the players) wanted Lopez to give him the opportunity. Feller had won 13 games and lost just three during the season, with a 3.09 earned run average.

"It's according to how we go," Lopez answered when queried before the Series as to whether Feller would be given the chance to nail down the one prize that had eluded him in a Hall of Fame career. "If we get out in front and get a chance to rest the Big Three, I'm sure Bob will get a start. If we have to keep coming from behind I'm not so sure. Art Houtteman [15–7] deserves a starting shot, too. He and Feller have both done fine jobs. But a short series isn't like a full season. You can't use everybody."[25]

The Indians hadn't gotten out in front. The Giants had pinned their backs to the wall, and, in a desperate attempt to avoid the embarrassment of a record-setting season culminating in a World Series sweep, Lopez ignored both Feller and Houtteman and started Lemon on just two days' rest.

"It was a regular thing a year ago," Lopez said, defending his decision to use his ace for the second time in four days, even though Lemon had pitched nine and a third hard innings in the first game. "In fact, he's better with too little rest than too much rest. We're really backed up to the wall and I have to use Lem. He told me yesterday he's ready to go anytime."[26]

Lemon's spirit was willing, but his arm wasn't up to the task, although he didn't get much help from his shell-shocked teammates. Lemon surrendered two second-inning runs on a walk, a double by Irvin (who Durocher allowed to bat for himself for a change) and errors by Wertz and Wally Westlake. The Giants added another run off the Indians' weary ace in the third on singles by Dark and Mueller and a double by Mays. New York reached Hal Newhouser and Narleski for four runs in the fifth to balloon its lead to 7–0. Mossi and Garcia mopped up with two scoreless innings apiece.

The Indians rallied briefly in the sixth when the Giants' defense collapsed temporarily. Errors by Liddle and second baseman Davey Williams put Sam Dente and Hegan on base, and Majeski, batting for Narleski, slammed one of Liddle's deliveries over the left field fence. In the seventh, Wertz and Hegan singled (Wertz's eighth hit in 16 at-bats) and Regalado, pinch-hitting for Mossi, singled Wertz home to cut the Indians' deficit to 7–4 and gave the crowd of better than 78,000 hope that their heroes might grab yet another come from behind victory and prolong the Series. Durocher summoned Wilhelm to put out the fire, and he and Antonelli combined to check the Tribe the rest of the way. The Indians could get no closer and the humiliating sweep was complete.

Feller, deprived of his last chance to win a World Series game, declined to fault his manager for leaving him in the bullpen. "We lost the first three games and that forced Lopez to go with his top pitchers all the way," said Bob, acknowledging that he was no longer among the top pitchers on the Cleveland staff. "It was a desperation deal. He had to go with his aces. If we had won today, I probably would have pitched tomorrow. Sure, I was disappointed that I didn't get to play, but I was just as disappointed that the Giants beat us."[27] Sentiment aside, would a well-rested Feller have given the Indians a better chance to beat the Giants than an obviously exhausted Lemon? Would Houtteman?

In the exuberant Giants clubhouse, the manager of the new world

8. The Catch, the Homer and Other Calamities

champions admitted he was intimidated by the daunting task his club faced just four days earlier, and not much intimidated Durocher. "I never thought we could do it in four straight," he readily confessed. "Frankly, I wasn't even sure beforehand that we could do it at all." Durocher then, without trying, may have put his finger on what happened to the seemingly invincible Indians. "We got all the breaks. That helped. Everything we did seemed to be right. Everything they did seemed to go against them."[28]

That, in a nutshell, may have summed up the collapse of the Indians. It may have been no more complicated than that. Dark had another take on his club's victory. "Don't be too hard on the Indians," said the Giants shortstop and inspirational leader, who undoubtedly reveled in the victory more than his teammates after having lost to the Indians as a member of the Braves in 1948. "They're a fine ball club. It's just that we had a ball club that simply wouldn't be beaten. I doubt if there was a club that could have beaten us in this series."[29]

A few days later, during the post-mortems, Dark added, "maybe we simply caught them at the right time. The Indians are a great ball club and don't let anyone tell you differently."[30]

Hank Greenberg visited the clubhouse to console the players. "We had a great season," he assured them. "It just lasted four games too long."[31]

Wertz, who batted .500 in the Series, was already looking ahead to 1955. "We're gonna come back next year and win 112 and then we'll beat these guys."[32]

The only happy face in the Tribe's devastated clubhouse belonged to Majeski, whose three-run blast was only the fifth pinch-hit home run in World Series history. "There'll never be anything like that again. The greatest thrill I ever had. I'm only sorry we couldn't have won to make it perfect. I still think we have a better team, and nobody will ever convince me otherwise."[33]

"The Giants beat us fair and square," wrote Wynn in his final column. "All I can say about how come we got blasted four straight is that the Giants played the coldest ball club I've seen in a long time. We were ice cold."[34]

Hegan used his last column to get some gripes off his chest. "I finally had a chance to read the papers yesterday," he wrote. The Series ended on a Saturday and the *News* didn't publish on Sundays, so Hegan's column obviously wasn't written until he'd seen the Sunday papers, filled with post-mortems and analysis.

> "It was the first time I've had an opportunity to sit down and read through them since the Series opened. Two things that were repeated several times irritated me very much:
> 1 — that the Giants sweep proves the American League is very weak.
> 2 — that we didn't try, that we didn't have any fight or desire.
> I can't buy either of these. Both these thoughts are way off base."[35]

To Lopez fell the unenviable task of trying to explain to writers (and fans) who had already anointed the Indians the 1954 world champions, how things went so horribly wrong so quickly —-as if he had the answers.

> "[The Giants] played championship baseball. They were good offensively and defensively and their pitching was terrific. Their relief pitching especially was great. We just weren't hitting, though. That may have had something to do with how good they looked. They were a hot ball club and we were cold.. We didn't hit —-at least not when it counted. We didn't have too much trouble getting on base, but we couldn't come up with as much as a fly ball to bring them in. I can't think of anything I would have done differently. I gave them my three best pitchers and then came back again with Lemon. They faced our best and still beat us, that's all there is to it.
> "I'm not crying about it, though. They were better than we were this time. It's hard to say if they're that much better. I think it's just more like the thing that happened to us in Chicago, just before the All-Star game. We lost two close ones and then went to pieces—-lost four straight."[36]

The morning after the Giants completed their sweep, Ed McAuley had breakfast with four fellow writers, each a member of baseball's scoring rules committee. Naturally, the five men tried to figure out what had happened to the seemingly invincible Indians. A writer McAuley declined to identify put it bluntly. "Let's face it. The American League is a lousy league. The Indians *are about as good as the St. Louis Browns of 1944* (italics mine.) Yet the Indians won 111 games. The Giants didn't come close to that figure. Their competition was too tough. So the Indians were made heavy favorites. But the Giants have a great ball club. That's why they won."[37]

8. The Catch, the Homer and Other Calamities

For his readers who weren't aware, McAuley described the 1944 Browns as a team of 4-F players exempted from the military draft (and thus available to play baseball) for various physical reasons who won the franchise's only pennant due to watered-down wartime competition. *"The Indians are about as good as the St. Louis Browns of 1944."*

The unidentified writer McAuley quoted may have been the same (also unidentified) writer quoted in the *Press* making the same argument: the Indians were a decent team that ran roughshod over an abysmal league. "This merely proves the Indians were just a fair ball club in a very bad league. They have good pitchers who ran through their league like a hot knife through butter. This just isn't much of a ball club, despite those 111 victories."[38]

About as good as the St. Louis Browns of 1944, considered by many baseball historians to be the weakest American League pennant winner ever. Even the Browns managed to win two games from the mighty Cardinals in the World Series. McAuley didn't accept that evaluation and defiantly said if the World Series were to be played over again, he'd still pick the Indians to win. He couldn't deny the fact, however, that for four straight days, at least, the Giants were the superior ball club.

Greenberg and Lopez took a day off to lick their wounds and went immediately back to work on October 4, putting their heads together to start preparations for the 1955 season, which, their World Series debacle notwithstanding, the Indians would enter as defending American League champions. As painful as it must have been, Lopez met with writers afterward and again reflected on his team's pratfall on baseball's biggest stage.

Echoing Dark's comments, Lopez offered the opinion that

> "Looking back, I don't believe that any team in either league could have beaten the Giants. It was a hot ball club, one that just didn't make mistakes. It's been said that Al Rosen and Bobby Avila weren't rested enough before the series but I can't buy that. Both of them had some rest and then wanted to play in the last few games to keep sharp. When Avila was out earlier in the season it took quite a while for him to get in stride, and the same for Rosen. Both of them felt that too much rest would take off some of their sharpness."

Lopez acknowledged that "it was a long season for Jim Hegan and Larry Doby. Perhaps they did feel a little weariness in the series."[39]

Weary himself, Lopez prepared to leave for his home in Tampa. He had no plans to return to Cleveland until the January Ribs and Roasts dinner, at which sportswriters and broadcasters wrote and performed satirical sketches inspired by the exploits of Cleveland's teams and athletes. The World Series had given the writers abundant material for those sketches.

"Guess the Series put new life into that affair, didn't it?" Lopez asked with a wry smile. "You see, something good comes from everything."[40]

Epilogue

It's difficult to accurately gauge the impact of the Indians' embarrassing pratfall in the 1954 World Series on the community and the future of the franchise itself. There are those who will argue that it took the team 41 years to recover, since the Indians didn't win another pennant, or even qualify for post-season competition, which became somewhat easier when the American and National Leagues split into divisions, until 1995. While the bottom line is that a series of well-meaning but dreadfully underfinanced ownerships were mainly responsible for the Indians' four-decade-long journey through baseball's wilderness, the seemingly unbeatable Indians loss in the 1954 Series reinforced a belief among Cleveland fans, which can be traced back to the franchise's earliest days, and which they hold to this day, that something was bound to go wrong. Some how, someway, the Indians would screw up and find a way to disappoint the city and their supporters. Only twice, in 1920 and 1948, had the Indians overcome the stigma and brought home a world championship. If the 1954 Indians, winners of a league record 111 games, couldn't win the World Series, what Cleveland team ever could or would? And none since has.

As noted elsewhere in this book, it took Clevelanders a long time to warm up to the 1954 Indians. Not until September 12, when 86,000 fans packed Municipal Stadium to cheer the Tribe on to a sweep of the Yankees, reducing the team's magic number for clinching the pennant to three and convincing even the most pessimistic fans that it was, indeed, the Tribe's year, did the city truly embrace the team. And the season attendance of 1,335,472 drew Hank Greenberg's attention. So did

.721

the crowd of 71,555 at the third game of the World Series. It was far short of a sell-out, as the Indians already trailed the Giants, two games to none, and a lot of Clevelanders, many of whom had jumped on the team's bandwagon only two weeks earlier, had jumped off. It doesn't take much to convince a Cleveland sports fan that the roof is caving in, and, in October of 1954, it was. Home cooking and the friendly confines of cozy League Park had been all the 1920 Indians needed to propel them past the Dodgers to the franchise's first world championship. The same recipe didn't work in 1954 (and there's no way Municipal Stadium could ever have been referred to as "cozy").

Al Lopez earned a new contract for bringing home a pennant. The 1955 Indians, with key performers Al Rosen, Larry Doby, Vic Wertz, and the "Big Three" of Early Wynn, Mike Garcia and Bob Lemon each a year older, blew a September lead and slipped back to their accustomed position of second place, three games behind the Yankees. The Indians held on to the runner-up spot in 1956, but they didn't seriously challenge New York, which won its seventh pennant in eight years by a comfortable nine-game margin.

The contract Lopez signed in the fall of 1954 expired after the 1956 season. Greenberg wanted Lopez to return in 1957 and professed to be stunned when his manager resigned on September 28. "These have been six rugged years, and I think a change might do us all some good," Lopez said.[1]

According to Gordon Cobbledick, Greenberg asked two writers he encountered in the catacombs of Municipal Stadium why Lopez quit. In unison, the writers replied "because of you!" Cobbledick contended that Lopez would've returned had Greenberg offered him a new deal anytime in September of 1956. But Greenberg stubbornly stuck to his belief that a manager should never be rehired during the season, and Lopez, weary of being left twisting in the wind each time he was in the final year of his contract, resigned.

Lopez denied that friction between himself and Greenberg led to his decision. "That isn't true at all. Hank and I may not have seen eye-to-eye on everything, but we managed to get along. The strain of six rugged years was the main factor in my decision. Another was the fact

Epilogue

that I was disappointed because I thought we could have done better in the last six years."[2] The fans, who came to Municipal Stadium in ever decreasing numbers in 1955 and 1956, thought so, too, and weren't shy about letting Lopez know it.

"This is like closing a chapter on a book," said Greenberg.[3] Despite the rigors of being a major league manager, which Lopez had told Frank Gibbons would lead to an early retirement, he signed with the White Sox for 1957 and led that club to its first World Series in 40 years in 1959. The "Go-Go Sox" lost in six games to a Los Angeles Dodgers squad some baseball historians consider to be among the weakest National League pennant winners ever. Lopez would manage the White Sox through 1965, finishing second in 1963, 1964 and 1965. He came out of retirement to pilot the White Sox again for 47 games in 1968 and the first 17 contests of 1969 before retiring for good.

Greenberg insisted Lopez's resignation blindsided him, and he had no candidates to replace him. He decided on Kerby Farrell, the manager of the Indians' top farm team, who lasted just one season. After employing only two managers, Lou Boudreau and Lopez, from 1942 through 1956, with the departure of Lopez, the club may as well have installed a revolving door in the manager's office. The Greenberg-Lopez partnership may have run its course. But Indians fans of longstanding can be excused for wondering what the team's future would have been like had Lopez stayed. Maybe the deterioration that began in 1957 would've begun anyway.

Greenberg noticed that the Indians' 1954 attendance was half of what it had been during the world championship season of 1948. The combination of a contender, owner Bill Veeck's promotional genius, a huge stadium and a booming post-war economy created what might today be termed a "perfect storm." The red-hot love affair between the city and its baseball team couldn't last. Cleveland cares about its Indians, but baseball isn't an all-consuming passion in northeastern Ohio, as it is in New England or on the north side of Chicago. Rather than receiving a pennant bump, Clevelanders were so turned off by the World Series flop that attendance declined to 1.2 million in 1955 and fell even further, to 865,000, in 1956. It was the first time since 1945 that the Indians had failed to draw a million paying customers. Greenberg was convinced that the steady attendance decline since 1949, interrupted only slightly by the 1954 pennant, indicated that Clevelanders were tired of baseball. If Cleveland would no longer support a major league team, Greenberg knew of a metropolitan area that would.

After the 1957 season, during which the Indians had fallen to sixth place, and again after the lackluster 1958 campaign, Greenberg, who owned 19 percent of the team's stock and sat on the board of directors, urged his fellow directors to move the Indians to the growing metropolis of Minneapolis/St. Paul. The directors rejected the idea in 1957 and fired Greenberg as general manager. Greenberg made another pitch in 1958 and was joined by brothers Andrew and Charles Baxter, who also owned 19 percent of the club's stock. The other directors put down the insurrection by purchasing the stock owned by Greenberg and the Baxter brothers and sending them on their way. Greenberg would join Veeck's front office in Chicago and (re-united with Lopez) be part of the White Sox's 1959 championship.

Both of the participants in the 1954 World Series soon fell on hard times. The Giants, who drew fewer fans than the Indians in 1954 (admittedly, with competition from the Yankees and Dodgers, but also drawing from a much larger population base) finished third in 1955, 18½ games behind the arch-rival Dodgers, and sank to sixth in 1956. Once the flagship franchise of the National League, the Giants were bound for San Francisco in 1958. The Indians, thanks to some civic-minded members of the board of directors, resisted the temptation to relocate to greener pastures and stayed in Cleveland. A succession of underfinanced and just plain unlucky ownerships (the team changed hands in 1962, 1966, 1972, 1975, 1978 and 1986) kept the club on the shores of Lake Erie but failed miserably to produce competitive teams until real estate moguls Richard and David Jacobs, natives of nearby Akron with extensive business holdings in Cleveland, purchased the team and convinced Cuyahoga County voters to approve financing for a shiny new park built exclusively for baseball in 1990. Jacobs (now Progressive) Field opened in 1994, and the following season ushered in the Indians' "Era of Champions" during which they won six division titles and two pennants, by far the most

Epilogue

successful stretch in franchise history. A World Series title continues to elude Cleveland, however.

Lopez's exemplary managerial record earned him election to the Hall of Fame in 1977. His teams won 1,410 games and fashioned a winning percentage of .584, but he always looked back on 1954, and the World Series in particular, which should've represented his crowning achievement, with regret. He called it the lowest point of his career.

Al Rosen's career peaked with his pursuit of the Triple Crown in 1953. Injuries, mainly the chip fracture of his finger, drastically reduced his effectiveness during the Indians' record-setting 1954 season, and his batting average continued to fall. After batting .244 in 1955 and .267 in 1956, combining for 36 homers (seven fewer than he'd hit in 1953) and 142 runs batted in (three fewer than he'd driven home in 1953), Rosen retired and became a successful businessman in Cleveland. He, along with another prominent Clevelander, George M. Steinbrenner III, put together a group that tried to buy the Indians from owner Vernon Stouffer in 1971. Stouffer rejected the $8.6 million offer. When CBS was looking to unload the Yankees the following year, Steinbrenner's group bought them instead. Rosen would serve the Yankees in several capacities, and once he'd had enough of Steinbrenner, he joined the front office of the San Francisco Giants. Thus, he was employed by both of the teams he tried mightily to defeat during his career with the Indians.

It will never be known if Bob Feller could've prolonged the 1954 World Series with a victory in the fourth game, had Lopez given him the chance. Feller had proven an effective "doubleheader pitcher" in 1954, but he had just four more wins remaining in his stout right arm. Feller appeared in 25 games in 1955, starting 11 and posting a 4–4 record and 3.47 ERA. He retired after going 0–4 in 19 games in 1956, leaving him with a career mark of 266–162. Feller was elected to the Hall of Fame in 1962 and remained an occasional coach and full-time goodwill ambassador for the only team he ever played for, until his death in 2010. A statue of Feller's classic high leg-kicking windup stands in Bob Feller Plaza outside Progressive Field, the Tribe's home park.

It was often speculated by writers in the off-season of 1953–1954 what it would take for Greenberg to break up the "Big Three." The

.721

answer turned out to be: more than Greenberg was ever offered. The trio of Bob Lemon, Early Wynn and Mike Garcia remained together through the 1957 season. Lemon's 18 victories would top the American League in 1955, and he'd win 20 more in 1956. Lemon slipped to 6–11 in 1957 and retired after posting an 0–1 record in 11 games (one start) in 1958. He'd return to the major leagues as a manager in 1970, taking the reins of the second-year expansion Kansas City Royals. Veeck hired Lemon to manage the White Sox in 1977, and was rewarded with a strong third-place (90–72) finish in the American League's West Division.

Weeks after Veeck fired Lemon, with the White Sox stumbling to a 34–40 start the following year, Steinbrenner turned to him to take over the Yankees from Billy Martin in July of 1978. Lemon's calm demeanor was just the tonic needed by a talented team whose nerves had been stretched to the breaking point, and he guided the Yankees past the crumbling Red Sox to the East Division title. New York then won a thrilling five-game League Championship Series from Lemon's former club, the Royals, and defeated the Dodgers in six games in the World Series. It was one of the most impressive jobs any manager has ever turned in, given the circumstances. It was also the high point of Lemon's managerial career. He was fired by Steinbrenner 65 games into the 1979 season, and returned to pilot the Yankees for the final 25 games of the second half of the strike-shortened 1981 campaign, replacing Gene Michael. The Yankees, under Michael, had been in first place in their division when the players walked off the job and were guaranteed a spot in the post-season when action resumed. Lemon led New York to a victory over the second-half champion Milwaukee Brewers in the division playoff to earn a spot in the League Championship Series, which the Yankees swept from Martin's Oakland Athletics in three games. The Yankees then won the first two games of the World Series from their ancient rivals, the Dodgers, before Los Angeles did what the 1954 Indians couldn't do. Down two games to none and heading home, the Dodgers won three one-run games before returning to Yankee Stadium and blowing Lemon's club out in the sixth and final game, 9–2. Steinbrenner dismissed Lemon after just 14 games in 1982, and although the Indians made no secret of

Epilogue

their desire to lure Lemon to Cleveland to manage the only club he ever played for, no deal was reached.

Wynn won 17 games in 1955 and 20 in 1956, but his numbers slipped to 14–17 in 1957 and he was sent to the White Sox, pitching them to the 1959 pennant with a record of 22–10. That left Wynn 29 victories short of the 300 mark, an achievement he coveted. He won 28 more games for the White Sox from 1960–1962 but was released after a 7–15 record in his final season in Chicago ... one victory short of 300. He signed with the Indians, who hoped Wynn's pursuit of history could boost attendance for an otherwise dull and mediocre team. Wynn notched the milestone victory in the second game of a doubleheader versus the Kansas City Athletics at Municipal Stadium on July 13, 1963. In what would today be termed a "five and fly," Wynn pitched the first five innings and exited with a 5–4 lead. Jerry Walker held the Athletics scoreless the rest of the way and the Tribe added a pair of insurance runs for a 7–4 victory. The 43-year-old Wynn made 15 more appearances for the Indians but didn't win another game, retiring with a career mark of 300–244. He was elected to the Hall of Fame in 1972.

Garcia's 2.64 ERA in 1954 was the lowest in the American League. It was his last big season for the Tribe. His spot in the starting rotation was taken in 1955 by a fire-balling young left-hander named Herb Score, who'd win 16 games in 1955 and 20 in 1956. Garcia's victory totals shrank to 11, 11 and 12 in the three seasons following 1954, and he'd be released after winning three and losing six for Cleveland in 1959. The Big Bear pitched in 15 games for the White Sox in 1960 and 16 for the expansion Washington Senators in 1961, winning none of them. He retired with a career record of 142–97.

Larry Doby's power numbers dropped dramatically in 1955. Although he raised his batting average from .272 to .291, his homers declined from 32 to 26 and his runs batted in plunged from 126 to 75. Greenberg had seen enough and traded Doby to the White Sox for outfielder Jim Busby and shortstop Chico Carrasquel. After two seasons in Comiskey Park, Doby was sent to the Orioles, who quickly traded him back to Cleveland for pitcher Bud Daley, infielder Dick Williams and outfielder Gene Woodling. Doby's second tour of duty with the Tribe lasted just 89 games and produced a .283 average, 13 home runs and 45 RBI. The Indians traded him to Detroit for Tito Francona in March of 1959, and the Tigers sold his contract to the White Sox in May.

Doby served as a coach on manager Ken Aspromonte's Cleveland staff in 1974 and made no secret of his desire to become a manager himself. When Aspromonte resigned with six games left in the season, Doby hoped he'd be considered for the job. He was disappointed when club president Ted Bonda and general manager Phil Seghi chose Frank Robinson, who'd been acquired by the team in mid–September while the Indians still harbored long-shot playoff aspirations, to become the first African American manager in major league history. Doby's chance to call the shots came in 1978, when Veeck elevated him from coach to replace his close friend and former teammate Lemon as White Sox skipper. Doby wasn't retained for 1979 after posting a 37–50 record and never got another opportunity to manage. He was elected to the Hall of Fame in 1998.

Maybe the 1954 World Series would have turned out differently had it been the American League's year to host the first and second games. Maybe it would've turned out differently had Wertz's clout eluded Willie Mays's glove, or bounced off of it. Maybe, as Lopez insisted, the Indians slumped at the worst possible time. Or maybe the 1954 Indians truly were no better than the 1944 St. Louis Browns and took advantage of a pathetic American League to post a historic season. Regardless of what happened in the World Series, the Indians broke the five-year pennant streak of the hated Yankees. They won 111 games, an American League record that stood until 1998, when the Yankees reclaimed it. Cleveland's winning percentage of .721 is still the best in American League history.

A team must win the championship of its sport to be considered among the all-time greats, and the 1954 Indians failed that test. Miserably. But their remarkable accomplishments deserve to be more than a mere afterthought ... or worse, something that Cleveland's baseball fans have been trying ever since to forget.

APPENDIX A.
THE PLAYERS' STATISTICS

Season Numbers

Player	G	AB	H	2B	3B	HR	RBI	AVG
Larry Doby	153	577	157	18	4	32*	126*	.272
Bob Avila	143	555	189	27	2	15	67	.341*
Jim Hegan	139	423	99	12	7	11	40	.234
Al Rosen	137	466	140	20	2	24	102	.300
Dave Philley	133	452	102	13	3	12	60	.226
Al Smith	131	481	135	29	6	11	50	.281
George Strickland	112	361	77	12	3	6	37	.213
Bill Glynn	111	171	43	3	2	5	18	.251
Vic Wertz	94	295	81	14	2	14	48	.275
Wally Westlake	85	240	63	9	2	11	42	.262
Rudy Regalado	65	180	45	5	0	2	24	.250
Dave Pope	60	102	30	2	1	4	13	.294
Hank Majeski	57	121	34	4	0	3	17	.281
Dale Mitchell	53	60	17	1	0	1	6	.283
Hal Naragon	46	101	24	2	2	0	12	.238
Luke Easter	6	6	1	0	0	0	0	.167
Rocky Nelson	4	4	0	0	0	0	0	.000
Mickey Grasso	4	6	2	0	0	1	1	.333
Joe Ginsberg	3	2	1	0	1	0	1	.500
Jim Dyck	2	1	1	0	0	0	1	1.000

At Bats: 5,222; *Hits:* 1,368; *Doubles:* 188; *Triples:* 39; *Home Runs:* 156*; *Runs Batted In:* 714; *Runs Scored:* 746; *Batting Average:* .262

*League leader

Source: *Cleveland Indians Encyclopedia*

Appendix A

Pitcher	G	GS	CG	IP	H	BB	SO	W–L	ERA
Mike Garcia	45	34	13	258.2	220	71	129	19–8	2.64*
Ray Narleski	42	2	1	89	59	44	52	3–3	2.22
Don Mossi	40	5	2	93	56	39	55	6–1	1.94
Early Wynn	40	36	20	270.2*	225	83	155	23–11	2.73
Bob Lemon	36	33	21*	258.1	228	92	110	23–7	2.72
Art Houtteman	32	25	11	188	198	59	68	15–7	3.35
Hal Newhouser	26	1	0	46.2	34	18	25	7–2	2.51
Bob Feller	19	19	9	140	127	39	59	13–3	3.09
Bob Hooper	17	0	0	34.2	39	16	12	0–0	4.93
Dave Hoskins	14	1	0	26.2	29	10	9	0–1	3.04
Bob Chakales	3	0	0	10.1	4	12	3	2–0	0.87
Jose Santiago	1	0	0	1.2	0	2	1	0–0	0.00
Dick Tomanek	1	0	0	1.2	1	1	0	0–0	5.40

Shutouts: Garcia 5, Wynn 3, Lemon 2, Feller 1, Houtteman 1; *Saves:* Narleski 13, Mossi 7, Newhouser 7, Garcia 5, Hooper 2, Wynn 2; *Innings Pitched:* 1,419.1; *Hits Allowed:* 1,220; *Bases on Balls:* 486; *Strikeouts:* 678; *ERA:* 2.78
*League leader
Source: *Cleveland Indians Encyclopedia*

World Series

Player	G	AB	H	2	3	HR	RBI	AVG
Vic Wertz	4	16	8	2	1	1	3	.500
Bill Glynn	2	2	1	1	0	0	0	.500
Early Wynn	1	2	1	1	0	0	0	.500
Rudy Regalado	4	3	1	0	0	0	1	.333
Al Rosen	3	12	3	0	0	0	0	.250
Al Smith	4	14	3	0	0	1	2	.214
Hank Majeski	4	6	1	0	0	1	3	.167
Jim Hegan	4	13	2	1	0	0	0	.154
Wally Westlake	2	7	1	0	0	0	0	.143
Larry Doby	4	16	2	0	0	0	0	.125
Dave Philley	4	8	1	0	0	0	0	.125
George Strickland	3	9	0	0	0	0	0	.000
Dave Pope	3	3	0	0	0	0	0	.000
Sam Dente	3	3	0	0	0	0	0	.000
Bob Lemon	3	6	0	0	0	0	0	.000

At Bats: 137; *Hits:* 26; *Runs:* 9; *Average:* .190
Source: *Cleveland Indians Encyclopedia*

The Players' Statistics

World Series Numbers

Player	G	IP	H	R	ER	BB	SO	W–L	ERA
Bob Lemon	2	13.1	16	11	10	8	11	0–2	6.75
Mike Garcia	2	5	6	4	3	4	4	0–1	5.40
Art Houtteman	1	2	2	1	1	1	1	0–0	4.50
Early Wynn	1	7	4	3	3	2	5	0–1	3.86
Ray Narleski	2	4	1	1	1	1	2	0–0	2.25
Don Mossi	3	4	3	0	0	0	1	0–0	0.00
Hal Newhouser	1	0	1	1	1	1	0	0–0	∞

Innings Pitched: 35.1; *Hits:* 33; *Runs:* 21; *Earned Runs:* 19; *BB:* 17; *K:* 24; *ERA:* 4.84

Source: *Cleveland Indians Encyclopedia*

APPENDIX B.
THE 1954 SCHEDULE

Date	Opponent	Score	Record	GB
4/13	at Chicago	8–2	1–0	—
4/14	at Chicago	6–3	2–0	+½
4/15	DETROIT	2–3	2–1	—
4/17	CHICAGO	1–8	2–2	1
4/18	CHICAGO	3–6	2–3	2
4/21	at Baltimore	2–1	3–3	½
4/22	at Baltimore	1–4	3–4	1
4/23	at Detroit	1–6	3–5	2
4/24	at Detroit	3–6	3–6	3
4/25	at Detroit	10–9	4–6	2½
4/29	at Boston	6–3	5–6	2
4/30	at New York	9–4	6–6	2
5/1	at New York	10–2	7–6	2
5/2	at Washington	6–4	8–6	1
5/2	at Washington	6–3	9–6	1
5/4	at Philadelphia	2–3	9–7	2½
5/5	at Philadelphia	7–2	10–7	1½
5/6	at Philadelphia	3–2	11–7	1½
5/8	at Baltimore	5–3	12–7	2
5/9	at Baltimore	1–2	12–8	2
5/10	NEW YORK	8–7	13–8	2½
5/11	NEW YORK	3–5	13–9	2½
5/12	NEW YORK	4–5	13–10	2½
5/13	WASHINGTON	8–7	14–10	2½
5/14	WASHINGTON	5–2	15–10	1
5/15	WASHINGTON	5–4	16–10	1
5/16	PHILADELPHIA	12–7	17–10	—

The 1954 Schedule

Date	Opponent	Score	Record	GB
5/16	PHILADELPHIA	6–0	18–10	—
5/18	BOSTON	6–3	19–10	+1
5/19	BOSTON	5–3	20–10	+1
5/21	BALTIMORE	2–1	21–10	+2
5/22	BALTIMORE	4–3	22–10	+2
5/23	BALTIMORE	14–3	23–10	+2½
5/23	BALTIMORE	2–1	24–10	+2½
5/25	at Chicago	2–4	24–11	+1½
5/26	at Chicago	4–5	24–12	+½
5/28	DETROIT	3–0	25–12	—
5/29	DETROIT	12–0	26–12	—
5/30	DETROIT	3–1	27–12	+1
5/31	CHICAGO	4–6	27–13	+1
5/31	CHICAGO	6–3	28–13	+1
6/2	at New York	8–7	29–13	+2
6/3	at New York	1–2	29–14	+1
6/4	at New York	3–8	29–15	—
6/5	at Philadelphia	4–1	30–15	—
6/6	at Philadelphia	2–1	31–15	—
6/6	at Philadelphia	7–5	32–15	—
6/8	at Washington	2–5	32–16	1
6/9	at Washington	1–0	33–16	1
6/10	at Washington	4–8	33–17	1½
6/11	at Boston	6–2	34–17	½
6/12	at Boston	4–3	35–17	+½
6/13	at Boston	4–1	36–17	+1½
6/13	at Boston	8–1	37–17	+1½
6/14	at Boston	13–5	38–17	+2
6/15	WASHINGTON	9–3	39–17	+3
6/16	WASHINGTON	5–1	40–17	+3
6/17	WASHINGTON	6–4	41–17	+3
6/18	BOSTON	2–0	42–17	+4
6/19	BOSTON	3–6	42–18	+3
6/20	BOSTON	3–1	43–18	+4
6/20	BOSTON	9–2	44–18	+4
6/22	PHILADELPHIA	1–4	44–19	+3
6/23	PHILADELPHIA	5–2	45–19	+3
6/24	PHILADELPHIA	1–5	45–20	+2
6/25	NEW YORK	0–11	45–21	+1
6/26	NEW YORK	9–11	45–22	+1

Appendix B

Date	Opponent	Score	Record	GB
6/27	NEW YORK	4–3	46–22	+1½
6/29	at Baltimore	5–1	47–22	+2
6/30	at Baltimore	2–0	48–22	+3
7/2	CHICAGO	3–2	49–22	+4½
7/2	CHICAGO	5–4	50–22	+4½
7/3	CHICAGO	5–4	51–22	+4½
7/4	CHICAGO	2–1	52–22	+4½
7/5	at Detroit	13–6	53–22	+3½
7/5	at Detroit	0–1	53–23	+3½
7/6	BALTIMORE	11–3	54–23	+3½
7/7	BALTIMORE	6–1	55–23	+3½
7/8	BALTIMORE	4–1	56–23	+4
7/9	at Chicago	3–8	56–24	+3
7/10	at Chicago	0–3	56–25	+2
7/11	at Chicago	0–3	56–26	+½
7/11	at Chicago	2–8	56–27	+½
7/15	at Philadelphia	4–0	57–27	+½
7/16	at Philadelphia	9–3	58–27	+½
7/17	at Philadelphia	6–0	59–27	+½
7/18	at Washington	3–8	59–28	½
7/18	at Washington	7–4	60–28	+½
7/19	at Washington	4–3	61–28	+½
7/20	at Boston	5–5	61–28	+½
7/21	at Boston	7–7	61–28	+½
7/22	at Boston	6–3	62–28	+½
7/22	at Boston	5–2	63–28	+½
7/23	at New York	8–2	64–28	+1½
7/24	at New York	5–4	65–28	+2½
7/25	at New York	3–4	65–29	+1½
7/27	BOSTON	6–3	66–29	+2½
7/28	BOSTON	2–1	67–29	+2½
7/29	BOSTON	2–10	67–30	+1½
7/30	WASHINGTON	8–3	68–30	+2½
7/31	WASHINGTON	6–0	69–30	+2½
8/1	WASHINGTON	3–1	70–30	+2½
8/1	WASHINGTON	5–4	71–30	+2½
8/3	NEW YORK	1–2	71–31	+1½
8/4	NEW YORK	5–2	72–31	+2½
8/5	NEW YORK	2–5	72–32	+1½
8/6	PHILADELPHIA	7–3	73–32	+1½

The 1954 Schedule

Date	Opponent	Score	Record	GB
8/7	PHILADELPHIA	5–1	74–32	+2½
8/8	PHILADELPHIA	7–2	75–32	+4
8/8	PHILADELPHIA	5–2	76–32	+4
8/10	at Detroit	0–4	76–33	+3
8/11	at Detroit	2–0	77–33	+3
8/12	at Detroit	10–1	78–33	+2½
8/13	BALTIMORE	9–4	79–33	+2½
8/14	BALTIMORE	4–3	80–33	+2½
8/15	BALTIMORE	5–2	81–33	+3
8/15	BALTIMORE	3–1	82–33	+3
8/17	DETROIT	4–3	83–33	+3
8/18	DETROIT	4–0	84–33	+3
8/19	DETROIT	4–3	85–33	+3
8/19	DETROIT	2–8	85–34	+2½
8/20	at Baltimore	7–2	86–34	+3½
8/21	at Baltimore	4–1	87–34	+4½
8/22	at Baltimore	12–1	88–34	+5½
8/24	at Philadelphia	1–4	88–35	+4½
8/25	at Philadelphia	4–3	89–35	+4½
8/26	at Washington	2–1	90–35	+4½
8/27	at Washington	2–3	90–36	+3½
8/28	at Washington	5–2	91–36	+3½
8/29	at Boston	6–2	92–36	+4
8/29	at Boston	8–1	93–36	+4
8/30	at Boston	5–4	94–36	+4½
8/31	at New York	6–1	95–36	+5½
9/1	at New York	1–4	95–37	+4½
9/2	at New York	2–3	95–38	+3½
9/3	at Chicago	3–2	96–38	+3½
9/4	at Chicago	5–8	96–39	+3½
9/5	at Chicago	8–2	97–39	+4½
9/6	at Baltimore	6–1	98–39	+4½
9/6	at Baltimore	2–3	98–40	+4½
9/8	PHILADELPHIA	5–2	99–40	+4½
9/9	PHILADELPHIA	5–4	100–40	+5½
9/10	BOSTON	4–2	101–40	+5½
9/11	BOSTON	3–0	102–40	+6½
9/12	NEW YORK	4–1	103–40	+7½
9/12	NEW YORK	3–2	104–40	+8½
9/14	WASHINGTON	4–2	105–40	+8½

Appendix B

Date	Opponent	Score	Record	GB
9/17	at Detroit	6–3	106–40	+8
9/18	at Detroit*	3–2	107–40	+8
9/19	at Detroit	4–2	108–40	+8
9/20	CHICAGO	7–4	109–40	+9
9/21	CHICAGO	7–9	109–41	+8
9/22	CHICAGO	3–1	110–41	+8
9/24	DETROIT	4–6	110–42	+8
9/25	DETROIT	11–1	111–42	+8
9/26	DETROIT	7–8	111–43	+8

*clinched pennant

Source: baseball library.com, baseball reference.com

Chapter Notes

Chapter 1

1. Cleveland *Plain Dealer*, March 28, 1948.
2. *Plain Dealer*, November 22, 1949.
3. *Ibid*.
4. *Plain Dealer*, November 11, 1950.
5. *Ibid*.
6. Cleveland *Plain Dealer*, September 16, 1953.
7. Cleveland *Press*, September 15, 1953.
8. *Plain Dealer*, September 17, 1953.
9. Cleveland *News*, September 17, 1953.
10. *Plain Dealer*, September 28, 1953.
11. *Plain Dealer*, September 29, 1953.
12. *Ibid*.
13. *Ibid*.
14. *News*, October 2, 1953.
15. *Press*, September 29, 1953.
16. *News*, September 29, 1953.
17. *Plain Dealer*, January 13, 1954.
18. *News*, October 7, 1953.
19. *News*, October 3, 1953.
20. *News*, October 13, 1953.
21. *Plain Dealer*, October 2, 1953.
22. *News*, October 3, 1953.
23. *News*, September 18, 1953.
24. *Plain Dealer*, November 30, 1953.
25. *News*, September 17, 1953.
26. *Plain Dealer*, November 30, 1953.
27. *Ibid*.
28. *Plain Dealer*, November 28, 1953.
29. *Plain Dealer*, October 8, 1953.
30. *News*, October 8, 1953.
31. *Plain Dealer*, December 1, 1953.
32. *Plain Dealer*, December 9, 1953.
33. *Plain Dealer*, December 17, 1953.
34. *Ibid*.
35. *Ibid*.
36. *News*, December 18, 1953.
37. *Plain Dealer*, January 19, 1954.
38. *Ibid*.
39. *Plain Dealer*, January 20, 1954.
40. *News*, January 13, 1954.
41. *News*, December 15, 1953.
42. *Plain Dealer*, February 11, 1954.
43. *Press*, February 12, 1954.
44. *Press*, February 2, 1954.
45. *Plain Dealer*, February 16, 1954.
46. *Ibid*.
47. *News*, February 15, 1954.
48. *Plain Dealer*, February 20, 1954.
49. *Plain Dealer*, February 21, 1954.
50. *Plain Dealer*, February 22, 1954.
51. *Plain Dealer*, February 25, 1954.
52. *Plain Dealer*, February 23, 1954.
53. *Plain Dealer*, February 24, 1954.
54. *Ibid*.
55. *Ibid*.
56. *News*, February 23, 1954.
57. *News*, February 24, 1954.
58. *Plain Dealer*, February 25, 1954.
59. *Plain Dealer*, March 4, 1954.
60. *News*, March 3, 1954.
61. *Plain Dealer*, March 4, 1954.
62. *Plain Dealer*, March 2, 1954.
63. *Plain Dealer*, March 5, 1954.
64. *Plain Dealer*, March 2, 1954.
65. *Press*, March 22, 1954.
66. *News*, March 6, 1954.
67. *Plain Dealer*, March 8, 1954.
68. *Plain Dealer*, March 5, 1954.
69. *News*, February 15, 1954.
70. *Ibid*.

Chapter Notes

71. *News*, March 24, 1954.
72. *Plain Dealer*, March 12, 1954.
73. *Plain Dealer*, March 15, 1954.
74. *News*, March 15, 1954.
75. *Plain Dealer*, March 15, 1954.
76. *Plain Dealer*, March 18, 1954.
77. *Plain Dealer*, March 22, 1954.
78. *Press*, Match 22, 1954.
79. *Plain Dealer*, March 26, 1954.
80. *Ibid.*
81. *News*, March 29, 1954.
82. *Ibid.*
83. *Plain Dealer*, March 17, 1954.
84. *Plain Dealer*, March 31, 1954.
85. *News*, March 6, 1954.
86. *News*, April 2, 1954.
87. *Plain Dealer*, April 2, 1954.
88. *Plain Dealer*, April 5, 1954.
89. *Ibid.*
90. *Ibid.*
91. *Plain Dealer*, April 10, 1954.
92. *Plain Dealer*, April 12, 1954.
93. *Ibid.*
94. *Press*, April 5, 1954.
95. *Ibid.*
96. *News*, March 6, 1954.
97. *News*, April 9, 1954.
98. *News*, April 8, 1954.
99. *Press*, April 14, 1954.
100. *News*, April 10, 1954.
101. *News*, March 13, 1954.
102. *News*, March 31, 1954.

Chapter 2

1. Cleveland *Plain Dealer*, April 13, 1954.
2. *Ibid.*
3. Cleveland *News*, April 12.
4. *Plain Dealer*, April 13.
5. *Ibid.*
6. *Ibid.*
7. *Plain Dealer*, April 15.
8. Cleveland *Press*, April 15.
9. *Plain Dealer*, April 15.
10. *Ibid.*
11. *Plain Dealer*, April 16.
12. *News*, April 16.
13. *Plain Dealer*, April 19.
14. *Ibid.*
15. *News*, April 27.
16. *Plain Dealer*, April 18.
17. *Ibid.*
18. *Ibid.*
19. *News*, April 17.
20. *Plain Dealer*, April 24.
21. *News*, April 22.
22. *Plain Dealer*, April 22.
23. *Plain Dealer*, April 25.
24. *Plain Dealer*, April 26.
25. *Plain Dealer*, April 27.
26 *News*, April 27.
27. *News*, April 30.

Chapter 3

1. Cleveland *Plain Dealer*, May 3, 1954.
2. *Plain Dealer*, May 7.
3. *Ibid.*
4. *Plain Dealer*, May 8.
5. Cleveland *News*, May 7.
6. *News*, May 17.
7. Cleveland *Press*, May 7.
8. *News*, May 8.
9. *Press*, May 8.
10. *News*, May 13.
11. *Plain Dealer*, May 12.
12. *Press*, May 17.
13. *Plain Dealer*, May 13.
14. *Ibid.*
15. *Ibid.*
16. *Ibid.*
17. *News*, May 14.
18. *Press*, May 14.
19. *Plain Dealer*, May 16.
20. *News*, May 17.
21. *Plain Dealer*, May 17.
22. *Plain Dealer*, May 19.
23. *Press*, May 19.
24. *Plain Dealer*, May 20.
25. *Ibid.*
26. *Plain Dealer*, May 24.
27. *Press*, May 24.
28. *Ibid.*
29. *Press*, May 24.
30. *Plain Dealer*, May 27.
31. *Ibid.*
32. *Plain Dealer*, May 29.
33. *Plain Dealer*, May 31.
34. *Plain Dealer*, June 1.
35. *News*, May 31.

Chapter Notes

Chapter 4

1. Cleveland *Press*, June 2, 1954.
2. Cleveland *Plain Dealer*, June 2.
3. *Ibid.*
4. Cleveland *News*, June 3.
5. *Plain Dealer*, June 4.
6. *News*, June 5.
7. *Ibid.*
8. *Ibid.*
9. *News*, June 5.
10. *News*, May 31, 1954.
11. *Press*, June 4.
12. *Press*, June 8.
13. *Ibid.*
14. *Plain Dealer*, June 6.
15. *Ibid.*
16. *News*, June 8.
17. *Press*, June 9.
18. *Ibid.*
19. *Plain Dealer*, June 11.
20. *Plain Dealer*, June 16.
21. *Plain Dealer*, June 17.
22. *Plain Dealer*, June 18.
23. *Plain Dealer*, June 19.
24. *Plain Dealer*, June 21.
25. *News*, June 28.
26. *Ibid.*
27. *News*, June 26.
28. *Plain Dealer*, June 28.
29. *Ibid.*
30. *Press*, June 28.
31. *Plain Dealer*, June 29.
32. *Press*, June 29.
33. *Ibid.*
34. *Plain Dealer*, June 30.

Chapter 5

1. Cleveland *Plain Dealer*, July 2, 1954.
2. Cleveland *Press*, July 1.
3. *Ibid.*
4. Cleveland *News*, June 29, 1954.
5. *News*, July 2.
6. *Ibid.*
7. *Plain Dealer*, July 3.
8. *Plain Dealer*, July 5.
9. *News*, June 30, 1954.
10. *Ibid.*
11. *Ibid.*
12. *Press*, July 7.
13. *Plain Dealer*, July 7.
14. *Plain Dealer*, July 8.
15. *Press*, July 8.
16. *Plain Dealer*, July 9.
17. *News*, July 8.
18. *Press*, July 9.
19. *News*, July 19.
20. *News*, July 9.
21. *Plain Dealer*, July 11.
22. *News*, July 12.
23. *Ibid.*
24. *Plain Dealer*, July 13.
25. *Plain Dealer*, July 14.
26. *Ibid.*
27. *Ibid.*
28. *Plain Dealer*, July 15.
29. *Ibid.*
30. *Plain Dealer*, July 17.
31. *Plain Dealer*, July 18.
32. *Plain Dealer*, July 20.
33. *News*, July 20.
34. *News*, July 24.
35. *News*, July 26.
36. *Press*, July 31.
37. *Ibid.*
38. *Ibid.*
39. *Plain Dealer*, July 31.

Chapter 6

1. Cleveland *Plain Dealer*, August 2, 1954.
2. *Plain Dealer*, August 5.
3. Cleveland *News*, August 6.
4. *News*, August 4.
5. *News*, August 6.
6. *News*, August 7.
7. *News*, August 9.
8. *News*, August 11.
9. *Ibid.*
10. *News*, August 12.
11. *News*, August 11.
12. *Ibid.*
13. Cleveland *Press*, August 12.
14. *News*, August 13.
15. *News*, August 16.
16. *Press*, August 16.

Chapter Notes

17. *Plain Dealer*, August 16.
18. *News*, August 17.
19. *Plain Dealer*, August 17.
20. *Plain Dealer*, August 18.
21. *Ibid*.
22. *News*, August 19.
23. *Ibid*.
24. *Ibid*.
25. *News*, August 20.
26. *Press*, August 24.
27. *News*, August 23.
28. *Ibid*.
29. *Plain Dealer*, August 26.
30. *Press*, August 26.
31. *Plain Dealer*, August 27.
32. *Plain Dealer*, August 28.
33. *News*, August 28.
34. *Plain Dealer*, August 30.
35. *Press*, August 28.
36. *News*, August 28.
37. *Ibid*.
38. *News*, August 30.
39. *Plain Dealer*, August 31.
40. *News*, August 28.

Chapter 7

1. Cleveland *Plain Dealer*, September 1, 1954.
2. Cleveland *News*, September 2.
3. Cleveland *Press*, September 3.
4. *News*, September 3.
5. *Press*, September 3.
6. *News*, September 3.
7. *News*, September 7.
8. *Press*, September 8.
9. *Plain Dealer*, September 6.
10. *News*, September 8.
11. *Plain Dealer*, September 8.
12. *Plain Dealer*, September 9.
13. *News*, September 8.
14. *News*, September 9.
15. *Plain Dealer*, September 9.
16. *Ibid*.
17. *Ibid*.
18. *Plain Dealer*, September 10.
19. *Plain Dealer*, September 12.
20. *Plain Dealer*, September 13.
21. *Plain Dealer*, September 14.
22. *Plain Dealer*, September 13.
23. *News*, September 13.
24. *Ibid*.
25. *Press*, September 13.
26. *Ibid*.
27. *Plain Dealer*, September 17.
28. *Press*, September 20.
29. *Plain Dealer*, September 19.
30. *Ibid*.
31. *News*, September 20.
32. *Plain Dealer*, September 20.
33. *News*, September 18.
34. *Press*, September 17.
35. *Press*, September 21.
36. *Plain Dealer*, September 21.
37. *Plain Dealer*, September 22.
38. *Plain Dealer*, September 23.
39. *Ibid*.
40. *Plain Dealer*, September 25.
41. *News*, September 27.

Chapter 8

1. Cleveland *Plain Dealer*, September 28, 1954.
2. *Plain Dealer*, September 29.
3. Cleveland *News*, September 22.
4. *News*, September 21.
5. *Plain Dealer*, September 29.
6. Cleveland *Press*, September 25.
7. *News*, September 20.
8. *News*, September 28.
9. *Ibid*.
10. *Plain Dealer*, September 30.
11. *Ibid*.
12. *Ibid*.
13. *Ibid*.
14. *Ibid*.
15. *News*, September 30.
16. *Plain Dealer*, October 1.
17. *Ibid*.
18. *News*, October 1.
19. *Ibid*.
20. *Press*, October 1.
21. *Plain Dealer*, October 2.
22. *Ibid*.
23. *Ibid*.
24. *Press*, October 2.
25. *News*, September 21.
26. *Plain Dealer*, October 2.
27. *Plain Dealer*, October 3.

Chapter Notes

28. *Ibid.*
29. *Ibid.*
30. *Press*, October 4.
31. *Plain Dealer*, October 3.
32. *Ibid.*
33. *Ibid.*
34. *News*, October 4.
35. *Ibid.*
36. *Plain Dealer*, October 3.
37. *News*, October 4.
38. *Press*, October 2.
39. *Plain Dealer*, October 5.
40. *Ibid.*

Epilogue

1. Cleveland *Plain Dealer*, September 29, 1956.
2. *Ibid.*
3. *Ibid.*

BIBLIOGRAPHY

Books

Appel, Marty. *Pinstripe Empire.* New York: Bloomsbury, 2012.
Berger, Phil. *Mickey Mantle.* New York: Park Lane Press, 1998.
Castro, Tony. *Mickey Mantle: Baseball's Prodigal Son.* Dulles, VA: Brassey's, 2002.
Feller, Bob, with Bill Gilbert. *Now Pitching Bob Feller.* New York: Birch Lane Press, 1990.
Hirsch, James S. *Willie Mays: The Life, the Legend.* New York: Scribner, 2010.
Honig, Donald. *The American League.* New York: Crown, 1983.
Leavy, Jane. *The Last Boy: Mickey Mantle and the End of America's Childhood.* New York: HarperCollins, 2010.
The New York Times Story of the Yankees. New York: Black Dog and Leventhal, 2012.
Schneider, Russell. *Cleveland Indians Encyclopedia.* Norwalk, CT: Easton Press, 2001.
Schneider, Russell. *Whatever Happened to Super Joe?* Cleveland: Gray, 2006.
Sickels, John. *Bob Feller Ace of the Greatest Generation.* Washington, D.C.: Brassey's, 2004.
Singletary, Wes. *Al Lopez: The Life of Baseball's El Señor.* Jefferson, NC: McFarland, 1999.
Snyder, John. *Cleveland Indians Journal.* Cincinnati: Clerisy Press, 2008.
Solomon, Burt. *The Baseball Timeline.* New York: DK, 2001.

Newspapers

Cleveland *Plain Dealer*, September 1953–October 1954.
Cleveland *News*, September 1953–October, 1954.
Cleveland *Press*, September 1953–October 1954.

INDEX

Abbott and Costello 123
Aber, Al 119
All-Star Game 98, 101, 105–106, 128, 141
Aloma, Luis 30–31
Alston, Walter 40
American Association 9
American League 5, 19, 23–24, 27, 35, 40, 43, 49, 67, 88, 91, 97, 103, 105–107, 122, 126, 131, 134–136, 140, 146–147, 151–152, 164–165, 173–174
Antonelli, Johnny 106, 155, 158, 161–162
Arizona 38–39, 44, 60
Arkansas 76
Aspromonte, Ken 174
Associated Grocery Manufacturers 8
Associated Press 19
Atlanta, Georgia 20
Atlantic Ocean 136
Avila, Bob 28, 30, 52, 54, 60, 66, 71, 83–86, 90, 101, 106, 108, 113, 116, 120, 122–125, 135, 140–141, 143, 146, 151, 157, 160, 165

Baltimore, Maryland 38, 67–68, 74, 95, 97, 114, 125, 127, 129, 136, 137
Baltimore Orioles 27, 41, 43, 51, 56, 58–59, 65, 74, 81, 91, 95, 101, 114–115, 120–122, 127, 136–137, 142, 152
Bang, Ed 26–28, 43
Barrow, Ed 12
Baseball Writers Association of America 52
Batts, Matt 56, 61
Bauer, Hank 83
Baxter, Andrew 170

Baxter, Charles 170
Baxter, Williams and Company 23
Beaumont (Texas League) 23
Belardi, Wayne 119
Bell, Bert 75
Berardino, Johnny 95
Berra, Yogi 65, 69, 83, 106, 116, 130, 141, 151
Berry, Charley 74
Bock, Wally 84–85
Bollweg, Don 25, 108
Bonda, Ted 174
Boone, Ray 56, 60, 143
Boston, Massachusetts 61–62, 88, 90, 99, 108, 123, 129, 136, 140
Boston Braves 161
Boston Red Sox 6, 10, 19–20, 22, 24, 45, 48, 51–52, 57, 61–62, 73–74, 76, 87–91, 93–94, 98, 107–108, 112, 117, 122–123, 125–126, 129–130, 137, 139–140, 142, 152, 172
Boudreau, Lou 7–9, 19, 22, 74, 86–88, 125, 139, 146, 152, 169
Bradley, Alva 42
Bragan, Bobby 17
Branca, Ralph 56
Brideweser, Jim 102
Briggs Stadium 101, 119, 142, 144
Brooklyn, New York 112
Brooklyn Dodgers 9, 12, 16–18, 20, 40, 52, 68, 93, 95, 112, 122, 145, 153, 170
Buffalo, New York 19, 90, 140
Burns, George 22
Busby, Jim 173
Byrd, Harry 25–26, 35, 65, 108, 118, 126

189

Index

Cain, Bob 116
Carey, Andy 77, 111
Carrasquel, Chico 57, 173
Cavarretta, Phil 47, 99, 146–147
Celebrezze, Anthony 54
Chakales, Bob 52, 71, 73, 81, 121
Chesapeake Bay 136
Chicago, Illinois 53, 101, 103, 136, 169, 170, 173
Chicago Cubs 12, 43, 47, 146–147
Chicago White Sox 10, 12–13, 16, 24, 26, 37, 47–48, 51–52, 54, 57, 73, 76–77, 85–86, 88, 91–94, 96–99, 103, 109, 111, 114, 117–118, 120, 126, 130–131, 134–136, 140, 145–147, 152, 155, 169–170, 172–174
Cincinnati Reds 12, 14, 24, 144
Cleveland, Ohio 5, 112, 118, 122, 129, 134, 139, 146, 153, 159, 166–167, 169, 170, 173–174
Cleveland Advertising Club 53
Cleveland Baseball Federation 111
Cleveland Browns 28, 75
Cleveland Naps 87
Cleveland News 14, 26, 35, 40, 44, 48, 50–51, 55, 100, 105, 136, 154, 156, 164
Cleveland Plain Dealer 7, 10, 19, 122, 135
Cleveland Press 14–15, 36, 39, 51, 84–85, 154
Cleveland Spiders 87
Cobb, Ty 17
Cobbledick, Gordon 10–11, 19–20, 24–25, 27–28, 42–45, 55, 66, 71, 75, 91, 137, 154, 168
Coleman, Jerry 83
Collins, Joe 65, 69, 82, 117, 133
Columbus (American Association) 17
Columbus, Ohio 90
Comiskey, Charles 55
Comiskey, Chuck 55
Comiskey Park 13, 54, 76–77, 79, 84, 100, 173
Connie Mack Stadium 66–67, 126–127
Consuegra, Sandy 99, 104
Corum, Bill 49
Courtney, Clint 27, 43, 60, 125
Cuba 34, 58
Cuccinello, Tony 38, 121–122, 124, 126, 154–155, 157

Cuyahoga County 170

Daley, Bud 173
Dallas, Texas 47
Dark, Alvin 52, 154, 157, 162–163, 165
Darvas, Lou 154
Daytona Beach, Florida 33, 39, 48
Dean, Dizzy 113
DeMaestri, Joe 72
Dente, Sam 87–88, 90, 110, 115–116, 120, 129, 134, 137, 146, 162
Detroit, Michigan 60, 100–101, 118, 120, 137, 156
Detroit Lions 28, 75
Detroit Tigers 5–6, 13, 31, 55, 59–60, 65, 77, 79, 82, 85–86, 92–93, 98, 108–109, 155–166, 118, 120, 123–125, 128–129, 134, 142–143, 147, 152, 174
DiMaggio, Joe 113
Dixon, Johnny 87
Doby, Larry 24, 28–29, 59–60, 62, 71, 77, 87, 91, 99, 101, 108–109, 111–113, 116–117, 124, 133, 135, 142, 151, 166, 168, 173–174
Dolin, Nate 78
Dorish, Harry 78
Dropo, Walt 56, 78
Durocher, Leo 39, 47, 51–52, 145–146, 153, 162–163
Dyck, Jim 58, 70, 81
Dyer, Eddie 12–13

Easter, Luke 16, 28, 41, 45–46, 56, 70, 91
Ebbets Field 112, 145
Effrat, Lewis 50
Ehlers, Art 27, 43, 60
Evers, Hoot 30

Fain, Ferris 24, 111
Farrell, Kerby 169
Feeney, Charles 50
Feller, Bob 13–14, 19–20, 22, 28, 34, 36, 54, 59, 65–66, 71, 75, 78, 81, 86–88, 90, 97–99, 102–103, 108–109, 113, 118, 120, 124, 128–130, 145, 161–162, 171
Fenway Park 86, 90, 109, 125, 129–130
Finley, Charles 38
Fisher, Geoffrey 154

190

Index

Flaherty, John 113
Florida 31, 37, 39, 41, 52
Forbes Field 95
Ford, "Whitey" 54, 62, 69, 83, 94, 105, 116, 134, 161
Fort Worth, Texas 47
Fox, Nellie 76, 106
Fracchia, Don 23–24
Francona, Tito 174
Fricano, Mario 107
Fridley, Jim 125

Gaedel, Eddie 116
Garcia, Merced 112
Garcia, Michael Martin 112
Garcia, Mike 20, 22, 28, 32–33, 41–42, 47, 56, 59, 61–62, 69, 71, 74, 76–78, 81–82, 84, 88–90, 93–94, 96, 100–102, 107, 112, 115–116, 118–119, 124, 126–127, 129, 133, 135, 140, 142, 144, 147, 159, 168, 172
Garver, Ned 60, 119, 143
Gaynor, Dr. Sidney 110
Gibbons, Frank 39, 49, 75, 85, 126, 154, 169
Ginsberg, Joe 27, 76–77
Glendale, California 11
Glynn, Bill 16–17, 34, 41, 45–46, 54, 56, 58, 60, 97, 101, 127, 134–135, 160
Goldstein, "Spud" 37, 44
Gomez, Ruben 160
Grabiner, Harry 5
Grasso, Mickey 29, 33–34, 43, 95, 112, 157
Gray, Johnny 126–127
Gray, Ted 144
Greenberg, Hank 5–10, 12–17, 22–23, 25–31, 35–40, 42, 44–45, 48, 54, 56, 60–61, 67–68, 79, 81, 87, 98, 103, 128, 143–144, 163, 165, 167–172
Grieve, Bill 83
Griffith, Clark 24, 29
Griffith Stadium 54, 65, 77, 108, 128
Grim, Bob 69, 94, 130, 160
Grissom, Marv 157
Gromek, Steve 77, 119–120
Groth, Johnny 76, 99

Hall of Fame 7, 161, 171–174
Hamey, Roy 38

Hand, Jack 19
Harder, Mel 41, 104–105, 116, 131, 140, 155
Harridge, Will 40, 83–84
Harris, Bucky 66, 71, 129
Harshman, Jack 54, 99, 104, 146
Hatfield, Fred 147
Hatton, Grady 76
Haynes, Joe 70
Hegan, Jim 28, 47, 62, 76, 78, 83, 133, 141, 143, 156–157, 159, 162–163, 166
Herbert, Ray 77
Herman, "Babe" 38
Hi Corbett Field 33, 37, 39
Hodges, Gil 16
Hoeft, Billy 123–124
Hollenden Hotel 8
Hollywood Stars 17
Holmes, Tommy 161
Holyoke, Massachusetts 18
Hooper, Bob 86, 89, 93, 104, 130
Hopkins International Airport 137
Hornsby, Rogers 105
Hoskins, Dave 30, 69–70, 73, 93, 101, 109, 138
Houston, Texas 45
Houtteman, Art 57, 59, 66, 68, 73, 75, 78, 81, 85, 88, 90, 92, 101, 103–104, 108, 111, 113, 116, 118, 121, 125, 130, 135, 140, 146, 160–162
Hurley, Ed 104–105, 112
Hutchinson, Fred 78, 118, 124

Indianapolis (American Association) 9–10, 57, 70, 77
International League 9, 16, 47, 67
International News Service 49
Iowa 102
Irvin, Monte 47, 157–158, 160, 162

Jackson, Ron 105
Jacobs, David 170
Jacobs, Forrest "Spook" 66
Jacobs, Richard 170
Jacobs Field 170
Jensen, Jackie 24, 112–113
Johnson, Walter 87–88
Jones, Harry 7, 12, 39, 44, 49, 58–60, 66, 69, 82, 86, 88, 90, 102, 118, 121, 123, 126, 128, 135–136, 154

Index

Joost, Eddie 91, 117–118

Kahn, Roger 50
Kaline, Al 56, 124
Kansas City (American Association) 17
Kansas City, Missouri 127
Kansas City Athletics 22, 36, 38, 57, 173
Kansas City Royals 172
Keefe, Tim 87
Keegan, Bob 57, 78, 104, 145
Kell, George 76
Kelley, Don Dr. 57, 84, 122–123, 137
Kellner, Alex 84, 107
Keltner, Ken 146
Kennedy, Bob 28–29, 43, 57, 81, 121
Kinder, Ellis 90, 130
King, Joe 50
Korea 69
Kremenko, Barney 50
Kress, "Red" 38, 124
Kretlow, Lou 75
Kryhoski, Dick 43, 74
Kuenn, Harvey 101, 119
Kuzava, Bob 69

Lake Erie 137, 170
Lane, Frank 25, 30, 76, 79, 87, 155
Larsen, Don 74, 121, 136
Las Vegas, Nevada 93
League Park 140, 159, 168
Lebovitz, Hal 14, 20, 49, 100, 112, 129, 137
Leja, Frank 18
Lemon, Bob 13, 20, 28–29, 32, 36, 54, 59, 62, 68, 76–78, 81–82, 85–86, 88, 90, 92, 94, 101, 105, 108–109, 112, 114, 117–118, 120, 122, 125, 127, 130, 134, 141–144, 147, 157, 161–162, 168, 172–174
Lemon, Jim 70
Lepcio, Ted 87
Lewis, Franklin "Whitey" 14, 43, 46, 91, 154, 159
Liddle, Don 155, 157, 162
Little World Series 9, 17
Lockman, Whitey 145, 160
Long Island Press 50
Lopat, Ed 20, 54, 69, 82, 94, 107, 109, 119, 133
Lopez, Al 5, 7–10, 12–17, 22, 27–28, 35, 37–38, 40, 42, 44, 45–46, 48, 50–51, 53–61, 66–71, 73–74, 81, 85–86, 88–91, 93, 95–98, 101, 103, 105–107, 111, 116, 119, 120, 122, 125–126, 130, 133–134, 136–138, 141–148, 153, 158–162, 164–166, 168–169, 171, 174
Los Angeles Angels (American League) 18
Los Angeles Dodgers 169, 172

Mack, Connie 32, 107
Mack, Earle 32, 107
Mack, Roy 32, 107
Maglie, Sal 155, 157
Majeski, Hank 88–91, 99, 130, 134, 142, 160, 162–163
Mantle, Mickey 53, 77, 111, 117
Marrero, Connie 89
Marsh, Freddie 30–31
Marshall, Willard 24
Martin, Billy 51, 172
Martin, Morrie 87, 99
Masi, Phil 161
Mathewson, Christy 87
Mays, Willie 47, 49, 113, 145, 154–158, 160, 162, 174
McAuley, Ed 26–27, 43, 46, 49, 136, 154, 164–165
McCall, John 43
McCarthy, Joe 12–13
McCulley, Jim 51
McDermott, Mickey 24, 71, 88, 127–128
McDonald, Jim 65
McDougald, Gil 77, 83, 111
McGraw, John 12–13, 105
McKinney, Frank 9
Memorial Stadium 59, 95
Mesa, Arizona 46
Meyer, Billy 9
Michael, Gene 172
Michaels, Cass 76
Miller, Bill 62, 65
Milwaukee Braves 52
Milwaukee Brewers 172
Minneapolis/St. Paul, Minnesota 170
Minoso, Orestes "Minnie" 58, 78, 100, 106, 140
Mitchell, Dale 24, 28, 33, 43, 56, 60, 108, 143

Index

Mize, Johnny 20, 25, 51
Montreal Royals 9, 16–17, 40, 67
Moore, Terry 113
Morgan, Tom 62–63
Mossi, Don 48, 51, 53, 57, 61, 81–82, 89, 93, 101, 103–104, 108, 116, 120–121, 125, 129, 135, 144, 146, 158, 162
Mueller, Don 52, 145, 160, 162
Municipal Stadium 6, 10–11, 13, 15, 17, 24–25, 36, 48, 50, 53, 55–57, 68, 70, 75, 79, 81, 89–90, 92, 97, 99–100, 113, 117, 120–121, 123, 126, 136, 139–140, 142, 146–147, 157, 161, 167–169, 173
Murray, Arch 51

Naragon, Hal 47–48, 68–69, 76–77, 121, 127, 138
Narleski, Ray 57, 66, 68, 81–82, 93, 100, 102–103, 107–108, 111, 116, 120–121, 124, 130, 143, 145, 147, 160, 162
National Football League 28, 75
National Journalism Fraternity 144
National League 40, 49, 93, 112, 122, 131, 145–146, 169–170
Nelson, Glenn "Rocky" 16–18, 24, 34, 40–41, 44–45, 47–48, 56, 58, 67–68
New England 169
New York City 79, 82, 85, 94, 98, 136
New York Daily Mirror 51
New York Daily News 51
New York Giants 12–13, 39, 41, 43–45, 47–49, 52, 54, 87, 93, 105–106, 112, 131, 141, 145–147, 153, 155–156, 159–161, 163–164, 168, 170
New York Herald-Tribune 50
New York Highlanders 74
New York Journal-American 50
New York Post 51
New York Times 50
New York World Telegram and Sun 50
New York Yankees 6, 10–11, 18–20, 22–23, 25–26, 38, 46, 48–53, 62, 65–66, 68–71, 76, 81–82, 85, 88, 91–92, 96, 100, 103, 105, 108–109, 114–118, 122, 124, 125–131, 133–138, 140–142, 144, 146, 151–152, 155, 160, 170, 172, 174
Newhouser, Hal 31, 40–41, 45, 48, 51, 60, 66, 68, 71, 81–82, 85, 88, 94, 99, 103–104, 115–116, 125, 141, 162

Nixon, Willard 130
Noren, Irv 82, 134

Oakland Athletics 172
Oklahoma City (American Association) 70
Oklahoma City, Oklahoma 44–45
O'Malley, Walter 9
O'Neill, Steve 140
Ottawa (International League) 70

Pacific Coast League 17
Paige, "Satchel" 38
Pascual, Camilo 142
Patterson, "Red" 62, 65
Paul, Gabe 15
Philadelphia, Pennsylvania 13, 83–84, 107, 127, 136
Philadelphia Athletics 14, 17, 25–26, 32, 40, 66–67, 71, 84–85, 91–93, 98, 107–108, 117–118, 120, 125–126, 137–138, 152
Philadelphia Phillies 106, 126
Philley, Dave 32–34, 38, 45, 51, 59, 60–61, 71, 84, 86, 91, 117, 130, 142
Pierce, Billy 54, 104
Piersall, Jim 49
Pillette, Duane 59
Pittsburgh, Pennsylvania 60, 95
Pittsburgh Pirates 5, 16, 44, 46, 68, 95
Polo Grounds 82, 112, 156
Pope, Dave 43, 60, 121, 142, 157
Porterfield, Bob 86, 115
Portocarerro, Arnold 86
Posedel, Bill 112
Power, Vic 25
Preston, Howard 26
Priddy, Jerry 14

Raschi, Vic 34–36, 51
Regalado, Rudy 40, 43, 45–46, 48, 51, 53, 60–62, 66, 70, 74, 76, 82, 95, 128–129, 133–134, 146, 157, 162
Renna, Bill 25
Reynolds, Allie 20, 34, 71, 82, 93, 107, 116–117, 119
Rhodes, Jim "Dusty" 154, 157–159
Ribs and Roasts Dinner 27–28, 167
Rice, Grantland 52
Richards, Paul 58, 76–77, 87, 97, 99, 104–105, 127, 136

Index

Richmond (International League) 70, 73, 81
Rivera, Jim 84
Rizzuto, Phil 65, 77
Roberts, Robin 106
Robinson, Eddie 25–26, 134, 146
Robinson, Frank 174
Rosen, Al 14, 20, 22–23, 28, 35–37, 56, 59–62, 66–67, 69, 71, 74, 77–78, 84–86, 88, 90, 98, 100, 102, 105–107, 113, 117–120, 122–124, 128–130, 133, 138, 142–143, 146, 151, 156, 160, 165, 168, 171
Rowe, Lynwood "Schoolboy" 109
Runge, Ed 123
Runnels, Pete 128
Ruppert, Jake 13
Russell, Allen 23
Ruth, Babe 23
Ryan, Ellis 6–7, 9, 42

Sain, Johnny 20, 25, 35, 69, 82, 111, 126
St. Louis, Missouri 136
St. Louis Browns 9–10, 27, 38, 57, 74, 116, 121, 164–165, 174
St. Louis Cardinals 12–13, 16–18, 34, 36, 53, 68, 95, 102, 105, 111–112, 143, 165
San Diego (Pacific Coast League) 70
San Francisco, California 170
San Francisco Giants 171
Santiago, Jose 48, 57, 70
Schmitz, Johnny 71, 115
Schoendienst, Red 105
Score, Herb 173
Scripps-Howard newspapers 52
Seghi, Phil 174
Shea, Frank "Spec" 114
Sievers, Roy 113
Sima, Al 87
Simpson, Harry 91, 104
Sipple, Charlie 95
Skowron, Bill 69
Slaughter, Enos 53
Smith, Al 27, 43, 61–62, 66, 70–71, 74, 76, 82, 84, 91, 94, 104, 108–109, 123–124, 127, 133, 158
Smith, Ken 51
Soar, Hank 14
Speaker, Tris 39, 139, 146

Sport magazine 52
Steinbrenner, George 171–172
Stanky, Eddie 112
Stengel, Casey 10–11, 16, 18, 20, 22, 35, 46, 62, 65, 77, 83, 94, 101, 103, 105–106, 109, 111, 114, 117–120, 133–134, 138, 146, 155–156
Stephens, Vern 9–10, 125
Stewart, Bill 161
Stewart, Bunky 89
Stobbs, Chuck 88, 129
Stone, Dean 105, 113
Stouffer, Vernon 171
Strickland, George 30, 54, 71, 75, 82, 85–87, 95, 107, 110, 116, 120, 122, 129, 137, 146, 160
Summers, Bill 124

Tampa, Florida 166
Texas League 23
Thompson, Henry 145, 158, 160
Tipton, Joe 29
Tomanek, Dick 48, 51, 57
Tomaro, Dr. A.J. 129
Topping, Dan 46, 146
Trice, Bob 66
Triple Crown 13, 22–23
Trosky, Hal 45
Trucks, Virgil 104, 106
Tucson, Arizona 5, 33, 35–37, 40, 44, 49
Tulsa, Oklahoma 44
Turley, Bob 59, 68, 75
Tuttle, Bill 56

Umphlett, Tom 24, 113
United Press 52
University of Southern California 45
Upton, Bill 32

Veeck, Bill 5, 7, 9, 25, 38, 169–170, 174
Vernon, Mickey 14, 128
Visalia, California 112

Wade, Gale 47
Walker, Jerry 173
Wapakoneta, Ohio 90
Washington, D.C. 54, 65, 86, 109, 127, 129–130, 136
Washington Senators 12, 19, 23–24, 26, 29, 51, 54, 66, 70–71, 86–87, 91–92,

Index

98, 105, 107–108, 113–115, 127–129, 135, 142, 152; expansion 173
Webb, Del 146
Weiss, George 11, 22, 25, 34–36
Wertz, Vic 81, 89–91, 95, 97, 101, 113, 120–121, 125, 133–134, 137, 146, 156–158, 160, 162, 168, 174
Westlake, Wally 43, 54, 56, 60, 66, 70, 87, 94, 99, 112, 142, 162
Westrum, Wes 160
Wheat, Leroy 32
White, Sammy 74
Whiz Kids 126
Wight, Bill 70
Wilhelm, Hoyt 160, 162
Wilks, Ted 95
Williams, Davey 162
Williams, Dick 173
Williams, Ted 20, 23, 45, 61–62, 73, 106

Wilson, Myron "Mike" 42–43, 142
Woodling, Gene 173
World Series 5, 7, 12, 19–20, 25, 49, 68, 126, 133, 139, 141, 145, 147, 153–154, 158–159, 163, 165, 167–172, 174
Wynn, Early 20, 24, 28–29, 32, 36–37, 54, 58, 60–61, 65, 67–68, 74, 77, 81–83, 86, 88–89, 92, 94, 99–100, 102, 107–109, 113, 115, 121, 123, 125, 127, 130, 135, 137–138, 141, 143–144, 147, 156, 158–159, 163, 168, 172–173

Yankee Stadium 10, 62, 77, 107, 122, 130–131, 134, 141, 172
Yost, Eddie 86
Young, Cy 87

Zernial, Gus 14
Zuverink, George 101, 120, 122

www.ingramcontent.com/pod-product-compliance
Lightning Source LLC
Chambersburg PA
CBHW021914180426
43198CB00035B/561